Business Communications

BARRON'S BUSINESS LIBRARY

Business Communications

Ray E. Barfield
  Clemson University

Sylvia S. Titus
  Clemson University

BARRON'S

General editor for *Barron's Business Library* is George T.
Friedlob, professor in the School of Accountancy at Clemson
University.

All inquiries should be addressed to:
Barron's Educational Series, Inc.
250 Wireless Boulevard
Hauppauge, New York 11788

Library of Congress Catalog Card Number 91-18079

International Standard Book Number 0-8120-4639-0

Library of Congress Cataloging-in-Publication Data

Barfield, Ray E.
    Business communications / Ray E. Barfield, Sylvia Titus.
        p.   cm. — (Barron's business library)
    Includes index.
    ISBN 0-8120-4639-0
    1. Business communication. 2. English language—Business
English.
    I. Titus, Sylvia. II. Title   III. Series.
    HF5718.B36   1991
    808'.06665—dc20   91-18079
                                                          CIP

PRINTED IN ITALY
2345 9929 987654321

Preface

The interests of two large reader groups meet in this review of business communications principles and techniques. Some readers will want a cover-to-cover review of the forms and procedures commonly used in corporate offices and in independent firms today. These steady readers will find that one chapter reinforces another through cumulative emphasis on key ideas and strategies—for example, on the adaptation of the indirect and the direct organizing patterns of letters, memos, or reports. Other readers—those who want a reference source for browsing or for spot-checking—should find sufficient background information to make each chapter relatively self-contained. Chapter introductions and conclusions, glossary entries, and other cues will aid the occasional reader in quickly establishing a context for a particular point.

In this book we have attempted a consensus coverage rather than an exhaustive one. That is, we have drawn on a number of years of experience in reviewing student and professional documents, in teaching business writing and oral communications, and in discussing communications issues with colleagues and acquaintances in the academic and business communities. They have helped us define what is central to the wide and varied enterprise of business communications.

Specific borrowings from printed materials (and a few unpublished ones) are credited at the appropriate places in the text. We express our thanks also to our students, who taught us to think through details and to improvise examples and solutions; to Harold Woodell and G. T. Friedlob, early inspirers of this project; to Kim Hunter and Bronson Beisel for assistance in preparing the manuscript; to Barron's editors Max Reed and Grace Freedson for careful reading and excellent advice; and to Claire Caskey, Sterling Eisiminger, Carl Henson, William Koon, Ray Sawyer, Robert Testin, Terry Titus, Richard Underwood, and Peter Vergano for a variety of courtesies and contributions.

Contents

Communication Basics

INTRODUCTION AND MAIN POINTS

The ability to communicate influences every professional's career. Exchange of information may involve two people in person-to-person, telephone, or memo dialogue, or it may draw a group of people together in committee discussions, oral presentations, or submission and consideration of reports. Weekly reports presented in triplicate, memos announcing action or requesting information, letters inquiring about products or responding to such inquiries, reports submitting test or study findings, quarterly sales updates—these and numerous other kinds of communication are standard operating procedure for independent business people and company employees. Your skill in conveying information plays a significant role in determining your value to your business—and, in fact, may influence the success of that business itself.

After studying the material in this chapter:

■ You will become aware of the role of nonverbal cues in business communication.

■ You will understand the importance of each stage of the communication process.

■ You will realize the necessity of defining your purpose and audience before you begin writing.

■ You will recognize those characteristics essential to successful business documents.

NONVERBAL COMMUNICATION

Awareness of the impact of nonverbal communication is essential to any person involved in business ventures and interactions. People transmit and receive "metamessages" almost constantly. Because of their unstated quality, the messages may not be reliable, but responders still "read" them. Furthermore, if the spoken and unspoken messages conflict, people will usually rely on the unspoken message, as illustrated by the adage "What you do speaks so loudly that I can't hear what you're saying." Certain nonverbal cues become acceptable in a given society, but, as the discussion of international communications in Chapter 18 illustrates, those current in one culture rarely translate to another.

In a work or social environment, people look to nonverbal cues to learn something of others' moods, temperament, self-confidence, sense of power, opinions on issues, and attitudes toward certain people. Messages are sent by one's tone of voice in conversation, choice of clothing, stance, expansiveness of hand gestures, and a host of other indicators.

Voice

Listeners can tell much about a speaker's mood, sense of self-confidence, and comfort in a situation by noting the quality of his or her voice. A person who feels confident and comfortable about a situation will speak with a full, rich voice, but tension, fear, and anger will alter that quality. A tense speaker may project a thin, reedy voice until her nervousness subsides. An infuriated coworker will have difficulty hiding his anger when his voice trembles. Just as the richness or reediness of a voice indicates mood, so does pace of speech: people who are emotional tend to speak more rapidly than do unemotional speakers. Voice quality and speaking pace indicate one's level of confidence. Thus, a person whose voice is reedy may want to concentrate on developing voice richness and depth, and one who speaks rapidly may choose to work toward slowing his or her speaking pace—to project a clearer image of confidence and self-control.

Objects

People also send messages to others by means of the objects with which they surround themselves—their clothes, desks, jewelry, cars, homes, art, gadgets, and "status" items. Clothing choices may range from chic to shabby, from austere to casual, from well-coordinated to mismatched. Clothing gives impressions about self-esteem. One person may seem to dress professionally but comfortably, indicating a healthy self-concept, while another may appear to place unusual emphasis on dressing "just right," suggesting a need to enhance self-confidence. Clothes also hint at one's attitude toward a job. If an employee wears casual, even sporty clothing when others wear tailored business suits, he or she may be "read" as flouting tradition or showing nonchalance about the job. In addition, prevailing dress within a company gives some impression about the formality of an organization's structure. Those companies in which people dress traditionally often maintain more distinct separation between the ranks, while companies in which employees dress more casually may soften the lines between ranks. Certainly size has much to do with this difference. Smaller companies can afford to operate in a more relaxed manner, but as companies expand, they necessarily become more formal in structure.

Desks are also message-senders, hinting at people's attitude toward organization and detail. One person's desk may reveal intermingled piles of memos, journals, letters, file folders, and paper clips, while another's will show a carefully planned array of desktop holders and trays with every item meticulously placed in its intended location. The organization of the desk (and, by extension, the home as well) may indicate one's appreciation for or dislike of orderliness and sequence. Certainly a person is not totally organized or disorganized but is instead systematic in some areas and not in others. Nevertheless, orderly desk arrangement probably illustrates a degree of attention to detail that is further expressed in terms of organizing conferences, programs, and studies. On the other hand, disorganized people are often stronger than detail people at being creative and conceptualizing projects.

Use of Time

People's use of time is a nonverbal cue about their patterns of organization. In attending meetings, some people always seem to run late, and others are consistently early. One who makes a habit of entering meetings well after they have begun will undoubtedly be perceived as disorganized and unbusinesslike. Conversely, the person who can be counted on to arrive fifteen to twenty minutes before the meeting starts creates an image of being exceptionally well organized (some might say almost compulsive). Most people gather a few minutes before a meeting starts or exactly on time. Meeting arrival patterns also seem to predict a person's approach to deadlines: often, but not always, those who run late to meetings are also late in meeting deadlines.

A person's efficiency in use of time also reflects on his or her organizational ability. One speaker may begin a meeting precisely on schedule, waste little time with irrelevancies, proceed in clear order down the agenda, and bring a session to a logical close within the allotted time frame. Participants in such a meeting are indeed fortunate. In contrast is the leader who begins five to ten minutes late, uses several minutes for small talk, approaches the first item on the agenda as a brainstorming opportunity

("What ideas do you have?"), and then either ends the meeting without finishing the agenda or runs an hour overtime to complete the business. Obviously, individuals differ in their approaches to time, but every business depends upon employees' efficient time use.

Use of Space

Space considerations are essential to successful interaction. People "own" the space surrounding them, and the entry of others into that space causes pleasure or discomfort, depending on who is entering the space. Proxemics, the study of these spatial differentiations, defines the space categories as: public distance—twelve to twenty-five feet; social distance—four to twelve feet; personal distance—eighteen inches to four feet; and intimate distance—eighteen inches or less. If a close personal friend stands within the intimate distance, you will react positively. However, if overcrowding in a room or an elevator forces a stranger into that same proximity, you will feel uneasy until the area clears and the person can move away. In such a situation, you are disturbed because the relationship conflicts with the distance definition. Although reaction is strongest when others get too close, friends experience some tension, too, when they are forced by the room setup to carry on a conversation across a distance of fifteen or so feet. In the same way, when large groups are crowded into a limited space, or when small groups meet in cavernous rooms, people may sense the awkwardness of the arrangements without actually being aware of the cause. Appropriateness in use of space is an elusive quality, but it is important to the business environment as people interact with others in personal conversations and meetings and as organizers of functions consider space requirements and suitability.

Body Gestures

Body language, or kinesics, is the facet of nonverbal communication that people are most aware of. One way people disclose their reactions to situations is by their stance. In an important interview session, the interviewee may at first sit stiffly upright with knees together and hands in lap. Then as the interview proceeds, he or she may assume a more natural sitting position, leaning toward the interviewer at times in a move that suggests openness and interest. Thirty minutes after the interview, the same person may sit slumped in an easy chair and recount the details of the interview for a friend.

Hand gestures are another form of body language freely used in our society. Many speakers cannot give a speech or carry on a conversation without "talking with their hands." Open-arm gestures, which suggest expansiveness; pointing or directional movements, which emphasize directions or steps; and downward motions of the hand or fist to underscore points are integral parts of people's speech. These gestures contribute much to a speech—unless they are overly animated or distracting.

Facial expression also provides valuable information about a person's mood, reaction, and thoughts. A cocked eyebrow expresses surprise or doubt, a smile that involves only the mouth and not the eyes suggests falseness, a grin hints at openness more than does a controlled smile, and widely-opened eyes with dilated pupils indicate interest in the matter at hand. Eye contact is significant, too. A direct look suggests honesty, and averted eyes hint at deviousness or lack of self-confidence. Facial expressions are extremely important to communication in our culture.

Parent, Child, or Adult Roles

A different kind of unstated message is transmitted by the "role" you predominantly play. The psychological theory of transactional analysis states that every person, at various times, plays the part of the parent, the child, and the adult. The parent is the authoritarian role, with the "you should," "I ought," "they must," phrasing that stems from one's upbringing. The child, on the other hand, is unconcerned about the consequences of actions and very impulsive, using "I want," "let's," "I wish we could" language. In contrast to these two roles, the adult is neutral, rational, and objective, weighing pros and cons and making decisions on the basis of facts.

Obviously the only role suitable to the business environment is that of the adult, with a reasonable, unemotional approach. Neither the self-centered, inconsiderate child nor the hypercritical, authoritarian parent has a place in this setting. You might see the supervisor-employee relationship as being close to the parent-child pattern, but it is much more successful as an adult-adult relationship. A manager encourages more cooperation from employees by decreasing parent-child requests ("You must," "I want you to," or "You have to") and increasing adult-adult comments ("As we look to increasing our sales volume by 5%, we might consider initiating....").

Nonverbal communications consistently influence business interactions. Speakers acknowledge the effect of voice quality and body gestures in successfully transmitting messages, managers and organizers consider people's spatial and time needs when planning meetings and functions, and employees know, at least subconsciously, that their actions and appearance make distinct statements about them. Each person responding to these nonverbal messages should, however, insist upon using these cues purely as indicators or as corroboration—not as facts.

COMMUNICATING IN THE BUSINESS ENVIRONMENT

Speaking and writing provide the more reliable avenues for communicating messages. The predominant form, to be sure, is the spoken word. People speak briefly or at length in hallways, stop by offices for casual chats or weighty discussions, complete numerous telephone calls each day to people inside and outside the company, consider issues with committee members, and make presentations to groups of various sizes.

Paralleling these spoken communications, many different kinds of written documents allow employees to transact company business. These documents include project bids, complaint letters, contracts, requests for cost estimates, meeting announcements, expense reports, and study findings.

Those documents most frequently written are memos and letters. Memos abound within an organization and cover a wide spectrum of lengths and styles—from conversational, single-paragraph requests to formally-presented reports. For the independent business person and the company representative, the letter is the principal means of communicating with clients, sponsors, and suppliers. Inquiries, responses to others' inquiries, requests for adjustment, sales letters, and transmittal letters accompanying reports top the list as the most often written letters. Others are sent to acknowledge orders, to convey congratulations, to offer recommendations, to request payments on bills, and to place orders.

Reports, documents also essential to company operations, include periodic updates on expenses and activities, instruction manuals and documentation, summaries of testing procedures and results, progress reports, and project/study reports. Specialized professionals may also write lengthy definitions, explanations of processes, technical summaries of observed data, legal briefs, and analyses of loan requests.

Employees from the most to the least powerful carry out many of their duties by speaking and writing, and business effectiveness increases with improved communication skills.

THE STAGES OF COMMUNICATION

The communication cycle, whether oral or written, follows a clear progression from the beginnings of an idea to the considered response from the recipient of the message. As you embark on this process, you will work toward three goals: successfully conveying your intended message, obtaining the response you wish from your recipient, and maintaining goodwill with the other person or persons throughout the exchange.

Need to Communicate

The first step in the process is discovering the need to relay a message: to notify employees of a change in travel reimbursement procedure, to commend your sales director for April's outstanding sales performance, to submit an expense voucher for last week's business trip, or to acknowledge shipment of a customer's order. People write business communications because the need arises.

Choice of Communication Form

Once you verify the need for sending a message, you will select the most effective medium.

Person-to-person conversation gives the most personal contact, but is time-consuming and often impossible or unfeasible. A phone call offers the same personal touch and quickness of response, but in order for a phone call to be successful, you must find the person at his desk. Sometimes you can play a game of telephone tag for several days and continue to miss the person.

In such a situation, a memo could be a better alternative. By sending a memo you lose the advantage of the personal touch, but may save yourself time spent in telephoning. The memo also provides a written record of the transaction, which may be necessary when you are working out complex conference or contract details and need written verification of the agreed-upon arrangements. In such a situation, you may want to telephone the person to coordinate details, then follow up with a memo to confirm them. The memo assures you, too, that the person receives a full accounting of complicated information that might be misconstrued in the telephone conversation.

Memos also offer the advantage of communicating with several people at one time. If you need all five committee members present at an upcoming meeting, you will need to call each one to arrange a mutually acceptable date and time. However, if you are simply calling the meeting, you may send a memo; and, of course, for sending information to large groups, you will certainly need to send memos.

For speedy transmission of printed material, you may choose to send your message by fax. You might, for example, receive a telephone request for technical assistance from a client in Iowa, then call your equipment supplier in California to ask for documentation and technical advice on the cause of your client's problem. If the equipment representative is in the office and has the information readily available, he or she can fax it to you within minutes. You can then phone your client with advice that ideally will solve his or her problem. With fax technology, this problem-solving can be accomplished within an hour.

You have many considerations to weigh as you select the appropriate message form. The primary factors are maximum clarity, personal contact, speed of transmission, and convenience of the medium to both your and your audience.

Message Transmission

Once you have chosen your message medium, you will compose and convey the information. You will stop by your supervisor's office to ask a question, call your regional office to make a request, or draft a memo to your public relations director. But difficulties may delay the communication. You may be unable to give a verbal message because your supervisor is not in his office, or there may be a language barrier between you and the person you reach by phone. You may find yourself reluctant to begin writing because of writer's block, or find a backlog of work in the office with higher priority. Your secretary may be out sick and unable to type your letter. When you encounter such barriers, you may find it feasible to change your medium of transmission. Instead of stopping by your supervisor's office, you may send him a quick memo, provided your message does not require an urgent reply. Or you may choose to call your public relations director rather than sending a memo, and so bypass the secretarial delay. In most cases some kind of substitution is both possible and feasible.

Message Reception

If you have chosen the best message medium and have clearly expressed your information, your coworker, client or manager should receive the message you intended to convey—and you will have achieved the first of your communication goals. You may encounter difficulties at this stage in your client's being out of town or being too busy to read your memo or return your call. You may find response delayed, too, if your coworker puts your memo aside because of lack of interest. Unless you have sparked your advertising manager's interest in developing a new ad campaign to target young adults, she may choose to consider your memo later and handle more pressing business first. You can do little about people's demanding schedules, but realizing that wordy phone calls and memos are unwelcome, you can help insure positive response to your message by keeping your calls and memos or letters brief, clear, and to the point.

Feedback

Once your customer reads your letter or your supplier returns your call and you have made your offer or request, your part in the communication cycle is complete for the moment. At this stage your associate has the opportunity to respond—to subscribe to your service, to accept your offer, to supply the data you requested. Once the person composes an answer, he or she enters the communication cycle at stage one. A "yes" response will mean that you have achieved your second goal in the communication: the person is responding as you wished.

If, as you have phrased your message, you have used reasonable, considerate language and your recipient has not felt coerced or patronized or belittled by your message, you will have achieved the last of your communication goals—maintaining your recipient's goodwill—and your exchange can be called successful.

DEFINING YOUR PURPOSE AND AUDIENCE

Once you generate an idea and determine your message medium, but before you begin writing, you need to determine precisely what your purpose is in sending the message. Do you want to inform or persuade? And what do you want your reader to do in response? You should be able to state your intent clearly: "In order to lessen the number of accidents in the shipping department, I am sending all department personnel a copy of the rules concerning safe vehicle operation."

Considering the composition and needs of your audience is also important. How knowledgeable is your audience about the information you are conveying? If you are writing to colleagues or coworkers in your field of specialization, you can use the jargon associated with your specialty, but if you are writing to a layperson, you will need to define terms or use simpler language.

What is the age level of your intended audience? If you are writing to teenagers, you will use a more informal approach than you would with a middle-aged group. What is the educational level of your target group? You will gear your word choice to the level of understanding of the majority of your audience. If you are sending information to members of a community organization, some of whom are not high school graduates, you will be especially careful to avoid using unfamiliar words that may confuse or insult them. On the other hand, if you are writing to a college official, you may assume more latitude in word choice.

What use will your audience make of your information? Will a purchaser learn how to operate a new video camera? Will community members be convinced to contribute to your fund-raising project? Will employees learn of a new project being initiated in your department? Will the staff member send you the files you request? Your audience needs to know very clearly what response is expected. Finally, what information does your audience need or want to know? You will select the material that is pertinent to your audience rather than including all details. Be wary of giving your reader more information than he or she needs to understand and follow through on the message. Unnecessary details confuse and dilute your message.

Frequently you will be writing to or for an audience unknown to you. You can only guess at the age, educational level, and technical expertise. Regardless of the amount of information you have on your audience and the number of people you are writing to, however, you should write as if to a single person—to encourage a more natural and personal approach.

ESSENTIAL WRITING CHARACTERISTICS

Many writing characteristics are important to business communications, but the most vital are five *C* qualities.

Clarity is by far the most important, whether the message is a purchase order for a computer system, announcement of an award competition, or preliminary market testing results. Understanding the message is vital because misunderstandings are costly to the company and the employee. If the reader has to call or write a follow-up to clarify some point, both time and money will be lost.

Conciseness easily ranks second as a valuable characteristic. With the considerable number of activities to be completed in each day's work, people appreciate conciseness in the messages they receive. Your aim in this environment is to convey your information in the fewest possible words—as long as you provide sufficient details and maintain a smooth style of expression. Make your request in one paragraph if that is all the space you need. Report your findings in two pages if you can include all the pertinent information in that length. Do not feel obligated to lengthen documents to impress your reader.

Completeness in supplying information is also important. You will supply all the details you consider pertinent to the situation at hand and may even provide answers to relevant questions that the other person may not have thought to ask. Business professionals depend on such completeness as a basis for sound decision-making.

Correctness in content, style, and form is vital to every document. To avoid making costly or embarrassing errors, you should double-check figures on costs, revenue projections, inventory, and processing weights as well as the computation of numbers and placement of decimal points. No professional likes sending out a second memo correcting the information given in the first, making a public apology for a misstatement, or explaining to the board the reasons for a major miscalculation. You can avoid such costly and image-damaging mistakes by diligently proofreading work before sending it out. Correctness in the use of language is also important in that it reflects on the writer, positively or negatively. Misuse of words, sentence structure errors, misspellings, and confusing punctuation lessen a writer's professional image. Any writer who has difficulty using language accurately will find it necessary to double his or her efforts in proofreading, to use computer spell-checks, and to ask other people to look over work before it goes out. No document should go out with such errors.

Coherence, the smooth flow of words, sentences, and paragraphs, is fundamental to the readability of a document. In testing for coherence, you can read through your document to detect gaps between thoughts and unclear points. Anything that causes your reader to stop—whether to determine your exact meaning, to wonder about the connection between two ideas, or to notice the abruptness between statements—can be considered a flaw in coherence. You may need to elaborate on an idea, add a transitional word, or combine two sentences to lessen abruptness. If your reader can read through your entire document without interruption, it is coherent.

Several other characteristics are significant to business communications, including the following abilities:

- to write quickly and meet document deadlines.
- to write *to* rather than *at* people.

■■■ to stay on the subject without digressing.
■■■ to revise until the document is right.
■■■ to insist on an attractive appearance for documents.
■■■ to consistently maintain a professional tone and manner.
These and other characteristics are discussed in greater detail in later chapters of this book.

CHAPTER PERSPECTIVE

Communication—nonverbal, oral, and written—sustains business and industry operating functions. Handling information exchanges successfully is vital to both the people involved and the businesses themselves. As a recent survey indicates, the major problems in writing frequently are deciding what to say, organizing the message, expressing information clearly and concisely, and translating technical knowledge into generally understandable terms.[1] These and other essential facets of written and spoken communication serve as the focus for this book.

FOOTNOTE

1 *Unpublished survey conducted by Clemson University Department of English, May 1986, soliciting opinions of 75 business professionals.*

Style

INTRODUCTION AND MAIN POINTS

> "She always does her job with such flair and *style*."
> "The car is fuel-efficient, but I can't abide its *style*."
> "The report is convincing, but its *style* is ponderous."

Style is an elusive concept, sometimes noticed for its presence, sometime for its absence. Anyone or anything (including a business document) can have it—or lack it. Although it is difficult to define, style is an essential consideration in business communications because it can influence the reader's response to any message.

This abstract quality called "style" incorporates a variety of elements, and it is manifested in many ways. When you look in your closet to select a suit for an important conference, you consider the combination of fabric, texture, color, and cut. No single quality entirely defines the suit's style, but any one element (heaviness, brightness, severity of tailoring) might cause you to pass by one suit and consider others. In the same way, word choices, voices of verbs, sentence patterns, and paragraph length contribute to the sense of style in writing. In discussing the relationships among these elements, we will necessarily touch on matters of wording, sentence structure, and organization that will receive closer examination in succeeding chapters.

After reading this chapter:

■ You will recognize writing practices that produce clarity, conciseness, and exactness.

■ You will be able to arrange material within sentences and paragraphs to emphasize focal points.

■ You will be able to tailor your language to produce the tone appropriate to your message.

CONCISENESS

Conciseness is essential to business writing. Although some writers apparently believe that length impresses readers, it is brevity that readers most appreciate. Because of the number of memos, letters, reports, bulletins, and pamphlets that cross a typical business person's desk each day, writers of these documents should strive for conciseness. Ability to convey complex and detailed information within a limited space is a valuable skill for any business writer.

In composing business documents, you can generally follow the guideline "less is more." Compare the effect of "the man who was our president last year" with "last year's president," or "I would very much like to express my appreciation for your participation" with "Thank you for your participation." Using fewer words gives each word increased significance and thus intensifies your style.

In editing for conciseness, however, you should guard against condensing to the point of either choppiness or incompleteness. If your style is so compact that it is abrupt, your reader will be distracted or irritated by the phrasing. Maintain fluidity as you edit, utilizing smooth transitions and a variety of sentence patterns to give balance. Be careful, too, to assure the completeness of your message. Do not omit essential information or leave questions unanswered solely in the interest of compactness. If your reader has to follow up with a query to clarify details, you lose the advantage of conciseness.

You can eliminate two of the major causes of verbiage by avoiding the redundancies common to speech and the wordy constructions of jargon or bureaucratese.

Eliminating Speech Redundancies

Although writers are frequently told to "write the way you speak," spoken and written communication forms do differ. Because we speak at a faster pace than we write, spoken language is necessarily more wordy and repetitive. Speakers need time to construct their flow of ideas, and listeners need time to comprehend information.

Written language, on the other hand, should be more compact. It omits or condenses many of the wordy phrases common to spoken language:

- *"It is important to note that"*
- *"There are* three sessions to be offered"
- "in *the month of* May"

▪ "consensus *of opinion*"
▪ "five *short* weeks"
▪ *"complete* stop"
▪ "off *of"*
It discourages such redundancies as:
▪ "due to the fact that" (because)
▪ "in the near future" (soon)
▪ "on the grounds that" (if)
▪ "for the purpose of" (to)
▪ "with regard to" (about)
▪ "in view of the foregoing circumstances" (thus)
▪ "in the event that" (if)

Wordy phrasing can benefit from even minor editing, as the following paragraphs illustrate:

Wordy:

> There is a need to give the employees of Bryant Steel a safer and healthier work environment. If we provide a cleaner, safer, and healthier work environment, the attitudes of the employees will become more pleasant. This is clearly a benefit to the company as well as to the employees. It is important to have a satisfied work force because this will reduce job turnover, which results in a savings from hiring and training costs. It also gives the company a reputation for being sympathetic towards the problems of its employees. (90 words)

Revised:

> Bryant Steel should provide a safer, healthier work environment for its employees. Benefits to the employees would be greater safety and improved morale, and those to the company would be reduced employee turnover, decreased hiring and training costs, and better management-employee relations. (43 words)

After you have drafted any document, you should reread it, listening for these weakening redundancies. Eliminate any phrases that are not vital to the meaning or sentence balance. Condensing gives your style more power.

Avoiding Jargon or Bureaucratese

In its limited sense, jargon refers to that language particular to any discipline or profession. However, it has taken on a wider meaning in referring to writing that is intentionally or unintentionally wordy, repetitious, and obscure. Often it is the badge of those who are "in," but anyone who develops the habit of writing in jargon is in danger of obscuring meaning for—and exceeding the patience of—all readers. Examples of such language include "negative cash-flow position" to refer to a shortness of money, "frame-supported tension structure" to describe a tent, and "therapeutic misadventure" to refer to a nurse's giving the wrong IV fluid to a patient and causing his death. Other examples abound:

> Simply stated, travel that is incident to travel that involves the performance of work while traveling means travel to a point at which an employee begins to perform work while traveling or travel from a point at which an employee ceases performing work while traveling.

> Having espoused ourselves as advocates of linkage [in our relationship with the Soviets], or having portrayed ourselves as advocates of linkage, I would not want to suggest that what we're talking about is a mechanistic score-keeping, day-to-day rundown of explicit reciprocity.

Some professions or agencies—for instance, law, medicine, government departments, insurance, education, and sociology—seem more inclined than others to use jargon. However, many people writing documents intended for the layman are attempting to simplify their language and decrease the reliance on jargon. The "Plain English" movement, supported by legislation in some states, is producing greater readability in state and local laws, insurance policies, contracts, wills, and other written agreements or directives. Granted, such documents must include all the details considered pertinent to transactions, but intended readers have a right to understand their meaning. When you are writing such documents, you should consider the knowledge level of your audience to determine the amount of specialized language you can safely use.

Business communications in general should use simple and direct language, without circular phrasing that confuses the reader or empty phrasing that offers little substance. One way you can avoid stilted language is to concentrate on action verbs and participles rather than on noun phrases. Use the verbs "analyze," "transport," and "complete," or the participles "analyzing," "transporting," and "completing," rather than the noun phrases "the analysis of," "the transportation of," and "the completion of." The shorter forms produce a livelier, more direct, more readable style.

Another way to keep your styling natural is to avoid the popular buzzwords and phrases that proliferate in business and communications:

- parameter
- at this point in time
- scenario
- cognizance
- interface
- policywise
- commonality of interests

and such "-ize" words as:

- finalize
- maximize
- prioritize
- strategize
- conceptualize

You should also omit such "business" language as "allow me to express," "as per your instructions," "we beg to acknowledge receipt," "thanking you in advance," and "please be advised that." These expressions, while they may have been a standard part of business communications in years past, sound outdated and stiffly formal. Read every document aloud before you send it, to test for conversational (but not colloquial) quality. If your style sounds stuffy, wordy, and circular, simplify. Letters and memos especially depend upon this conversational quality to maintain a natural and congenial tone.

Another way to avoid bureaucratese is to use active voice rather than the passive. Active voice constructions begin with and focus on the actor: "After *you* developed the projections...." Passive voice, on the other hand, focuses on the receiver of the action: "After the *projections* were developed...." The active voice is concise and straightforward: "I *appreciate* your prompt attention," "Please *send* me a copy of last month's expense report," "Bender and Howells *sent* us their project proposal on May 15." Active-voice construction identifies and credits the actor: "Sandra Caughman *reports* an error in the March gross figures."

In reports, the writer may de-emphasize his or her role in collecting data, making projections, or trouble-shooting a problem—and focus on the substance of the report. Thus, reports often use the passive voice to emphasize the results, omitting reference to the actor: "Cost estimates *were* derived from last year's figures," "Respondents *were* surveyed by means of a three-page questionnaire," "The contract *was* delivered by its October 30 deadline." However, because passive voice creates distance between writer and reader and slows the pace of a document, you should use it sparingly. If you can use active voice, do so—changing "It *was* determined by the study that...." to "The study *shows* that...." and "It *can be* concluded from this study that...." to "This study *indicates*...."

EXACTNESS

Because corporate decisions are based on facts, the documents that guide those decisions must present detailed and exact information.

One way to be exact is to use specific references. The following entries show a general-to-specific flow:

▬ business person...manager...sales director...John McAuliff
▬ equipment...office machine...copier...Duplicraft 5000... #5301456

As you refer to objects and people, use the most exact reference feasible for your situation. Offer exact dates, figures on costs and projected savings, and names of personnel involved. Change references like "sometime in April" to "April 18," "significant savings" to "35% savings," and "substantial cost" to "$15,000"—or whatever the actual figures are. Give full and specific details on transactions and situations:

General:

> The representatives to the benefits committee have made some recommendations.

Specific:

> Our representatives to the ad hoc Benefits Enhancement Committee—Robert Epting, Julia Hastings, and Romero Cassada—have received responses from twenty-five employees in our department and have offered the following recommendations to the group:
> 1. Adoption of the dental coverage option
> 2. Elimination of the limited cancer coverage option
> 3. Elimination of the six-months' delay in the effectiveness of the major medical policy

Concentrate, too, on using specific verbs. Use action verbs rather than "to be" verbs. For "The report *is* on solid waste disposal," substitute "The report *centers on/concerns/focuses on/discusses* solid waste disposal." Use precise verbs: replace "go" with "vanish" or "extend" or "withdraw" or whatever verb exactly defines your meaning. Consistently offer specific language for greater value.

Exactness also comes from using concrete details. The mind can process images more effectively than it can handle abstractions, so references like "weekly call report," "3.5-inch diskette," "oily black liquid," "beetle-infested pine tree," "Facilities Maintenance Office" are easier to assimilate than are abstractions like "personnel," "professionalism," "bureaucracy," "administration," "environment," and "productivity." Abstract discussions lack readability and solid substance. Such language forces the reader to supply the specific examples, and the reader's mind might conjure images very different from those in the writer's mind. The writer takes a risk in leaving the reader to fill in the details. Every document needs a balance between abstractions for overview and concrete details for illustration.

Exactness in both phrasing and content is essential to writing for the business community. Few people have time for generalized discussions that omit the precise information necessary for drawing sound conclusions.

EMPHASIS

Emphasis also plays a part in writing clarity. By using the strong initial position, short sentences, and effective formatting, you can more precisely target the central points of your message.

Emphatic First Position

Because the beginning position in sentences, paragraphs, or entire documents is the strongest, you should use this position for important material. First words in sentences receive major emphasis, so sentences like *"It is important to note that* costs are increasing steadily" or *"There are* three employees from our department attending the meeting" are awkward because they focus on the insignificant *it* and *there*.

Sentences should open with a significant word:

- "Costs are increasing steadily."
- "Employees from our department attending the meeting are James Jackson, Bill Williams, and Janet Bonwell."
- "Six concurrent sessions will be offered."

■■■ "Next, place Part C over Part B at the juncture of the two pipes."

■■■ "Two new policies concerning extended leave will be implemented in June."

Just as the first word in a sentence is significant, so is the initial sentence in a paragraph. The first sentence is frequently the topic sentence, which serves as a guide to both the writer and reader because it provides the focus of the paragraph: "The potential benefits of the purchase are many," or "The DataLife program can be divided into three distinct segments," or "Our present check-in procedure causes a number of difficulties."

For the document as a whole, the first paragraphs provide direction. You may open a report with the purpose statement: "This study was designed to gather information on employees' reactions to and participation in the carpool incentive program instituted last January." In a memo or letter you will also indicate the substance of your message early: "The third meeting of the Finance Committee will take place on November 18 in Room 428," "Please note the following changes proposed by the Advisory Committee," or "Ryan, will you send me information on our agreement with Conrad and Associates to supply them information on our marketing research."

Whether in the sentence, the paragraph, or the document, the second most emphatic position is the close. You should end strongly. Do not close with phrasing that seems like an afterthought. Place transitional or parenthetical phrases like "on the other hand," "I believe," "so to speak," "at least thus far," in the middle rather than in the opening or closing. The final section is used for climactic points, offering summation and giving a sense of closure—as well as making closing requests. If you require follow-up action from your reader, state your request in the last paragraph so the person picks up on it. Then close with personal or public relations comments important to maintaining goodwill.

Short Sentences for Emphasis

Sentence length also influences emphasis. Short sentences are emphatic. They suggest action. Because their sound is abrupt, they receive more attention than do longer sentences. If you want to emphasize a point, state it in a short sentence. If you want to list several simple steps in a process, use a series of brief sentences to set up a rhythm. Realize, however, that short sentences—unless used singly to emphasize one point or used in a series to set up a rhythm—may create a choppy, fragmented effect. Use short sentences deliberately and selectively rather than accidentally.

Visual Formatting Techniques

In addition to word position and sentence length, there are several formatting techniques you can use to emphasize wording or points. The most frequently-used techniques are:

(a) underlining:	Place <u>all</u> parts in the basket provided.
(b) boldface:	**Warning: Allow the plate to cool before you attach Part B.**
(c) all capitals:	PLEASE COMPLETE THIS FORM BY AUGUST 15.
(d) tabulating:	The following departments will partic-ipate in the program:

      1. Accounting
      2. Marketing
      3. Transportation

You may also emphasize material by setting off single words, phrases, sentences, or entire paragraphs from the rest of the paragraph:

Please send me the following items:

1 French conversation manual with 3 cassettes		$34.95
1 French-English dictionary		<u>$21.95</u>
	Total	$56.90

Memo and report headings also use formatting techniques to show the relationship between sections. First-, second-, and third-level headings (discussed fully in Chapter 10) may be used in a presentation such as this:

EVALUATION OF FACILITIES
PARKING
Metered Parking. That area designated as metered parking....

These visual formatting techniques, like short sentences, are strong, so you should use them sparingly. Overuse leads to a tiring or strained style. Emphasis is an aspect of writing that escapes inexperienced writers, but by using these guidelines you will produce cleaner, more readable work.

WORD CHOICE

Word choice allows you much control over the tone of your document. Degree of formality, complexity and originality of phrasing, connotations as well as dictionary definitions of words, and sexist associations are among the factors you must consider in choosing words.

Degree of Formality

The degree of formality and informality of the language you choose depends largely upon the relationship between you and your readers. You will use a more formal style when writing to a large group of people, to people you have not met, and to your superiors, especially if you work in a large corporation. On the other hand, you may use an informal or even casual style when writing to a coworker or client whom you know well, or to your supervisor if you work in a small company that encourages informality and close working relationships.

The purpose of your document and its importance also influence the formality of your language. Because memos and letters often focus on immediate matters and goodwill among employees or between the company and its clients, their style may be moderately informal and personal. Reports, on the other hand, often present more substantive information that places them in a department's permanent files. Because of their long-lasting importance, and because they are frequently sent to supervisors, they usually employ a more formal style.

In a formal style, you will avoid contractions and use more multisyllabic words, long paragraphs, third person ("he," "she," "they"), and more passive voice. Informal phrasing, on the other hand, approaches a conversational style in using simpler words, shorter paragraphs, first and second person references ("I," "we," "you"), active voice, some contractions, and sometimes the person's name within the message. To illustrate, formal phrasing might read:

> Assessment of the water quality in the Lanyon region was based on tests to determine trace amounts of the following pollutants:
>
> 1. Lead and mercury
> 2. Arsenic
> 3. Nitrates

4. Phosphates
5. Bacteria

Informal expression of the same information might read:

> Jim, we checked the water in the Lanyon area for lead and
> mercury, arsenic, nitrates, phosphates, and bacteria.

On either level, you need to be wary of extremes. When you choose formal language, do not lapse into a stilted style, and when you are using an informal style, do not become *too* casual. Phrases such as "great" (to mean "very good"), "a lot" (for "much" or "many"), "you" to refer to people in general and slang expressions are appropriate to conversations but not to written messages. Your writing should maintain a professional manner at all times. If you choose to use a slang or coined word for effect, use quotation marks to show that you are using it deliberately: "The shelter was designed to survive a 'nuclear event'."

Your language in a document always affects your reader's reaction to the message, and sometimes your choice of phrasing may be inappropriate. If you use stiffly formal phrasing in a memo to a close coworker, you may offend the person because the tone suggests some cooling in the relationship. On the other hand, if you use a casual and flippant tone for a feasibility report that you send to the president, you may provoke a negative reaction, even if the data and conclusions are worthwhile and convincing. The tone of the document should clearly illustrate the writer-reader relationship and the purpose of the document.

Simple Phrasing

Although you may be tempted to use complex, Latinate phrasing ("articulate" rather than "say") to create a favorable impression on your reader, realize that most people appreciate clean, simple phrasing that is easy to read quickly. Documents that transact business should maintain clarity and readability, and these qualities rely on simplicity.

Simple language offers two distinct advantages: it is lively and it is easy to understand. If you consistently use multisyllabic words, you run the risk of people's not recognizing the meaning of the words. Your readers may be both confused about the meanings and offended by your use of words unfamiliar to them. As you write, concentrate on using the language your audience knows and on simplifying complex wording to develop a readable style. Make such substitutions as "equal" for "equivalent"; "aware" for "cognizant"; "decide" or "determine" for "ascertain"; and "begin" or "start" for "initiate." Although certainly you will use some words of three or more syllables in your writing, you should focus on achieving a natural and congenial style, especially in memos and letters.

Sometimes complex phrases need to be rearranged for clarity. Those such as *"limited duration protective/reactive* strikes," "materials for *product-water contact* surfaces," *"minimum nutritional quality* guidelines" are so compact that they are unwieldy. In situations such as these, a writer can break up the phrases into smaller, more readable units: "protective/reactive strikes of limited duration," "material for any surface providing product-water contact," and "guidelines for minimum nutritional quality."

Clichés

Clichés, overused phrases or sayings, such as "time and time again," "climbing the corporate ladder," "the lion's share," "bat around an idea," and "it's in the bag" weaken a writer's style because of their staleness. Original wording, even if it is less descriptive than the cliché, is preferable to trite, overworked expressions.

Neutral, Positive and Negative Phrasing

You choose some words because of their connotations. The denotative meaning of a word, its dictionary definition, is objective, with no emotional associations attached. For example, "nurture" is defined as "fostering, educating, or providing with nourishment." However, the connotative meaning of the word— its emotional association—suggests warmth, concern, and guidance. Emotionally-charged words are almost impossible to use in only their denotative sense; their connotations follow them. In business communications, though, the language you select for reports should be objective and neutral in connotation. When you do use phrasing with emotional associations (in letters and memos), choose words with positive rather than negative implications.

Reports, on the whole, aim at objectivity. A researcher/writer is expected to present an unbiased report on such matters as the procedures and results of testing, the findings of a study, or the subjects discussed at a meeting. In writing such a report, you will remain neutral both in attitude and language and avoid interjecting your personal opinions by using such words as "admirable," "excellent," "efficient."

Memos and letters, on the other hand, may use words with positive connotations to persuade and to generate acceptance and a sense of goodwill. Words like "genuine," "improvement," "benefit," "aspire," "admirable," "reasonable," "satisfactory," "notable," "expedite" evoke positive responses and aid in persuasion. One of the major writing characteristics of memos and letters is enthusiasm and a positive attitude, so your message benefits from using words with an upbeat tone.

Negative phrasing, on the other hand, produces negative responses. Words like "reject," "must," "allege," "squander," "impossible," "flimsy," "fault," "waste," "wrong," "cheap," "insincere," "extravagant" elicit unfavorable reactions from readers and should be avoided in business communications. Negative comments that may be acceptable when spoken often become unacceptable when written because the negative quality is intensified once a statement is put to paper. With this fact in mind, you would be wise to moderate the tone of any negative message that you must write. Instead of saying dismissively, "This is not the kind of data I want," you might say, "Please redirect your survey to emphasize...." In addition, you may make some of these substitutions:

> you must—you should, we require, we suggest, please (do)
> wrong—incorrect, erroneous, unsubstantiated
> cheap—inexpensive, cost-efficient, economical

Although making a conscious effort to rephrase harshly negative language means taking additional time in writing, the results are gratifying. Using a neutral or positive tone cannot guarantee acceptance, of course, but using a negative tone will surely produce an unpleasant reaction—and in all situations writers should avoid using language that is abusive, sarcastic, or insulting.

Sexist Language

Intentional or unintentional use of sexist language is offensive to many people. Because the English language has no generic pronoun except the awkwardly impersonal "one," we have usually used "he" for generic references. However, as our business community becomes more sensitive to the implications of such usage, we have looked for alternatives.

One option is converting singular constructions to plural. Changing "each manager...he" to "managers...they" or "the nurse...she" to "nurses...they" removes the implications that all managers are men and all nurses are women. Another alternative is the phrasing "he or she" and "he/she" if you need to draw on the construction only sparingly. Repeated usage, however, becomes irritating and distracting. Occasionally writers have chosen to alternate use of "he" and "she" for successive references, and that technique may prove to be a workable alternative. A third option is to rephrase a sentence to avoid the pronoun altogether. Rather than "Each employee should submit his expense voucher by May 10," you may write "Employees should submit expense vouchers by May 10."

Certainly some people go to extremes in attempting to purge the word "man" from the language, resulting in such awkward phrasing as "personhole cover," "waitperson," "sportsperson," and "personkind." However, every writer should be careful to avoid using references that explicitly or implicitly suggest sexism.

CHAPTER PERSPECTIVE

Writing style is unique to each person. Your style is yours alone, but you need to adapt it to the audiences and circumstances you encounter. The principles presented in this chapter provide means to sharpen the facets of style. Basically, these principles are insistence on strong, concise, exact wording; use of short sentences, first position, and active voice for emphatic points; and adoption of neutral language for reports and positive language for letters and memos. As you incorporate these practices into the fabric of your style, you will improve your writing as a whole.

Organization

INTRODUCTION AND MAIN POINTS

If you have ever had difficulty following the sequence of someone's speech or report, you are well aware of the fact that brilliant content can be undercut by confused organization. In fact, the value of the information can be lost entirely if the reader or listener is required to work too hard to decipher its meaning.

In every kind of presentation, the obligation of the writer or speaker, in addition to offering quality content, is to arrange the material—the phone inquiry, the quarterly sales report, the meeting agenda, the test results, the memo request—in an order easy for people to follow. This chapter will focus on the logical organization of information at every level of the document.

After reading this chapter:

■ You will be able to choose sentence patterns that encourage the logical flow of information in sentences and paragraphs.

■ You can develop a logical and workable progression of points in paragraphs and documents.

■ You can use phrasing techniques that illustrate the connections between segments of the document.

COMPOSING EFFECTIVE SENTENCES

Excellence in communication begins with sentences that present words and phrases in a comprehensible order. Documents that contain mangled sentence constructions, interruptions in sentence flow, and confusing arrangement of points both distract the reader and damage the writer's reputation. In contrast, documents using accurate syntax, balanced sentence rhythms, and a logical progression of segments produce favorable impressions of both the writer and the organization.

Sentence Types

As you deliver any message, you have three sentence structures from which to choose—simple, compound, and complex. In the makeup of your sentences, you will use both phrases and clauses, and the distinction between the two is clear: phrases are groups of words with no subject-verb set, and clauses are groups of words with at least one subject-verb set. Independent clauses, as their name implies, form complete statements, and dependent clauses do not.

Simple sentences contain only one independent clause and no dependent clause. Any of the units may be compound: "*Marion and Beatrice attended* the seminars in St. Louis and Kansas City." Most writers have little difficulty writing simple sentences, pairing singular subjects and singular verbs ("The *wisdom* of the decision *is* clear") and plural subjects with plural verbs ("The *figures indicate* sharply rising costs"). Occasionally, however, a complicated sentence will cause a writer to mismatch the subject and verb ("The projected *figures* on sales for next quarter *and* their *effect* on the budget *has* become a topic of concern to management"). Diligent proofreading should catch such sentence structure errors.

Compound sentences contain two or more independent clauses with no dependent clauses and, again, any of those elements may be compound: "This month's reports have just been completed, and they illustrate strong growth in our region." The two clauses are joined by a comma and a conjunction (*and*, *but*, *or*, *nor*, *for*, *yet*, *still*). All the ideas presented in compound sentences receive equal importance because of the balanced sentence construction.

Complex sentences contain one or more independent and one or more dependent clauses. The compound sentence above might be converted to a complex sentence by changing one of the independent clauses to a dependent one: "This month's reports, which have just been completed, indicate strong growth in our region." Complex sentences allow you to subordinate one or more points by placing them in dependent clauses and to emphasize other points by phrasing them as independent clauses.

Sentence Purposes

Within paragraphs, sentences serve three purposes: they introduce topics, they support discussions, and they conclude sections. A topic sentence introduces the subject being discussed in a particular paragraph, and most frequently in business communications this sentence begins the paragraph, enhancing document readability and reader understanding.

Supporting sentences offer examples, contrast issues, elaborate on points, and cite statistics. Every topic sentence needs from one to six supporting statements to develop and illustrate it.

Concluding sentences draw information together and provide a sense of finality. Not every paragraph will need a concluding sentence because some sections provide continuation of discussion from one paragaraph to the next. However, concluding remarks are necessary at the ends of sections to give a sense of completeness and closure.

Sentence Patterns

English is a language that depends on word order to show meaning. "The dog bit the man" and "The man bit the dog" use the same words, but the actions described are quite different. We are most accustomed to the patterns subject-verb-object ("Barnes initiated the investigation") and subject-verb ("Data collection was completed on August 29"). Sometimes a writer will seek variety or rhetorical emphasis by changing the expected pattern: "Coming in last today were the Belmont Stakes and the Kentucky Derby winners." This reversal does carry with it, however, the possibility of slowing the reading pace and making sentence errors such as this subject-verb disagreement: "Involved in the heated discussion *was* the chairman of the benefits committee and the insurance representative."

Sentence order also enhances organization by indicating points of emphasis. When you realize that the opening of a sentence is its most emphatic position, a theory discussed in Chapter 2, you will begin sentences with significant words—"Power struggles suggest...," "The Sony, in contrast, offers...," "Costs for July indicate...."—rather than beginning with inessential words such as "There is...," "It is notable that...," and "I wish to indicate that...."

Parallel structures, too, promote continuity in flow of points. When you group related subjects or ideas, when you show a progression, when you balance two points, you underscore those relationships by utilizing a series: "*Personnel Management Journal* has an appropriate number of photographs, *The Journal of Administrative Management* borders on having too many, and *Personnel Administration* has too few."

WRITING COHERENT PARAGRAPHS AND DOCUMENTS

Just as sentences contribute to paragraph integrity, so paragraphs determine the success of the whole document as they direct and develop the presentation of material.

Paragraph Clarity

Like sentences, paragraphs introduce, support, and conclude discussions. Introductions are usually short and definitive: one to three sentences for letters and memos and several paragraphs for reports. Opening sentences in letters and memos may offer congenial comments, and those in reports may discuss background information—but then they move quickly to stating the purpose of the document. A letter might begin, "Jim, I appreciated talking with your group in Dallas last week. Could you send me some additional information on the networking plan we discussed?" A report introduction might read:

> Midway Daycare Center, serving the Liberty Hill area, has seen a 50-percent increase in enrollment in the past four years, and its staff has grown comparably. The purpose of this study is to survey parents of children served by the center concerning the success of the operation. All aspects of the daycare operation were surveyed, including facilities, services, supervision, and child care.

Supporting paragraphs provide the richness and depth of content essential to the quality content of any document, and you have several different paragraph arrangements available. You may enumerate points:

> The log book should contain all of the following:
> 1. date and time the problem was noticed
> 2. description of the problem
> 3. serial number of the damaged hardware
> 4. name of the operator reporting the problem.

You may compare and contrast:

> UV-A and UV-B rays differ in their roles in tanning. UV-B rays trigger the tanning process by encouraging the production of melanin. Only a minimum of UV-B is required for this process, and overexposure will result in the all-too-familiar sunburn. UV-A rays, the safest and most effective of the rays emitted by the sun, promote tanning without sunburn by causing the melanin to darken.

You may classify:

> Class A fires involve wood, paper, fabrics, upholstery, plastic and similar common combustibles, which water, available in sufficient quantity, would ordinarily extinguish. Class B fires involve burning grease, oil, paint, solvents and other flammable liquids. This is the type of fire most likely to break out in or around a kitchen stove, or in a garage. Class C fires involve electrical wires, motors or other equipment where non-conducting extinguishing liquids, powders or other agents are required.[1]

You may define a concept, explain a term, or describe an object:

> Fragile X [is] the most common inherited form of mental retardation, with symptoms ranging from mild learning disabilities to severe mental retardation. It's found in one of every 1,000 males and one in 660 females.... Fragile X is named after a mutation of the X chromosome, the tip of which under a microscope sometimes appears to hang by a thread. The defective gene is located within that "fragile" site. The Fragile X gene may produce a faulty protein unable to carry messages among brain cells. That would cause impaired mental functioning.[2]

Concluding paragraphs offer closure to any discussion. Letters and memos often end with a request for action and make suitable public relations comments: "Can you let us know your response by September 1? Our Rotary Club members would appreciate hearing about your initiation of the adult literacy program and its success in the Amarillo area." For a report you will close, without adding new information, by summarizing important points, drawing conclusions from information presented, or making recommendations for future actions. Your survey of daycare patrons might conclude with statements like:

> The parents' overall response to the Midway Daycare Center was positive. Most (68 percent) gave the center an overall rating of *above average*. Facets of the operation they commended

continues on next page

were playground and playroom supervision, playground facilities, the after-school program, and workers' care and concern for the children, all of which at least 60 percent of the parents rated as *above average* or *excellent*. Areas they considered slightly less satisfactory were the kitchen and nap area, TV instruction, and supervision during meals. These areas, as this survey indicates, need at least moderate improvement and upgrading to allow Midway to continue providing excellent care to the children of Liberty Hill.

Logical Document Arrangement

Coherent organization of document segments is central to the success of your message, and although the whole document is the culmination of the writing process, deciding on your order of points is, in fact, one of your first considerations.

Your initial steps in preparing to write, of course, are determining your purpose and analyzing your audience, the stages discussed in Chapter 1. Once you have clearly recognized your purpose, you will jot down the major points you will use in your discussion and organize them into what seems to be the most logical order.

As you consider this arrangement, you will weigh the merits of direct and indirect order. In most documents you will use direct order—progressing from general to specific—making clear in your initial section the purpose of your presentation. Then you will elaborate on your points, offering sufficient illustration and statistics to convince your reader or listener of the validity of your message.

In some documents, however, especially those asking people for favors, money, or time commitments, you will find that using indirect order is more conducive to a positive response. You will reverse the direction—moving from specific to general—enumerating your points, such as problems associated with working with a limited staff, then offering your proposal, such as the employment of temporary workers to ease peak-season work loads.

Once you decide whether to proceed directly or indirectly, you will choose the most sensible arrangement of points within that order. Proceeding through enumeration of points allows you to develop your discussion by citing illustrations or examples. This pattern is appropriate to both direct order, in which you state your purpose or overview at the outset, and indirect order, in which your examples culminate with a proposal or recommendation. Enumeration is appropriate for presenting such information as the causes of stress among employees, the difficulties associated with the present shipping procedures, the results expected from implementing after-hours foreign language classes, salary averages in the region, and readings on test results.

Order of importance, progressing from most to least important, is preferable for situations in which you want to show ranked order—short lists of candidates for a position, members' preferences for the site of the next regional professional meeting, recommendations for equipment purchase, or rankings of priorities.

Climactic order, which allows you to build to the most significant or final point, is useful for such situations as evaluating the effectiveness of each stage of your production line, noting the spread of a plant disease in various areas of the state, or proposing incentive programs for lowering employee absenteeism.

Spatial arrangement, which describes or refers to a particular object or structure, uses a clear sequential order—right to left, top to bottom, inside to outside, or front to back. This order is suitable for describing, room by room, the renovation of a building, the installation of electrical lines, or the offices assigned to employees. It is also useful for describing objects such as a proposed protective suit for firefighters, or for showing geographical layout.

Chronological arrangement is best for presenting information in the order in which it happened or will happen: trip or meeting reports, test procedures or results, agendas, instructions, or description of a process. Use a chronological sequence, however, when it promotes maximum understanding, not simply when it is the most convenient order to use. Even though you carry out projects and studies by completing functions sequentially, you should not necessarily arrange project or study reports in chronological order. It may well be more effective to present the material by enumerating points (apartment comfort, facilities, parking, maintenance), showing order of importance (first- to last-ranked), or using climactic order (order of increasing importance).

DEVELOPING COHERENCE BETWEEN SEGMENTS

After you select the kind of organization most logical for your discussion, you will use phrasing that insures uninterrupted flow from point to point. Judicious repetition of key words is one method that creates coherence between sentences. Use of pronouns is another:

Power is the currency of all office relationships. *It's* the ability to cause something to happen or not to happen. *It* involves influencing and negotiating with coworkers to get the job done. In most organizations, getting others to cooperate is at least as great a challenge as doing the work. *Power* facilitates cooperation because, if people believe you have influence, they will work with you more readily. Most people covet *power* in work situations because *it* means having control over events.[3]

Selected use of transitional words and phrases provides a third reliable method for providing connection between statements. You have a choice of several different kinds of transitional words to illustrate relationships between ideas:

Addition — also, too, in addition, second, third, finally, another, furthermore, moreover

Contrast — on the other hand, but, in contrast, however, though, although, yet, still, on the contrary

Result — therefore, as a result, thus, in summary, as a consequence, hence, in conclusion

Condition — granted, it is true, certainly, of course, provided that, even though, although

Time — afterwards, until then, henceforth, at the same time, as soon as, while, in the meantime, currently

Example — for example, in particular, for instance, namely, that is, to illustrate, specifically

Parallel structures also promote coherence. When you express a group of ideas in parallel structure, you set up a rhythm that enhances smoothness and increases readability: "People may not seek counseling for stress for a variety of reasons: denial of the existence of a problem, belief that adults should be able to cope with their own stress, fear of damage to their reputation, and lack of awareness of counseling services available."

As you read through your completed document in testing for coherence, you will listen for breaks between statements and paragraphs. You may need to add transitional phrasing to bridge gaps, you may change a noun to a pronoun to eliminate repetitiveness, you may convert several short sentences to one sentence with a series, or you may add phrasing to "round out" the rhythm of the sentence. Your aim is to keep the flow of information connected in both content and expression.

CHAPTER PERSPECTIVE

Whether at the level of thinking or of composing, disorganization is a key area of difficulty in any kind of presentation. Unclear organization fails to represent hard work done on a project, undermines worthwhile suggestions, and causes reader confusion. Selecting logical arrangements and establishing clear connection between segments will enhance your success in conveying your message because readers and listeners can focus on the content itself, and this, of course, benefits you and your organization.

FOOTNOTES

1 *Bernard Gladstone, "Home Improvement,"* New York Times, *March 9, 1978, p. 22.*

2 *"Medicine,"* Newsweek, *June 10, 1991, p. 61.*

3 *Marilyn Moats Kennedy, "How to Build a Power Base,"* Business Week's Guide to Careers, *[n.d.], pp. 21-22.*

Frequently Made Errors

INTRODUCTION AND MAIN POINTS

You have written a fine proposal. You send it for your supervisor's review and (you expect) enthusiastic approval. It comes back to your desk virtually without comment, but the reader has underscored three punctuation marks and two misspelled words on the first two pages and has drawn a line from a circled "everyone" to a circled "their." While a slip of the pen (or of the fingers on a keyboard) might be understandable in a hastily written interoffice note to one of your peers, you are responsible for the correctness of anything that leaves your office under your initials or over your signature. If glaring syntax, grammar, or word choice errors cause the reader to question the quality of your written communications, he or she will next begin to wonder about the general accuracy of your work. Is a careless writer also a careless thinker? Perhaps the inference is unfair, but appearances do count. Many a job application has landed in the wastebasket because it was addressed to the "Personal Officer" rather than the Personnel Officer. Some mistakes cause delays and provoke impatience, and other mistakes can be even more costly.

This chapter offers a selective review of common errors in grammar and punctuation, word choice, the placement of words and phrases, and spelling. The assumption here is that your increased awareness of some potential trouble spots will stimulate your overall watchfulness.

After reviewing the material in this chapter:

▬ You should feel secure in handling familiar grammar and punctuation choices.

▬ You will know how misplacing a word or a phrase can mislead the reader.

▬ You will avoid many of the common confusions of one word for another that is similar in sound, spelling, or meaning.

CLEAR CHANNELS

Two people meet and extend their right hands in a gesture of greeting. In this widely used ritual, offering the left hand would be either a sign of ignorance or a deliberate insult. Like body language and gestures, communicating in words is a social phenomenon, dependent on mutual understanding of conventional meanings, patterns, and contexts. As some physical cues (a wink, a confidential nod) suggest close or casual acquaintance, others (folded arms, a deep bow) define ceremonious distance. In the same way, some levels of language are best suited to everyday speech and to casual notes, while others reflect the polished detachment required in the public arena. Over the telephone you wish your partner "a lotta luck" in negotiating the deal, but in a letter you wish your client "much success" in building an investment portfolio.

Some choices in grammar and wording are simply right or wrong, but other kinds of choices convey subtle, deliberate gradations of meaning and intent. For instance, you might occasionally have a good reason to include a colloquial expression in a generally formal context. Your first responsibility is to know exactly what you mean to say and why—and to say it in a way that every reader should understand. In other words, you will try to keep your communications channels free of the annoying static that comes from faulty punctuation, inconsistencies in grammar, unclearly structured sentences, vague or ambiguous wording, and incorrect spelling.

Punctuation Errors

To avoid errors in punctuation, you must know what kinds of clauses and phrases you are working with. Do you need a terminal mark of punctuation (period, question mark, exclamation point) because you are at the end of a sentence? Or do you need to show the relationships within a compound or complex sentence with an intermediate-level punctuation mark (colon, semicolon) or a minor mark (comma)?

Two major punctuation errors, the sentence fragment and the comma splice, result from confusion about what a sentence is. To have a complete sentence, you need at least one main clause (a subject and a verb). A sentence fragment occurs when a phrase ("assuming the accuracy of the figures") or a subordinate clause ("after you have completed your arrangements") is punctuated as if it were a full sentence. A comma splice results when a comma, the weakest mark of punctuation, stands alone between two main clauses: "His sense of direction had failed, he was lost." You can correct a comma splice in three ways:

Create separate sentences:

> "His sense of direction had failed. He was lost."

Use a semicolon between parallel or closely related ideas:

> "His sense of direction had failed; he was lost."

Subordinate one of the clauses:

> "Since his sense of direction had failed, he was lost."

Many comma splices are caused by the presence of the adverb "then" or the conjunctive adverbs "however" and "therefore" between clauses.

incorrect:
> Set the left margin, then measure the right one.

correct:
> Set the left margin; then measure the right one.
> Set the left margin, then the right one.
> > (original second clause now reduced to a phrase).

incorrect:
> Use a justified left margin, however, leave the right one unjustified.

correct:
> Use a justified left margin; however, leave the right one unjustified.
> Use a justified left margin. Leave the right one unjustified, however.
> > (The changed position makes "however" a minor parenthetic element, to be set off by a comma. It is no longer a conjunctive adverb between clauses.)

Colons and semicolons are useful for showing relationships between ideas. They show balanced contrasts and cause-effect patterns, or they create lists within sentences. *Semicolons,* as you see in the examples above, allow you to balance equally important ideas, often expressed in parallel phrasing. When one a, b, c series is contained within another, semicolons clarify the groupings: "Also invited are Continental's President, Angela Rourke; First Federal's Vice President, Daniel O'Connell; and Capital Investment's Executive Secretary, Vladimir Rudowski." *Colons* introduce restatements and brief examples:

> Only one action is left to us: we must complete the merger.

> Trade imbalance has hurt many traditional economic strongholds: textile production, car sales, and steel exports have suffered.

Use a colon to set off a list *added to* a complete clause, but do not use the colon when the list functions as *a part of* the clause:

incorrect:

> For the next leg of the trip, bring only: light clothing, your wallet or purse, your passport, and, if you wish, a camera.

correct:

> For the next leg of the trip, bring only light clothing, your wallet or purse, your passport, and, if you wish, a camera.

> For the next leg of the trip, bring only these things: light clothing, your wallet or purse, your passport, and, if you wish, a camera.
>> (In the second version, "these things" completes the clause. The list of items is now appended to the statement.)

Dashes and parentheses are interrupters. The *dash* signals surprise—or simulates a conversational burst of added thought. (Using *parentheses* to enclose a phrase or a clause suggests a lowering of the voice to make a confidential remark or to define a term in passing). Overuse of dashes, parentheses, colons, and semicolons can make your writing seem nervous and jerky. Save these punctuation marks for the sentences in which they will be truly effective.

The *apostrophe* is the most troublesome punctuation mark for many writers. Remember to make a noun singular or plural before adding the apostrophe as a sign of possession, as these examples show:

> The *company's* employees notified their *union's* officers.
> (one company, many employees, one union)
> The *companies'* employees notified their *unions'* officers.
> (several companies, many employees, several unions)

the child's choice (one child)
the children's choice (a group of children)

the woman's choice (one woman)
the women's choice (a group of women)

the people's choice (one collective city, state, or
national population)
the world's peoples' choices (one world, many
peoples, many choices)

Do not add an apostrophe to the possessive case of a personal pronoun: his, hers, its, yours, ours, theirs. The idea of possession is built into the spelling of these pronoun forms. Remember that "its" means "something belonging to *it*"—"The train moves on *its* track"—while "it's" never means anything except the contracted form of "it is": "The train has started its run, but it's (it is) running late." Similarly, do not write the interrogative pronoun "whose" ("Whose book is this?") when you mean to use the contraction of "who is" ("Who's coming now?")

Opinion is mixed on whether or not to use an apostrophe in forming plurals of letters, numbers, and references to some types of groups or sites, especially historical ones. In referring to a decade, some writers prefer "the 1990s," while others use "the 1990's." Local custom or the trademarked form of a name often dictates the choice between "The People's Bank" and "The Peoples Bank," "Farmers' Hall Restaurant" and "Farmers Hall Restaurant."

Quotation marks distinguish direct quotations from indirect ones:

direct quotation:

> She said, "I'll be there in a minute."

indirect quotation:

> She said that she would be here very soon.

selective quotation:

> She said that she would be here "in a minute."

Note that a comma follows a "verb of saying" (said, read, muttered, opined) when the verb introduces a direct quotation, but the comma is omitted before an indirect quotation. Follow these other conventions when you close a set of quotation marks.

1. Place a period or a comma before closing quotation marks:

   ". . . nattily attired," he said.

2. Place a question mark or (an exclamation point) inside closing quotation marks when only the quoted part of the sentence is a question (or an exclamation):

   She asked, "Are you ready?" He replied, "Yes, I'm ready!"

   Conversely, if the full sentence is question or an exclamation incorporating a quoted statement, the question mark or exclamation point follows the quotation marks:

   Did she say, "I'm ready"?

3. Never use two marks of terminal (end) punctuation at one time. In the incorrectly punctuated sentence

   He asked, "Shall we vote now?".

   the period is redundant, because the question mark terminates both the quoted question and the full sentence.

Agreement Errors

The process of matching singular subjects with singular verbs, plural subjects with plural verbs, singular pronouns with singular antecedents, and plural pronouns with plural antecedents seems easy—until certain distinctions come into play. While simple carelessness creates a sentence such as "Every person have their own opinion," one class of nouns, including "sports," "mathematics," "politics," and "news," causes many writers to pause, because these nouns look plural in form but name fields of endeavor in singular or collective senses. Politics "is," not "are," a risky profession.

Some company names cause similar problems in subject-verb and pronoun-antecedent matching. If the name ends in an -*s* (General Motors) or in "and Company" (Levi Strauss & Co.), the writer's ear hears a plural noun and signals the use of a plural verb (are) and plural pronouns (their products, their employees), even though the name refers to a single organization. Correct forms include:

> General Motors is introducing new models.
> Levi Strauss & Co. is increasing…(singular subject)
> Employees at Levi Strauss & Co. are celebrating…(plural subject)

The generally undesirable filler constructions "there is" and "there are" open temptations to subject-verb disagreements too. If you are unsure of the matching of subject and verb in a sentence like "There is several solutions available," drop "there," place the other elements in their normal order, and you will readily match "solutions" with the plural verb form "are."

Often a writer is thinking one way but transcribes the idea slightly differently, causing a disagreement of sentence elements. Inverted sentence order and phrases intruding between subject and verb are frequently troublesome here. A front-page newspaper story about the closing of a notable Atlanta high school included the sentence "Among the alumni attending were U.S. Sen. Wyche Fowler, Jr." Although the reporter was *thinking* "Sen. Fowler and other alumni were present," that is not how she *wrote* it. The prepositional phrase "Among the alumni" has no bearing in the matching of the original sentence's subject, "U.S. Sen. Wyche Fowler, Jr." and the appropriate verb form "was." In matching singular to singular and plural and plural, disregard any phrase (often beginning with "along with" or "as well as") appearing between the grammatical subject of the sentence and its verb. In saying "John as well as Marty is attending the 2:30 conference," you have chosen to make "John" the center of attention and thus the subject of "is"; Marty is a bystander whose intentions have already been established.

Colloquial or popular usage, including the influential tyrannies of newspaper, radio, television, and billboard advertising, condones some relaxations of grammatical correctness, but business writers will want to keep clear distinctions between the simulations of everyday speech in advertising and the more formal uses of most letters, memos, and reports. In announcing a national photography contest, a major film manufacturer defines eligibility this way in its newspaper ads: "An amateur *photographer* is any*one* who derives less than five percent of *their* income from photography." The subject "photographer" and the predicate nominative "anyone" are singular, while "their" is plural. Surely the photography giant's formal reports will use more formal matching of pronoun and antecedent: "Amateur *photographers* derive less than five percent of *their* income from photography," or "An amateur *photographer* is *one whose* income from picture-taking is less than five percent."

"Who" (subject) and "whom" (object) are especially confusing pronoun forms, and popular speech has further blurred their distinctions by using "who" for both subjects and objects.

correct:

>Who was elected?
>>(The pronoun is the subject of the verb).

colloquial:

>Who would you give the job to?
>>("You" is the subject of the sentence; the object of "to" should be "Whom").

correct:

>...for whom the bell tolls
>>(The pronoun is the object of the preposition "for").

correct:

>I am willing to work for whoever is elected company president.
>>(When a pronoun is both subject and object in a single sentence, its use in its own clause takes precedence. "Whoever" is the subject of "is elected," although the pronoun is also the object of the preposition "for").

correct:

>I am willing to work for whomever you ask to lead the company.
>>("Whomever" is the object of the verb "ask" and of the preposition "for").

Other Verb Problems

Verbs begin as infinitives (to be, to write, to create, to act, to buy) that are essentially indexes to a variety of forms through which an individual verb can express its subject's action or state of existence. Any verb form defines several qualities:

tense—

>is, are, shall be; buys, bought, will buy
>>(time relationship)

voice—

>active: "Our company bought General Tool."
>passive: "Our company was bought by General Tool."

mood—

>indicative: "We bought General Tool."
>>(fact)
>subjunctive: "If we had bought General Tool last year..."
>>(speculative idea)

imperative: "Complete the paperwork on buying
General Tool."
(command, with understood "you" as subject)

Although the forms of many verbs follow regular patterns, some
are irregular, and others come from confusingly similar infinitives. A person sits, but the same person sets an agenda, a table,
or a clock. The sun seems to set, not to sit, at the horizon. "To
lie" is doubly confusing, for it can mean "to recline" or "to fib,"
and it can be confused with "to lay," which means "to place"
(that is, to cause to lie down) in human actions, but for birds it
means "to produce eggs." As a noun, "lead" names a chemical
element, a weight, or the first in order; as an infinitive, it means
"to go first" or "to show the way." More confusingly still, the
simple past tense form of "to lead" is "led," which in turn is pronounced like the name of the metal. To clarify the principal parts
(present, past, past participle) of similar-sounding verbs, check
the beginning of the appropriate entry in a desk dictionary. A
grammar handbook will often outline further forms of troublesome verbs.

Word Choice: Saying What You Mean

A lawyer advertises an initial consultation "at no cost" to the
would-be plaintiff. A medical clinic offers a blood pressure check
"at no cost." Neither claim is exact, for either kind of consultation will require time, expertise, materials, and facilities that
carry some cost value. The lawyer means that the first consultation will not result in a billing for services rendered. The screen-
ing clinic and its sponsors will absorb the expenses of the health
test, which often has promotional value.

Some writers are content with the approximate rather than the
exact word, but approximations blur the picture. A second thought
would prevent many an error. If you write that someone "has
returned again" or that you have had the feeling of "déja vu again,"
you have created a twofold return, because "déja vu" and the prefix
"re-" mean "again." Banners in supermarket windows seldom distinguish between "everyday low prices" and "low prices every
day," although these are different constructions that call for different spellings of a key word. "Everyday," spelled as a single word,
is a modifier and should be followed by the noun it modifies.
However, in the sentence "We offer low prices every day," the
noun "day" is modified by the adjective "every." Maintain distinctions between "amount" and "number" or "among" and "between."

An amount is measured; a number is counted. "Between" links two persons or items; "among" links three or more.

Be especially careful of wording that suggests rank or group distinctions. You might "talk to" your subordinates, but you "talk with" someone whose rank is equal to or higher than yours. ("Talk to" carries the connotation of lecturing or talking down to someone.) Until very recently, a social or a racial "minority" meant only a group. Using "a minority" to refer to a single member of a minority group ("He is a minority") is gaining some colloquial currency, but it is far from being universally accepted usage.

Choose the proper member of a set. In medicine, an intern(e) is a student or a graduate who is gaining supervised experience in a hospital or another setting, but an internist specializes in internal medicine. In reference to school graduates, "an alumni" is an oxymoron because the singular article "an" does not match the plural designation "alumni." The traditional distinctions in this group are:

an alumnus — one male graduate
an alumna — one female graduate
alumni — a group of graduates (especially, male graduates)
alumnae — a group of female graduates

Academic institutions and academically trained professionals especially tend to maintain such distinctions.

Misunderstood expressions and mixed metaphors sometimes produce unintentionally ludicrous pictures for those who see the difference between what is said and what is meant. When a television weatherman advised his hearers to "button down the hatches" for an impending storm, he substituted a rather delicate small-scale operation for the nautical drama of battening down the hatches. To accuse someone of "feathering his own bed" is to confuse the union practice of featherbedding (padding the payroll with nonessential employees) and the domestic image of setting up housekeeping. On the other hand, the man who improved a cliché in saying "in one ear and gone forever" may have been more inspired in his word choice than he realized. The happy verbal accident is rare, however.

As you attempt to choose exactly the right word, watch out for homonyms—words that are similar in sound but markedly different in meaning. You will be able to add your own examples to this basic list:

affect	influence, act on
effect	result
allude	hint at
elude	evade a pursuer
capital	an upper-case letter; a city that is the center of a government
capitol	the building that houses a legislature
complements	goes with, completes, enhances
compliments	favorable comments
continually	repeatedly—"He continually insisted that we cancel the project."
continuously	in an unbroken line or sequence—"He worked at the computer continuously for five hours."
creditable	worthy of praise, worthwhile
credible	believable, convincing
farther	distance from an object—"The canteen was farther from her office than from mine."
further	continuation or extension of an idea—"He was further convinced by the latest figures."
immigrate	settle in a new country
emigrate	leave one's homeland
imminent	forthcoming, about to happen
eminent	important, prestigious
imply	suggest
infer	draw conclusions from—"You imply that the company is considering a change, and I infer from your comments that you favor that change."
incredible	unbelievable—"His story was incredible."
incredulous	unbelieving—"I was incredulous when I heard his excuse."
ingenious	clever, witty
ingenuous	innocent, childlike, unpretentious
stationary	fixed in place
stationery	writing paper

Problems in Syntax

Some problems in meaning come not from the choices of words but from their placement. Consider the distinct changes in meaning and emphasis that occur when the position of one modifier is shifted:

Only he called her today.	(Only one caller dialed her phone number.)
He only called her today.	(He called but did not write or drop in for a face-to-face visit.)
He called only her today.	(He called one person but no others.)
He called her only today.	(He had not called before today.)
He called her today only.	(He called today and no other day.)

The innocent word "only" is often said to be the most frequently misplaced element in English sentences, but many other everyday violations of syntax (the way that words are clustered into phrases) do occur. Infinitives, always beginning with "to," carry the sense of being one phrasing unit, and most formal writers are reluctant to split infinitives by wedging modifiers between "to" and the verb form: "to cover expenses in part" (infinitive intact), "to partially cover expenses" (infinitive split).

Perspective Shifts

Some kinds of confusions of syntax lead to blurring or awkward shifting of a sentence's perspective. Double negatives ("He hasn't got no sense") are crude examples of the inconsistency created when a speaker or a writer establishes one phrasing expectation and shifts to another—changing anchors in midstream, so to speak. If you begin a contrast with "not only," you should complete it with "but also." The correlative conjunctions "either... or" and "neither... nor" are matched pairs that should not be mixed.

A dangling modifier superimposes one perspective on another. "Rounding the corner, the building was falling down" would be an amazing event indeed if the statement were literally true, but the writer probably means, "As I rounded the corner, I saw the building collapsing." When you begin a sentence with a verbal phrase such as "To begin the meeting" or "Opening the meeting," you should follow that introductory phrase with a main-clause subject that is capable of performing the action described in the phrase: "Opening the meeting, Hilfinger distributed copies of the proposal."

Although dangling modifiers most often appear as opening phrases, a misplaced verbal phrase elsewhere in the sentence might also create a perspective shift. Consider the announcement "Blood donor cards will arrive a few weeks after donating." The cards themselves did not perform the donating; the donors (not the cards) should be told, "You will receive a donor card a few weeks after you donate." Some dangling modifiers occur when the writer shifts in mid-sentence from an active-voice introductory verbal phrase ("Opening the meeting") to a passive-voice main clause ("the proposal was distributed"). The proposal itself cannot open the meeting; a person must do that.

Squinting modifiers also inhibit the reader's clear sense of a sentence's direction. When the report of a department store managers' meeting says, "We decided for convenience to issue no rain checks," the placement of the phrase "for convenience" is ambiguous, because it could reasonably modify either the words immediately before or those immediately after it. Does the statement refer to a decision reached for the store's convenience, or do the managers want to avoid burdening the customers with inconvenient rain checks? The reader should not be left to guess.

Still other mixed constructions include sudden shifts of tense:

> Bob has been running for the council seat and enjoys it.

or of person:

> If the user is finished, you should turn off the machine.
> (If "the user" and "you" are the same person, the number has illogically shifted from third person to second.)

or from direct to indirect discourse:

> We were asking about the construction delay and will it be resolved in time.

> After thirty years, we must decide whether to stay or go?
> (heading in a clothing store advertisement)

or from a personal to an impersonal pronoun:

> You should be careful of one's spelling.

Avoid the double-exposure effect that such mixed statements cause.

Spelling Problems

Some people are naturally better spellers (or baseball players or diplomats) than others, but compensating effort can do much to remedy the problem. Reading widely will improve your awareness of how words are spelled, and mnemonic devices will remove uncertainty. For instance, if you are tempted to use the ending -_ence_ for your spelling of "attendance," lock the correct spelling in your memory by holding it in a rhyming or an echoing phrase: "atten_dance_ at the _dance_."

Some common spelling errors have been noted in earlier sections, particularly those dealing with homonyms and verb forms. You might find the following groupings useful in recognizing other danger spots in spelling:

-_able_ and -_ible_ endings:	accept_able_; fall_ible_
-_ain_ and -_ian_ combinations:	vill_ain_, Brit_ain_; Christ_ian_
-_al_ and -_le_ endings:	vertic_al_, princip_al_ (major or first); princip_le_ (law, rule, belief), partic_le_
-_au_ and -_gu_ combinations:	_gu_arantee, ton_gu_e; _gau_ge
-_ei_ and -_ie_ combinations:	Generally _i_ precedes _e_ (p_ie_ce) except after _c_ (re_ce_ive, per_ce_ived)
letters that should be doubled:	a_cc_o_mm_odate, o_cc_u_rr_ence, roo_mm_ate
letters, often mistakenly doubled, that should remain single:	bu_s_iness, occa_s_ional, unti_l_
optional _e_ between syllables:	judg(e)ment

unacceptable spellings:	"alot" for the informal phrase "a lot (of)"; "alright" for "all right"; "midevil" for "medieval"
troublesome vowels:	benefit (not i); immediately (sometimes mistakenly omitted); optimistic (not o); separate (not e)
spelling options (Be consistent):	"focused" or "focussed"; "gray" or "grey"; "traveled" or "travelled"
commonly confused pairs:	bare (uncovered), bear (endure, support; animal)
	canvas (heavy cloth), canvass (survey)
	cite (refer to), site (place); also, sight (vision)
	desert (arid land), dessert (sweet last course)
	later (future time), latter (last mentioned)
	lose (give up unwillingly), loose (not secure)
	manner (way, style), manor (estate)
	pastime (hobby, recreation), past time (old days)
	precede (come before), proceed (go ahead with)
	sole (only), soul (the spirit)
	taught (instructed), taut (tense, tight); also, taunt (tease, jeer)
	their (group possession), there (direction to a place)
	vain (proud, useless), vein (fissure, tubular vessel, direction)
	wares (commodities for sale), wears (dresses in)

Keep a standard desk dictionary near your work station, and when you check for a possible spelling error, do not be satisfied with noting that the word is listed under your anticipated spelling. Glance at the definition to be sure that you have found the word that you need, not its homonym or another illusory form.

CHAPTER PERSPECTIVE

Consideration of your reader and your self-interest are united in the care that you take in the language basics of grammar, spelling, word choice, smooth syntax, and consistent sentence perspective. Errors make a reader impatient with the writer and raise doubts about the validity of the material. The more you write, the better you will be able to avoid mistakes. A good dictionary and a well-organized handbook of grammar and style will prove to be wise investments when a wording, spelling, or placement crisis arises.

Memos

INTRODUCTION AND MAIN POINTS

The opening four chapters have considered the qualities that mark the work of any accomplished business writer: an awareness of audience, a sense of the appropriate style and organizational pattern to fit the occasion, and a freedom from distracting grammar and spelling lapses. The major forms of business writing, including memos, letters, and long or short reports, offer many opportunities to apply the principles already discussed. This chapter and those immediately following suggest ways of closely matching the medium to the message. The strengths and occasional weaknesses of the standard business communication forms are explored in detail. The memo, an unglamorous but practical and easily mastered form of everyday business writing, is a good starting point.

Memoranda (some users prefer to call them "memorandums") are an efficient way of getting a message into the proper hands within a company. Formatting a memo requires making only a few choices within a small range, and the body of a memo may be as brief as a few lines of praise and congratulations for a job well done, or as long as a dozen or so pages offering a resources report or detailed proposal. For the moment, we will focus on shorter memos, reserving full discussion of the memo-report for Chapter 11.

After studying the material in this chapter:

■ You will be aware of the formatting choices that allow you to adapt each memo to its audience and purpose.

■ You will consider the potential "double life" of each memo, for every memorandum can have both immediate and longer-term usefulness, especially in a rapidly changing situation.

■ You will know how to use the brief memo for making announcements or issuing assignments.

■ You will see how the memo format encourages turning complex data or sprawling details into easily assimilated material.

THE MEMO'S PURPOSES

While "an army marches on its stomach," many a business organization pushes forward on coffee and memoranda. Particularly in a large and diverse enterprise, the memorandum (more familiarly, "the memo") is a basic communications tool for matters handled *within* the company. This usually concise but expandable means of *internal (in-house) communication* carries information or questions upward, downward, or across the organizational chart. A supervisor who detects a frequent snag in the assembly line can "put it in writing" for the engineering department's consideration. Employees located in branches, regional distribution centers, and main offices can be drawn together through a single memo's focus on a company issue or a technical problem, and that memo can be sent selectively or circulated widely. A manager's or a secretary's memo can leap the physical barriers of office tower floors and work station cubicles to draw employees' attention to a new, a revised, or an unwisely neglected policy. Memos announcing company social gatherings, promotions, well-earned retirements, or the successes of the firm's amateur softball team not only perform their immediate objectives but also create a sense of mutual endeavor, agreeableness, and goodwill.

Why not simply use the telephone? Why bother putting your message into memo form? The busy signal and the hold button are two immediate answers to these questions, but other reasons lie beyond momentary inconvenience and frustration. Certainly the phone is useful for initial contacts or for handling emergencies, but the transient nature of a phone conversation makes it less than ideal for substantive proposals, precise directives, legally binding approvals, cautions, and other matters that frequently involve third, fourth, or many further parties, often days or weeks later. You will often pursue tentative in-person or telephone contacts in memos that begin something like "After our August 8 conference call...." or "When we talked last Thursday, I understood you to say...." A follow-up memo can clarify a position, point out a previously overlooked factor, or enlarge a proposal. The memo can also be distributed to solicit opinion, to establish areas of responsibility, and to keep interested parties informed.

The Latin original of the English word *memorandum* offers a hint about the memo's multiple uses: the memo prompts its reader to *remember*. For the moment or for the near future, then, your memo asks someone else, or someone else's memo asks you, to make a mental note ("By the 14th please give me your estimates of...."), to store an idea until further notice ("The company's maximum for expense account gratuities is...."), or to take action ("Please recheck all smoke detectors on the first Monday morning of each month"). When your supervisor's memo stares back at you from your desk, you are unlikely to forget that your project draft is due before noon on Wednesday, whether or not the message explicitly begins with the phrase "Remember to."

While the memo is a useful prompt to immediate action or short-term memory, it can be equally useful in the longer term. A memo drawn from your files can clear the air when the office atmosphere is tense with accusation ("I told you to...."), counteraccusation ("You only said to...."), and helpless lament ("But I thought you meant...."). The wisely saved memo is a buffer against wrongfully directed blame. If appearances suggest that you neglected a detail that caused a project to go awry, you should be able to retrieve a memo in which you clearly delegated responsibilities, with further memos and progress reports showing that you made reasonable efforts to monitor your assistants' progress. A memo can be a buffer against career-damaging events, and in many situations it offers legal or quasi-legal protection. As time passes, a company's memo files also become a valuable part of its collective memory and, if read and heeded, a shield against repeated mistakes.

MEMO FORMAT

The memo's basic format is simple and easily adaptable to personal taste or company preference. Under the general heading "Memo" or "Memorandum" or "Interoffice Correspondence," the conventional double-spaced indicators of date, recipient, sender, and subject are either listed vertically or boxed near the top of the page, leaving the remaining space for the message. To encourage brevity and consistency, and thus to save processing time and paper, many companies supply memo forms printed on whole or halved $8\frac{1}{2}$ by 11-inch sheets, with the "Date," "To," "From," and "Subject" elements immediately followed by fill-in blanks. You can achieve much the same effect on a typewriter or a word processor:

Memorandum	
Date:	October 6, 1996
To:	J. M. Ridley
From:	A. B. Dean
Subject:	Power Shutdown for Rewiring

or

> **MEMO**
>
> To: Andy Summers
> From: Colleen Arne
> About: Seasonal Fabric Pricing
> Date: 10 June 1994

or

> *Logan*
> Research
> Division
>
> INTEROFFICE CORRESPONDENCE
>
> DATE 10/21/92   SUBJECT Annual Report Printing Delay
>
> TO Hilda Kroner   FROM Curry Webster   *CW*

As you see in these examples, the conventions of memo formatting allow the writer or the company document designer some discretion in placing the elements, in capitalizing, in expressing dates, and so on. Some firms turn their memo forms into two-way devices by dividing the message space into rectangles, the first reserved for the sender's statement and the second for the recipient's reply. (See example on page 57.)

While the "Date," "To," "From," and "Subject" lines are essential to the memo format, some communication channels call for the addition of check boxes, "Through" lines, reference numbers, and other elements. We'll review each of the basic memo headings and also consider some conventional options.

The date is most often presented with the month name spelled out (January 31, 1994), less often given in all-numerals form (1/31/94), and even less often shown in military style (31 January 1994). When placed in the vertically arranged double-spaced sequence of headings beginning at the left margin, the "Date" line can appear first or last (as above), or it can fall between the "From" and the "Subject" lines. Alternately, to achieve economy of space, you can shift the date to the right side of the page (opposite the first of the three remaining essential elements).

FROM		FYI _____Urgent Please __respond __note and file. DATE _____
TO		**SUBJECT**
MESSAGE	INITIALS	
RESPONSE	INITIALS DATE	

With the latter placement, the word "Date" is often omitted.

As a matter of conventional business courtesy, the "To" line precedes the "From" one, no matter whether these elements are listed on a single line or on adjacent lines.

These "To" and "From" components raise questions of formality and informality in the treatment of names and in the inclusion or omission of job titles and division or unit names. If Aubrey Dean's office is three doors away from Jim Ridley's, and if these vice presidents have worked together on friendly terms for months or years, a memo from one to the other might be directed

To: Jim Ridley
From: Aubrey Dean

or even, in a small and casual business or department,

| To: | Jim |
| From: | Aubrey |

However, if these two executives are on more formal terms—aggressive competitors for a top position, perhaps, or simply stationed so far from each other that they have had little opportunity for personal acquaintance—their names will receive more formal treatment. First names or nicknames will be replaced by initials, and titles might be added:

| To: | J.M. Ridley, Vice President, Operations |
| From: | A.B. Dean, Vice President and Head, Security |

In the "To" and "From" lines, you should treat names, job titles, and unit or division names in parallel ways. That is, if the recipient's name is to be followed by title and department designations, you should not leave the sender's name naked, without indications of rank and location. Thus the shipping room clerk should write "From: Bradley Zauner, Clerk, Shipping Department" if he addresses a suggestion memo "To: Thomas Willimon, Head, Physical Plant Services." If the recipient's name, title, and department address are compact enough to fit on a single "To" line, that arrangement will produce a fine economy of spacing as long as the sender's name, title, and division will also fit easily on a single "From" line. On the other hand, if the recipient or the sender has a long surname, an elaborately specific title, a lengthy department designation, or a combination of these, you will use two lines for identifying each. Note that you should single-space within each unit and double-space between units:

To:	R.W. Wagenbusch, Assistant Comptroller
	Financial Services Department
From:	H.G. Hammersmith, Vice President
	Computer Operations and Ancillary Services

When a person's name, title, and department are listed on a single line, these elements are separated by commas, but if the "To" and "From" elements are split into two lines each, the comma falling at the line break is dropped.

A further wrinkle in the conventional use of "To" and "From" lines occurs when the writer (or the recipient) is seen not as an individual worker, secretary, or executive but rather as a spokesperson for a committee, a board, an action group, or another aggregation. When Jim Ridley sends his memo "From: J. M. Ridley, Operations," he identifies himself as the decision-making, responsibility-taking person in charge of his department or unit. On the other hand, "From: Katherine G. Willis, for the Grievance Committee" means that Ms. Willis has functioned more nearly as a recording secretary than as the sole or primary shaper of the memo's commands or demands. Also, an individual might address a memo to a group:

To:	All Employees
From:	Alicia Jackson

or a group might petition an individual:

To:	A.R. Wright, President
From:	Ad Hoc Committee on Employee Benefits

or one group can direct its concerns to another:

To:	The Board of Directors
From:	Celebrations Committee

To ease memo distribution and to show what persons have been included, committee titles are often followed by listings, in parentheses, of members' names:

From: Site Selection Committee (R.C. Lester, C.M. Sawyer, I.M. Wyzocki)

or

To: Honors Day Committee (Profs. Dubin, Miller, and Rochester)

If you are sending a memo to a number of persons (too many to list parenthetically without having the "To" line swell out of proportion), you can address the message "To: Distribution" or "To: See below" and shift the names to the left margin following the body of the memo. Alphabetize according to surnames, and treat all names in the same way: first plus last names, initials plus last names, or, when a single courtesy title applies to all members of the group, the standard abbreviation of that title (such as "Drs." for "Doctors" or "Profs." for "Professors") followed by surnames.

When a person at one end of the organization chart directs a memo to someone at the other end, company protocol might dictate that the message be routed through an intermediary, usually the supervisor of the lower-ranking person. For instance, when Charlie Handy notices a safety problem affecting not only his department but also the plant's full work force, he wants the unsafe condition to be known "at the top," yet he does not want to seem to be going over his supervisor's head. To avoid even a hint of insubordination or a slight, he addresses his memo this way:

To: H. C. Anderson, President
Through: M. B. Walters, Department Coordinator
From: C. F. Handy, Technician II

In this arrangement Mr. Anderson receives useful information, Ms. Walter's local authority has been recognized rather than implicitly challenged, and Mr. Handy will receive the Delco battery plant's monthly Safety Watch award, with a handsome check.

In a less happy situation, a company executive might use a "Through" line in a memo warning a worker that he or she is subject to dismissal because of habitual lateness or unsatisfactory performance:

To: William Roush
Through: Charlene Weitz
From: Charles Cheng
Subject: Unmet Quotas for District 5

Here Mr. Cheng not only warns Mr. Roush that he is in danger of losing his job, but he also, in effect, notifies Ms. Weitz that she is to monitor Mr. Roush's work very carefully during the probationary period specified in the memo.

For the "Subject " line, you should choose a brief phrase or even a single word that pinpoints a reasonably specific problem, opportunity, list of operating procedures, set of principles, or other topic. While "Subject" is the most commonly used designation for this line, some memo writers prefer the Latin "Re" or its English equivalent "About," and others use "Concerning" or "Regarding." No matter which of these words you use before the colon, you should complete the "Subject" line with a few words that tell not simply "what" ("1990 U.S. Census") but "what's up about what" ("Severe Undercounting of Midwest Rural Areas in 1990 Census"). The topic "Sales" is too broad to suggest an emphasis or a direction, but the phrase "Declining Fur Sales" gives a good idea of what a department store manager has in mind as he addresses memos to buyers, space designers, and clerks. While "Engineering Problem on I-20" is too general a heading for a State Highway Department memo, "Difficulties in Achieving Proper Join to Major-Artery Traffic Flow at Oak Street Connector" is awkwardly overburdened with lumpy phrases. "Oak Street Connector Redesign" is specific enough without being too long.

Sometimes a department head will have several items of moderate importance—neither urgent announcements nor trivia—to circulate at the same time. Rather than send out four or five short, single-subject memos covering one job opening, two promotions, the need for higher cleanliness standards in the coffee lounge, and a reminder of next week's awards banquet, the secretary or manager can issue one memo under the subject designation "Miscellaneous Items" or "Notes and Timely Reminders." The body of a several-matters memo usually begins with a very brief general admonition ("Please note these current needs and opportunities"), followed by numbered paragraphs for the unrelated items.

For a brief memo announcing a meeting on short notice, you should not try to put all the essentials into the "Subject" line. "Personnel Committee Meeting Called for Friday, September 16 at 2:30 p.m. in Conference Room A" certainly conveys the information, but it is unwieldy. "Subject: Emergency Personnel Meeting" or "Subject: Mandatory Meeting on Friday" will alert the reader to the memo's significance, and, of course, he or she will find details of place, time, and specific agenda in the body of the memo.

A brief memo often contains all the information necessary to direct its recipient's verbal response or physical action. At times, however, the memo's main or secondary purpose is to call the reader's attention to contract terms, legal requirements, or other matters detailed in previously distributed materials. Here you might choose to supplement the "Subject" line with a "Reference" line:

> Subject: Driveway Grading, Newton House
> Reference: ORDER # RZ-22-6067

The indented or centered "Reference" line is an economical way of saying "Make sure that you meet all the buyer's specifications, as detailed in the signed order" or "Take note of these contractual penalties for late delivery." In a law office the "Reference" line might refer to "FILE # 9206" or "Case # 95-220," while in a manufacturing firm it might be expressed as "Code # AB 401-2276" or "REFERENCE: 27496." (Alternately, the "Subject" line can become a "Reference" line: "Subject: Order # RZ-22-6067.")

No matter which of the options you choose in phrasing the Reference line, you will find it useful when you must draw someone's attention to a defining document. For instance, suppose that a machine shop has promised to fabricate a device and ship it to a major customer by April 15, only to find that the necessary raw materials (specified in the file contract) are unavailable from the usual supplier. Someone within the machine shop will need to find an alternate supplier (or seek permission to use alternate materials) and then notify coworkers of the expected delivery date. Someone else must reschedule production. And someone in the office will then need to notify the customer, apologizing and letting him know when to expect shipment of the finished goods. The machine shop foreman, the production manager, and the secretary communicate with each other through memos referenced to a contract, a transaction, or an order number.

No memo would seem properly formatted without the "Date," "To," "From," and "Subject" lines, and, as we have seen, the "Through" line is sometimes useful as a bridge between "To" and "From" lines. While those elements are conventionally listed at the top of the memo sheet, optional codes signifying the typist, any enclosures, and copies sent may be placed at the lower left margin, beginning three lines below the final line of the message. For economy, these elements are single-spaced:

> brp
> enclosures: "Study in Europe," application form
> cc: Mr. Charles Brittan, Academic Advisor
>
> or
>
> COE: krz
> enclosures (2)
> xc: Mary Briggs
> Bethany Dunn
> Roger Lowery

(For a detailed discussion of these information notations, please see Chapter 6).

Most memos are authenticated by the writer's initials handwritten in ink after the typed name on the "From" line. Some memo authors insist on signing their names rather than using initials there. An increasingly rare alternative is to use a signature block (complimentary close, handwritten signature, typed name, and optional title, as illustrated in Chapter 6) following the body of the memo. The formality of the signature block seems at odds with the memo's tendency toward economy and crispness; most memo writers are content to initial the "From" line.

THE MEMO'S MESSAGE

A few handwritten lines on a printed interoffice form may be called a memo. A several-pages-long report prefaced by the standard "Date," "To," "From," and "Subject" headings may be called an extended memorandum or, more and more often today, a memo-report, useful for the medium-length presentation of proposals, policy statements, or research results. (Chapter 11 treats the memo-report in detail). Between these extremes are the countless three- and four-paragraph variations that are the workhorses of internal business communication. In short, you can adjust the length, tone, and pattern of each memo to fit your purposes.

In the simplest terms, a memo's task is to deliver a plain in-house message plainly, without waste of time and paper. Most of your memos will be no-nonsense bearers of project assignments, requested data, departmental or company-wide announcements, and other useful material, and you will write under the assumption "we're all focused on getting work done here; there's nothing personal about this." In sending a memo to a colleague or an assistant, then, you can usually afford an economical crispness that might seem slightly abrupt if the same phrasing were dropped into a letter to a customer or a tax auditor.

On the other hand, maintaining a cheerfully efficient office pace might depend on remembering that staff members have bad days and hidden insecurities just as customers and regulators do. Your awareness of your reader's convenience and sensibilities might be secondary to the functional purposes of your memo, but these factors may still influence your tone, wording, and even sentence lengths as you seek the best way to ask the reader to undertake a difficult task or accept an unpleasant idea. The softening word "please," placed before the command "get me the figures on last quarter's sales in the West," can make a difference in how a resourceful but weary research assistant perceives your message at the end of a particularly hard week. Obviously, the researcher is there to provide the figures that you need, but, when she is already juggling your own earlier assignments as well as tasks given her by others, she will appreciate a sympathetic allowance of breathing room ("After you finish the Portnoy data, Sandra, would you take a few minutes to find the file on....")

You will notice that a memo assigning a task often opens or closes with a sentence containing the phrase "would you," and you will also observe that the sentence does not necessarily close with a question mark. Using a period to finish a "would you" sentence reinforces the suggestion that this is a polite but reasonably firm directive, not an opening to a "yes," a "no," or an "I don't have time to do that" answer. "Would you" suggests a reasonable balance between inappropriate groveling ("Could you possibly find the time in your busy day to look this up for me?") and inconsiderate bluntness ("Get these figures ASAP").

Your reader's response will depend not only on how you have phrased your memo but also on how you have organized it to fit your purpose. Good news and neutrally informative memos conventionally follow the direct approach: the key announcement appears in the first sentence, and supporting details follow. "I am happy to report that the board of directors unanimously approved a greatly expanded employee benefits package this morning," the manager's memo might begin, and he will continue by detailing the improved medical and dental plans, longer vacation periods, and enlightened maternity and paternity leave policies being introduced. Conversely, bad news and persuasive memos work toward—rather than opening with—their key statements. "I know you've worked very hard this year, Clark, but I'm not able to bump up your salary because the profit margin is extra thin right now" is a poor beginning for a memo telling a valued employee that he will not receive a merit raise in January. Using the indirect approach, the manager might first carry his reader through convincing details about new-product disappointments, profit shortfalls, voluntary pay cuts in upper management circles, and more favorable projections for next year, when the company will be able to take a fresh look at the salary levels of loyal, patient, innovative employees. A bad news memo, as you see, is often simultaneously a persuasive one, leading the reader to accept something "now" with the hope of gaining something different or better "later."

Information memos announcing personnel changes or reminding their readers of upcoming events in the company calendar are usually brief and often require no direct response. When the company is ready to announce the results of a key job search, an executive will send out the word to all concerned:

I am happy to tell you that Carole Coke has agreed to become our new Comptroller, succeeding Russell Merritt. She will be moving here to Santa Fe next week and will take her place at her new desk on April 17.

Carole's appointment, as some of you know, is essentially a homecoming, for she started her career in our offices not very many years ago, and her subsequent work for Colorado Frontier and for Sundwellers has confirmed her early signs of promise.

Please join me in welcoming Carole Coke to the executive ranks at Southwestern Industries.

A reminder memo might include last-minute details about plans for a company social occasion:

The softball teams have been chosen, and the beer and soft drinks will soon be iced down. Everything else is ready for the department's 4th of July family picnic, to be held this year at Legion Park.

We have reserved the picnic area nearest the softball field. Because of heavy demands on public recreation areas this holiday week, the Parks Department has asked that we delay setting up in this site until 4:30. This arrangement, coupled with a few vivid memories of mild food poisoning from too-long unrefrigerated food last year, suggests that we should begin eating at 5:00 and hold the softball game until afterward. If the game goes into extra innings, we'll try out the newly installed field lights.

Many information memos are vehicles for distributing schedules, committee appointments, rankings, and other kinds of material better suited to listing in columns (or some other graphic arrangement) than to sentence and paragraph form. In listing data, you will want to determine the most precise way of offering information at a glance. If you are responsible for urging your company's employees to try the newly opened branch of the City Area Rapid Transit System, you might produce this memo draft:

Mayor Wilkins's announcement in today's *Journal* confirms the on-time June 18th opening date of the Brookwood CARTS station. Since we have all grumbled for years about the increasing traffic congestion in Brookwood, and since the station is right across the street from us, I join the Public Transportation Department in urging you to give the high-speed commuter trains a try. The patrolled and fenced Safepark lots in Sylvan Hills, Sandy Springs, and Avondale will be paved and opened by June 18th, and if you plan to catch the train at the Decatur or the Fairplace station, you can do so after June 25th. Parking areas in Pace and Union counties will be ready for public use on July 9th and 14th respectively.

To arrive here by our 8:30 a.m. opening time, you will need to catch CARTS at 7:40 in Fairplace, 7:50 in Decatur, 8:00 in Avondale, 8:10 in Sylvan Hills, and 8:20 in Sandy Springs.

The details are there, but the memo is already getting to be hard going, and you still need to list times trains arrive at the station nearest the office, starting very early in the morning and continuing with those close to 8:30. Then you must spell out afternoon departure schedules for a system spreading web-like toward the suburbs.

A more effective approach would be to start your memo with a brief appeal for employees to try the rapid transit line for various reasons. That short paragraph can be followed by a list of opening dates for different stations:

The city's growth and our own convenience will be enhanced by the June 18 opening of the Brookwood CARTS station, practically at the Hillman Building's front step. You'll save on gas and high downtown parking fees if you leave your car at one of the guarded and well-lighted Safepark lots.

The Safepark lots will open on this schedule:

June 18	Avondale
	Brookwood
	Sandy Springs
	Sylvan Hills
June 25	Decatur
	Fairplace

After completing this schedule, you can provide a list or a grid on which each potential commuter can identify convenient arrival and departure times:

FOR ARRIVAL AT BROOKWOOD STATION BY:	TAKE THE TRAIN DEPARTING FROM YOUR STATION AT:						
	Avon-dale (red line)	Mid-town (blue line)	Sandy Springs (red line)	Sylvan Hills (red line)	Decatur (blue line)	Fair-place (red line)	Union County (red line)
7:30 a.m.	6:50	7:15	7:00	7:10	6:55	6:30	6:30
7:50 a.m.	7:05	7:30	7:15	7:25	7:10	6:45	6:45

In a single-page memo, you will have room for the standard headings, an opening statement, the list of station openings, and selected arrival and departure schedules pegged to the opening and closing times of your firm's business day (with allowances in your listings for those who prefer to arrive early or leave late). Alternately, you can expand the memo to a second page, where you can list the full daily and weekend schedules of the rapid transit line. A further option is to obtain a supply of the Public Transportation Department's printed CARTS schedules and attach a copy as an enclosure item to each employee's memo. Is it your responsibility to provide the greatest amount of information available or to select the most useful? Your answer determines the scope of data you include, perhaps in list or table form.

While the memos just discussed call only for the actions of interested recipients (no direct written response is expected), other memos invite optional or mandatory verbal responses. The reader is directed to fill out and return an attached form, check a "yes" or "no" line at the bottom of the memo and return it, or otherwise supply the data or opinion asked for. Similarly, a memo announcing a company-sponsored workshop on advanced computer applications might begin with a brief statement of purpose, listings of the lecturers' qualifications and affiliations, and, of course, specifications of dates, times, and places. The three- or four-paragraph body of the memo might be followed with a tear-off section:

I am interested in attending the workshop New Computer Worlds on January 15–16.

Name _____

Department _____

Topics of special interest you want to suggest, in addition to those listed on the agenda:

_____

_____

The detailed conference schedule can be listed on a second page.

When companies send their employees forms to be filled out and returned, those forms are often prefaced by explanatory memoranda. For instance, in a large organization where distribution of paychecks by hand or through mailboxes has become a cumbersome and risky process, the payroll office might want to persuade employees of the advantages of direct deposit. The office manager's memo begins with a brief definition of the program, followed by convincing reasons for accepting the service and acting promptly through an attached form, "Authorization for Deposit of Net Pay" (see page 69). Mr. Henson's memo is highly persuasive in its reminder that the service is free ("at no cost to you") and in the implied contrast between those who already enjoy the convenience of direct deposit (second paragraph) and the reluctant holdout who only makes life difficult for himself (third paragraph). The option of calling for further information (fourth paragraph) should set the doubter's mind at ease.

Large companies and government agencies use yearly, quarterly, or other periodic memos to inform employees of the changing status of their retirement accounts, credit union contributions, medical plan activity, and other record-keeping matters. Often starting with formula phrases such as "Attached you will find," "Enclosed is your annual record of," and "Please review the attached report of," the memo continues with a general explanation of the benefits covered, with an emphasis on any changes in procedures or stipulations that have become effective since the last report. The benefits update memo usually closes with directions for reporting a suspected or a confirmed error.

Office of Payrolls and Employee Benefits

MEMORANDUM

TO: All Employees

FROM: Carl Henson
           Payroll Manager

SUBJECT: Direct Deposit of Payroll Check

DATE: November 4, 1992

   This memorandum is a reminder that you may have your net pay directly deposited each biweekly payday. This service is available for most banks, savings and loans, and credit unions, at no cost to you. Direct deposit may be to either a checking or a savings account.

   This benefit is valuable for several reasons: you avoid the long line at your bank on Friday afternoon, you won't lose your paycheck during your round of errands, and you enjoy the security of knowing that your money is available on payday no matter where you are. You will continue to receive your check stub in your department showing your gross pay, all deductions, and the net pay deposited to your account.

   According to our records, you do not presently have direct deposit of your pay. We encourage you to consider this valuable benefit. If you would like to take advantage of this service, please complete the attached authorization form, sign, and return it to the Payroll/Benefits Office, 224 Calhoun Street. Be sure to read the important information contained on the back of the form.

   Should you have any questions, please call the Payroll/Benefits Office at 677-2543.

CH/dl

Attachment

The in-house nature of such memos is commonly confirmed, for better or for worse, by the presence of acronyms, abbreviated department names, and other verbal shortcuts: "Please report any errors on the attached STBO printout to the SEB office within ten days."

While general announcement, policy statement, and benefits report memos are often distributed directly from a central office to all employees—or at least to those interested or affected—other memos are directed from upper to middle management, with instructions that the message be passed on to members of various departments in digest form or in a summary adapted to the needs of each unit. Sometimes "passing the word along" simply amounts to photocopying the original memo and adding a handwritten endorsement (with signature or initials) of the department head or local manager. Alternately, the departmental official can endorse and urge attention to a "sent from above" memo by stapling a flag strip memo (about two inches wide) to the top of each duplicated copy of the original message.

A task-assignment memo rarely creates such distribution problems. Much of the time the assignment is directed to a single reader, and seldom will more than a few be involved—a committee, a small support staff, or narrowly designated vice presidents or district managers. As you ask for library research or field reports, you will need to determine how much detail to include about your needs and purposes. An old-hand research assistant can respond productively to the simple directive "Please bring me all the growth data you can find on Sunpower Spas," while a less experienced researcher would work best with a little guidance: "Before I can propose the acquisition of Sunpower Spas to the board of directors, I need to develop projections of its aggregate worth, its expansion possibilities, and its fit with our own enterprises. Please develop details of Sunpower's franchise expansions (locations, numbers of memberships sold) for 1988 through 1991."

Many assignment memos will fall readily into the three-paragraph direct pattern. The opening paragraph will establish the basic need, the second paragraph will suggest the scope or depth of the material wanted, and the short concluding paragraph will indicate a deadline for the report. In a travel agency specializing in packaged trips for hobbyist groups, a manager might give his assistant this task in this way:

Justin Prince wants to shift his 1994 Winter Photographic Workshop from his customary Southwest locations to the Gulf Coast of Florida, both for his own professional growth and in the hope of encouraging repeat attendees. We will need to rewrite our Sanibel and Captiva Islands shell collectors' brochure to catch the interest of the camera fans. Please brainstorm on ways to adapt our four nights, five days package.

Specifically, I will need material on optional daytrips to the Ding Darling National Wildlife Refuge and other nearby scenic sites. Check with the Sanibel/Captiva Chamber of Commerce (813/472-1080) about film availability and developing services and also about water taxi service in mid-January. Confirm winter season 1994 projected rates for a party of twenty-five at the West Wind Inn and at the Song of the Sea.

I want to put something together for Justin Prince before he leaves for Yugoslavia on the 29th, so please let me have your suggestions and cost figures by next Tuesday.

The tone of this memo suggests that the writer and the recipient are accustomed to working together and share a general knowledge of the information resources available for their purposes. One of them does the general planning, the other doing the legwork. The researcher's response to this memo will be simply to find the needed material.

In a large and formal workplace, however, the staff researcher, when asked to write a formal report, might quickly send an assignment-acceptance memo. Although it is highly unlikely that she will decline the information request, the researcher responds for both diplomatic and practical reasons. In the brief opening paragraph she will express her thanks for the endorsement of her abilities implied in the assignment. Even if she is gritting her teeth as she types, she will try to suggest a reasonable degree of enthusiasm for yet another task. At the same time, she will phrase the opening sentence so that she defines the center of the subject, as she understands it from the received request: "Thank you for the challenging assignment of tracing the growth of Levi Strauss and Co. advertising budgets in recent years." This sentence might be sufficient for the opening paragraph, or she might want to add a further expression of her interest in the subject or her confidence in producing an excellent, useful report. The second paragraph will allow her to detail her intended approach, again shaped by her perception of the reader's needs. "Since your request emphasizes recent years," she might say, "I plan to devote most of my efforts toward the period since Levi Strauss's going private, a little more than a decade ago, and I will use selective figures from the Walter Haas, Jr., management era and from the Grohman retrenchment period only for comparison purposes. I understand that you are interested in both print and broadcast media expenditures, but not in festival, concert, and in-store promotions." After one or two further suggestions of coverage options—in effect asking "How much or how little do you want me to include?"—she will add a brief paragraph that invites any needed correction in the approach she has described. The memo will end with a reference to the date her report is due: "If you require any further material, please let me know by January 28. If I do not hear of needed changes by then, I will proceed with the approach outlined here, and the completed report will be on your desk on the morning of February 2." In stating the assigned subject, reviewing her plans for complying with the assignment, and offering to adjust her approach as necessary, the researcher has used the memo not only as an instrument of business courtesy but also as a protection against the unhappy complaint, "No, no, that's not what I needed at all!"

Memos offer another kind of protection to workers at all levels of business. Not only will a young executive keep copies of key memoranda, but he, his secretary, or his office neighbor might have occasion to address a memo "To: FILE." Here the memo becomes, in effect, a diary entry, written when its author senses that she or he is being led by circumstances or by a superior into a potentially compromising, unwise, illegal, or any other undesirable situation, or even the appearance of having engaged in sexual harassment, bribe-taking, or betrayal of trust. If young Mr. Wells is finally forced to dismiss sixtyish Mr. Prescott on the grounds of habitual drunkenness on the job, Mr. Prescott might lash out with a countercharge of age discrimination. Mr. Wells's chances of holding his ground will be enhanced if he can produce a memo, sent to his own files, detailing his attempts to deal with Mr. Prescott's problems. "On March 4, 16, 19, and 23, and again on April 4 and 7, Ms. Stewart reported before 10:00 a.m. that Mr. Harold Prescott was intoxicated and unable to do his work. On each of these occasions I invited Mr. Prescott into my office and attempted to suggest remedies for the family and financial problems that he readily identified as motivators of his drinking. Each time I also warned him that failure to find help through AA or another agency might lead to his dismissal." This account, brought into public view only when necessary, is likely to persuade an objective observer that Mr. Wells has been more than fair in handling a repeated disruption of the office's work.

The memo is widely adaptable to many business functions, but two cautions are in order. First, as many business veterans will attest, the phrase "CONFIDENTIAL MEMO" is more often than not a misnomer, no matter how neatly the typed words are centered near the top edge of the sheet. Memos travel from files for various reasons, and the results are often damaging. A second try-it-at-your-own-risk action is to calculate rising to the top through something called "memo strategy." The phrase was a favorite of newspaper business columnists a few years ago, but it has proved transient. Some businessmen and women do have a gift for timing fresh, even exuberant proposals and using memos to build networks of allies for their projects. But if the memos sound a false note, the person producing them is likely to be resented as an opportunist wasting company time and paper.

CHAPTER PERSPECTIVE

Memos, short or expanded, carry much of the written interoffice communication load. Hirings and firings are accomplished by formal letters, because these events find the recipient with one foot inside and the other foot outside the company confines. If a manager sends a note of commendation to one of his subordinates, the writer might choose a letter format because the message is likely to be meant for public as well as in-house consumption. Conversely, a memo might be lifted out of the office context and placed in the annual report or in company advertising to dramatize the skill and initiative of the staff. These "larger-world" uses of memos are rare, though. Most memos carry instructions, offer proposals, and otherwise facilitate the day-to-day tasks of the office or manufacturing plant.

Using the standard memo format (with its few options and variants) is an easily acquired skill, and through practice a writer learns how to adjust a memo's wording, its length, and its paragraphing to the simple or complex nature of its subject and to the anticipated audience of one, a few, or many readers.

Letter Format

CHAPTER

6

INTRODUCTION AND MAIN POINTS

In the opening chapters, we reviewed the characteristics that make all forms of business writing readable (or not), and in Chapter 5 we began to apply the principles of good writing to that internal communication medium, the memorandum. Like most memoranda, the majority of business letters are brief, often a single page or less. However, lapses that are merely sad in the relatively closed context of a memo's interoffice rounds can become embarrassing and costly in a letter sent on your company's letterhead into the larger world. If an occasional careless word choice or spelling lapse makes your manager wince or your secretary lift an eyebrow, that's one thing. If an ungrammatical or misspelled letter greets your creditor or potential customer and spoils the welcome of your message, that's quite another and more serious problem. In preparing a memo, you make only a few formatting choices. In composing a letter, you have a greater number of options for balancing the page, and your choices are more likely to make a distinct impression.

In this chapter we will review your options—partly matters of mechanical placement, and partly a blending of personal taste and conventional practice—in formatting any business letter and preparing its envelope. The layout of each letter should ultimately mirror its purpose. The next several chapters will explore what this means.

After reading this chapter:

■ You will know the advantages and disadvantages of using the modified block and full block formats.

■ You should be able to gauge the pleasing placement of a letter on plain or letterhead stationery.

■ You will know the traditional as well as the recently revised U.S. Postal Service addressing styles.

■ You will know how to fold the letter for correct insertion into its envelope.

THE VALUE OF LETTERS

"Does this mean that the business letter is finally going the way of the carrier pigeon?" That question returns with every round of postal rate increases and the introduction of each new electronic message-whizzing device. Adding the cost of materials and postage to the paid working time needed for writing, keyboarding, and proofreading a letter, you might conclude that letter-writing is not an inexpensive means of reaching customers, competitors, creditors, critics, and others. The ultimate cost of an important, carefully prepared letter can run to twelve dollars or more, according to some estimates.

On the other hand, some of the newer message-bearing devices have proved expensive to own or lease as well as costly and inconvenient to maintain. Ironically, too, the same technology that has introduced rival communications media can be applied to making the business letter more cost-effective than it was a few years ago. In short, the letter will remain a principal form of communication for the foreseeable future, and anyone who expects to function efficiently in business should have a sure command of current letter-writing standards.

The underlying idea here is a conventional one: your letter is your stand-in when you cannot be "there" in person. Your paper-and-ink representative should be as neat and polished as any diplomat. Not only should the wording, the factual accuracy, and the paragraphing reflect your best skills, but you should also enhance your message by creating an eye-pleasing placement of elements on the page. The reader's first-glance impression can make a difference.

GENERAL LAYOUT

As a framed picture often seems raw and unfinished until it is bordered by a mat, your letter should be "contained" by margins of at least one inch on all four sides of the standard 8½ by 11-inch page. (Please note that the sample letters that follow have been photographically reduced for presentation as whole pages. Margins may appear narrower than in reality). You can extend the top and bottom margins for brief letters, and you can adjust for space-consuming decorative letterheads.

In all letters the left margin is justified—the first letter in every line begins at the same distance from the edge of the sheet. For the right margin, however, you may choose between greater and lesser formality. At a minimum, you will not allow the widest line on the page to intrude into the one-inch right border, but you might choose to set your keyboarding controls to produce those subtle within-the-line spacing adjustments that create right-justified margins, as shown on page 90. Although right-justified margins convey a sense that the letter is carefully planned, they can also seem cold and too fully calculated. For this reason, they are most appropriate to crisp missives about legal matters, lost factory orders, unpaid bills, and other highly impersonal subjects. Where a greater degree of human warmth is needed, the non-justified ("rag") right margin will seem to be a "normal" concession to convenience, at least as long as the majority of writers and readers are acquainted with the products of manual and early electric typewriters. You will certainly want to avoid the rugged coastline effect; the right ends of your lines should not appear to be a series of deep channels, inlets, and jutting promontories. By occasionally breaking long words at syllable divisions and by paraphrasing short words into long ones or vice versa, you can maintain approximately equal line widths. This "neat raggedness" of the nonjustified right margin says to many readers, in effect, "There's a real person behind this letter, whether or not the content is 'strictly business'." For most business letters, a general symmetry of parts is preferable to a clinical consistency of line widths.

Plain paper (nonletterhead) business letters are most often written by individuals to companies, while company-to-company, company-to-lawyer, and company-to-customer correspondence is "authenticated" by letterhead. Beyond these obvious distinctions, company manuals often caution employees against using letterhead stationery for private purposes. Naturally, the president of a chemical company will use letterhead to address the editor of a local newspaper whose factually careless reporters have misrepresented his company's landfill practices. A non-executive employee of the same company would be taking a risk, however, if he appropriated a sheet of letterhead to write a fiery letter to the editor about the newspaper's political stance, selection of comic strips, or amount of sports coverage. Use letterhead if your position empowers you to speak on your company's behalf. Do not use letterhead, which implies company endorsement of content, for the unapproved expression of political or social views or for the solicitation of contributions to causes not explicitly endorsed by your employer. Leave it to the chairman of the board to use company letterhead to trumpet the good works of the United Way, especially if he is local chairman for that charity; use plain paper for the schedule of your Pigeon Club meetings.

Letterhead stationery may be lavishly or modestly decorated, depending on the image the company wishes to project. Near the upper right corner of its fine-textured stationery, IBM uses only the company initials in medium-shade gray against a faintly gray background, giving an immediate impression of corporate stability and controlled power. The heavy-load carrier Overnight, Inc., centers its company name in a simulated rubber-stamp image printed in purple ink on gray paper, with the Minneapolis headquarters address and telephone number relegated to vaguely deco-style type at the bottom of the page. The slightly rough edge of the rubber-stamped logo says immediately, "This company is on the move; our systems are in place and are working; everything is 'go'." Although Procter & Gamble came to grief a few years ago when a segment of the public mistook some features of its corporate logo for traditional symbols of Satanism (and protracted lawsuits followed), most identity-rich companies such as Coca-Cola, Levi Strauss, many sports and entertainment organizations, and various national charities try to use their logos in creative ways. The rainbow-hued bitten-apple logo appears at the top of Apple Computer's letterhead, while the cursive script in the Ford Motor Company and Coca-Cola logos recalls the handwriting style prevalent in those corporations' earliest days, and thus evokes tradition and stability as company traits.

Occasionally the letterhead designer's fancifulness creates problems for the users of his product. It's a clever idea to simulate a yellow legal pad page on the letterhead of a law firm, but the ruled lines tend to fight against the typed lines, producing a jarring effect. Oversized logos call for adjusting top or bottom margins, and divided letterheads (part of the printed material at the top or side of the page, the remainder at the bottom) can help or hinder the vertical placement and right-left balancing of the page. One way or another, the keyboarded elements must be sited so that they appear to be neither crowded together nor floating away from each other. We will review these problems and possibilities of placement as we examine the standard parts of the business letter, from the top of the page to the bottom. Then we will consider ways to pull the elements together into a page that seems well-balanced in both vertical and horizontal dimensions.

LETTER COMPONENTS

The single-spaced return address block is composed of the full address needed for a reply and the letter's mailing date, divided as follows:

▬ street address or Post Office box or drawer number
▬ city, state (Post Office abbreviation), and zip code + 4
▬ date

If the return address has been included in the typeset letterhead, only the date need be added. The typed return address (or any portion thereof) may begin as near as two typing lines below the last printed letterhead line (page 90), but for a short-bodied letter the typist may use four or five returns in the interest of vertically balancing the page (page 91). Similarly, in a full-page plain paper (nonletterhead) letter, the return address block can begin just below the one-inch top margin, but if the body of the letter requires only about half of the sheet, the return address may be shifted several lines below the margin (page 88). This prevents the "floating balloon" effect that occurs when most of the letter's components seem pushed toward the top margin.

For a full-page letter, you should double-space between the return address block and the inside address block. For a shorter-text letter, you may further add two or three blank lines.

The inside address block begins with the name and the title (if any) of the addressee, followed by the name and address of the firm. Tradition suggests that the inside address should use the same abbreviations, spacing, courtesy titles, line divisions, and other features that will be used on the envelope, although this has become questionable since the U.S. Postal Service has recently urged adoption of a simplified envelope-addressing format (to be discussed later in this chapter). Letter writers may eventually become accustomed to the addressing style recommended to accommodate the Postal Service's mail-sorting optical scanning machines, but most current writers will find the all-capitals addressing style unsuitable for use in the inside address, where it should be set out within more conventionally capitalized and punctuated elements.

Names and titles sometimes create problems in addressing letters, as this checklist of considerations illustrates:

1. *Courtesy Titles.* Some writers like the brusque "modern" quality achieved by omitting "Ms.," "Mr.," "Miss," "Prof.," and other courtesy titles before names, while more conservative stylists see these omissions as rudely abrupt. Some women find "Ms." practical and prefer it to a wrong guess about "Miss" or "Mrs." But others consider "Ms." a dreadful innovation.

Too, some names are not really reliable clues as to gender: Tracy, Robin, Kim, Pat, and other given names are used today for males and females. Beverly may be "Mr." and "Mrs.," and a country-music lyric celebrates "a boy named Sue" and his difficulties.

Ideally, you will know your recipient's gender and preference as to title. If you don't, omitting the courtesy title is generally preferable to guessing.

2. *Correct Names*. People much prefer being addressed by name to being labeled "Occupant," "Homeowner," or "Anyone Residing at." The other side of that coin is that people are irritated by incorrect assumptions made about their names by strangers. If the name Frank Cooper appears on a mailing list you have leased, you might decide to add the flourish of treating the name formally, addressing him as "Mr. Franklin Cooper." However, he may have been named for a favorite uncle, Richard Frank Marshall—no Franklin about it. Ray is most often a nickname for Raymond, but not where Rayford is concerned.

Be careful also about spelling variants: Francis (conventionally male) and Frances (conventionally female); Sherry, Sherri, Sherrie, Sheri, Cherree; Betty, Bettie; Sean, Shawn.

Particularly in the South, you should respect the tradition of double first names: a recent governor of Georgia is Joe Frank Harris— "Joe Frank" to supporters and opponents alike, and tonally very different from "Joe F. Harris." Similarly, Miss Georgia Lee Fountain is Georgia Lee (double first name, not first plus middle name) and Fountain (surname).

Unless you know how an individual prefers to be addressed, use the form of the name that you found in a directory or a mailing list. Resist the temptation to add formalizing or casual touches to strangers' names.

3. *Job Title*. Business professionals, especially those of higher ranks, expect to be called by their correct titles as well as their correct names. The academic Department Head won't like being called the Chairman, because the two titles distinguish differing degrees and sources of authority. A chairman is usually elected for a few years to the leadership role, while a department head is often seen as a more strictly administrative individual who will carry the burden for a

longer time span. Likewise, notice that the "Manager of Human Resources" in one company might be crisply styled "Manager, Human Resources" in another or simply "Personnel Director" elsewhere.

Aside from the matter of accurate designation, the most common problem with a job title is whether to place it on the same inside address line that carries the addressee's name, or to place only the name on the first line of the inside address block and the title on the second. Use the simple length test: will the title, added as an appositive to the name on a single line, create a much longer line than the others in the block? If both the name and the title are compact enough to fit on the first line without running too far into the middle of the page, follow the name with a comma and then add the title: "Monica Jacks, Head Nurse." If only the name appears on the first line and the title follows on the second, you no longer need the comma:

> Ms. Monica R. Jacks
> Coordinator of Nursing Services

The comma occurs between the name and the title *only* when both appear on the first line.

4. *Options for Listing Names.* Some corporate letter writers prefer to address the letter to a company and add an "Attention" line:

> Young Baking Company
> Attn.: Robert Steele
> 124 Auburn Avenue

This style might be efficient, but it also seems dehumanizing and is not recommended here.

The 1991 edition of the Postal Service's official *National Five-Digit ZIP Code and Post Office Directory* illustrates still another way of specifying an individual recipient within a company:

> ATTN SUE MOBLEY
> SOUTHERN CORP
> LOUISIANA INDUSTRIAL PK
> 1725 E BEAUREGARD AVE
> NEW ORLEANS LA 70124-1299

Once you have made your choices for handling personal names and titles, the remainder of the inside address block is easy. Use a line for the company's name, expressed in the same way that the company represents it on its own documents: "Levi Strauss & Co.," not "Levi Strauss and Company," is the San Francisco-based clothing-maker's preferred form of its name, used that way on its letterhead (if not always in its most informal advertising). After listing the company name, use a line for the street address, Post Office box number, or route, suite, or apartment number. Place the city, state (in the standard abbreviation), and zip code + 4 on the last line of the inside address block.

Double-space before and after the next component, the greeting (also called the salutation). In a business letter, the greeting ends in a colon, not in the comma used in the same position in a personal or "friendly" letter.

In the greeting line, the question of how to treat the courtesy title arises once more. If you have made a solid choice in the first line of the inside address, stick with it here. If you are still debating whether to call the addressee "Miss Kay Harding" or "Mr. Kay Harding" or "Mrs. Kay Harding" or "Ms. Kay Harding," you might consider the increasingly frequent (but not universally liked) solution of phrasing the greeting "Dear Kay Harding."

Most one-page business letters will divide their messages into two to five short to medium-length paragraphs. Single-space within each paragraph and double-space between one paragraph and the next. If you prefer, you may indent the first line of each paragraph five character spaces. Indented paragraphs are more appropriate to letters arranged in modified block format (page 88) than to those laid out in full block. Indentions would be especially out of place in a letter having a right-justified margin (page 90).

Double-space between the last line of the body and the complimentary close, and capitalize only the first letter of the conventional complimentary close phrases "Sincerely yours," "Truly yours," or "Yours truly." Note that "Very truly yours," which initially seems more appropriate than "Yours truly," ultimately seems more formal and distant, and the three-word phrase is seldom used today. Some writers omit "yours" after "Sincerely," but traditionally-minded writers and readers find the result a bit abrupt and trendy. Of course the elaborate flourish of "I am, madam, your most humble servant and most truly yours," terraced across two or three lines, went out with the horse and buggy. It's best to choose among the two-word phrases listed above. The complimentary close ends in a comma, leading the eye to the handwritten signature.

Since signatures vary in height and in general elaborateness, you may leave two to four lines blank to accommodate the disciplined intensity or the splashy, loopy flourish of the signature.

Because many signatures are little more than blurs of inky effusion, the typed name of the writer follows, and it in turn is followed (single-spaced) with the title (if any) of the letter's author. The company division or office name may be added

> Jim Parker
> Chief
> Accounting Division

if it has not already been identified in the printed letterhead.

Even more often than in a memo, the lower left side of a business letter might carry abbreviated identifiers of the typist, any enclosures, and copies distributed to third parties. In a tightly laid-out letter, you will double-space after the last line of the signature block (usually the writer's title), while vertically balancing the page might mean adding two or three additional lines before inserting the typist-enclosure-copies lines. However, the last identifying line should fall above the one-inch bottom margin. You may use one, two, or all three of the identifyng elements, but you should maintain the conventional order of those you include.

The first of these is the set of typist's initials, listed in lower case letters without periods. Since the author's name is clearly printed in the signature block, it is redundant to include his or her initials in all-capitals on the typist identification line. The typist line on page 90 needs only "ms" for Margaret Smith, not "RB/ms" or "RB:ms" for "executive Rodney Banks dictating to Margaret Smith from the typing pool."

The enclosure(s) line tells the recipient to look for supplemental material such as application forms, schedules, maps, brief articles or reports, or any other printed matter needed to fulfill the letter's purpose. The simplest form of the enclosure line merely counts the number of supplemental items to be found in the envelope: "Encl. (2)." Alternately, you may expand the enclosure indicator to two or more typed lines that specify, by generic term or by title, what the enclosures are. A high school junior or senior might receive a warm and encouraging response to an initial college admissions inquiry, and the Admissions Director's letter might end with this enclosures designation:

> Encl.:   application forms
> "Adventures of the Mind" brochure
> SAT test schedule

Where only a single item is enclosed, the standard abbreviation "Enc." or "Encl." will suffice.

Like the enclosure line, the copies line might actually require several typed lines—as many as eight or ten. The copies element lists the one or more persons who, so to speak, read over the shoulder of the writer or the addressee. If a judge commands an irresponsible father to pay child support, he will address his orders to that parent, with copies to the mother and her attorney, to the husband's lawyer and his probation officer, and to the local sheriff, who will have to act if the child support payments do not arrive regularly and promptly.

Similarly, when a major downtown street must be closed to traffic for emergency tunnel repair, and when this closing occurs only a few days before the city's biggest annual event, the Rose Festival, the mayor might write the head of the contracted engineering firm, urging that the work be finished as expeditiously and safely as possible so that the traditional parade route can be used. Mindful of civic responsibilities and reelection hopes, the mayor will send copies of the letter to the festival chairperson, the chamber of commerce head, the city engineer, and any other key figures who should know that the head of the city government is doing everything possible to minimize disruption:

> Copies to: Mrs. Frank Bayless, Festival Coordinator
> 1227 Gordon Avenue
> Mr. Howard Stiffakis, Director
> Thomasville Chamber of Commerce
> Mr. Tom Sutton, City Engineer
> City Hall

Of the three copy recipients listed here, Mr. Sutton, the City Engineer, might have the most immediate practical concern in the repair problem, but courtesy dictates that he, as a city employee, be listed after the volunteer chairperson and the head of the quasi-public agency. Street and office addresses have been included in this designation for the secretary's convenience, but where space is at a premium, the listing can be reduced to:

> cc: Mrs. Frank Bayless
> Mr. Howard Stiffakis
> Mr. Tom Sutton

When copies are being directed to three or four persons of the same rank and standing, the names should be listed in alphabetical order.

THE UNITED EFFECT

Earlier in this chapter we reviewed the standard margin requirements and considered the placement of a letter's typed body in relation to printed letterhead. In examining the business letter's standard components, we have noted those places where spacing may be varied to achieve a pleasing vertical balance: before and after the return address block (or the date line, if the return address is preprinted), in the signature block spacing, and before and after the cluster of typist, enclosure, and copies identifiers. A few other considerations will strongly influence the general impression a letter makes when the recipient unfolds it.

An experienced typist will be able to take the handwritten draft of a two- or three-paragraph letter and closely approximate its ideal centering in the finished page, making almost instinctive allowance at the variable-spacing points. However, if the body of the letter is very short—a brief confirming response as the last in a series of letter exchanges—the typist will not aim for bull's-eye centering on the page, because the typed portions of the letter would be pulled too far from the letterhead. Rather, the text will be positioned in the upper two-thirds of the page, so that the signature block and, if at all possible, the last lines of the body will fall below the vertical midpoint of the sheet.

In general, though, we can say that a letter whose body alone requires two-thirds to three-quarters of the length of the page can be easily adjusted (by varying spacing where that is possible) so that it seems to fill but not crowd the page. Sometimes, despite the author's most economical wording and the typist's best spacing efforts, a relatively brief business letter must be continued on a second page. In this case, the skilled typist will plan for the page break, not merely let it arrive where it will. The second page should seem to justify itself; it should contain more than the last line or two of the letter's body followed by the signature block. To have only a fragmentary part of a letter continue on to a second page suggests wastefulness and lack of planning. Knowing that the letter will have to be continued onto a second sheet, the typist will begin adjusting her formatting in keyboarding the first lines of the first page.

While the first page of a company's letter will appear on its letterhead, the second and any succeeding pages should be typed on nonletterhead sheets. Many companies keep stocks of unprinted paper of the same weight, tint, and texture as the letterhead pages. Smaller companies often "make do" with plain typing paper for continuation pages.

If the second page of a letter becomes separated from the first when an "in" basket falls to the floor or a file is spilled, the pages can be most easily reunited if the continuation page carries, just below the top margin, an identifying legend that distinguishes it from all other letters in a stack, folder, or computer disk. This legend may be arranged horizontally or vertically:

Mrs. Mary Beamer   page 2   May 16, 1994

or

Mrs. Mary Beamer
May 16, 1994
page 2

In the typical single-page letters that follow, you will notice differences in the way the left and right sides of the pages are formatted. Mrs. Josephine Jewell's complaint letter (page 88) and the shorter version of Rodney Banks's reply (page 90) are arranged in modified block format, in which the return address block and the signature block appear on the right side of the page. In Mrs. Jewell's well-balanced page, the initial characters in each line of both blocks occur five inches from the left edge of the sheet, and the longest line in either block does not break into the right margin. The return address block at the top of the page is vertically balanced against the signature block at the bottom, and the line ends of both blocks roughly accord with the right ends of the message lines. The indentions are most appropriate to this arrangement. Mr. Banks's shorter reply slightly compromises the modified block format by beginning the return address block (or, in this case, the date) and the signature block in the precise horizontal center of the lines used. Although this arrangement nods toward establishing left-right balance, the effect is somewhat mechanical. Mrs. Jewell went to only a little more trouble in placing the return address and signature blocks, and she achieved a more natural balance.

Of course the easiest horizontal treatment to type is the full block format, which begins each line of every element at the left margin. For design-conscious writers and readers, this format (page 89) might conjure the image of a lame vessel listing to port-side, but typing convenience and familiarity have accustomed many eyes to this page arrangement.

With only modest success, some professional management associations have sponsored a streamlined format (page 91), which is basically the full block arrangement with a subject line replacing the greeting and with the complimentary close omitted. While satisfactory for business-to-business letters, this format lacks the friendly warmth that most business writers want to convey to their customers (and politicians to their constituents).

The letters on the following pages are offered as general examples, not exact models. The first three arrangements are more often seen than the last, but any of them might be used in one circumstance or another.

THE FINAL STEPS

You have chosen the best page arrangement, you have found the most appropriate words to produce the desired tone, and you have turned your letter draft over to the typist. Except for adding your signature to the final copy, your responsibility is over, right? No. You are responsible for every detail of any business document that you have signed, whether it is a contract offer or a sales letter. Nearly everyone knows of the rare lapse of care in the U.S. Government Printing Office that left a decimal point before rather than after two zeros in a revenue bill and cost the federal government thousands of dollars before the mistake was noticed by those responsible for it. Few errors are that costly in dollar amount, but even a transposition of letters in a hastily typed letter can register as carelessness in the reader's mind. Proofread before you sign.

The now-retired college teacher C.H. Watson likes to recall the astonishment and chagrin of his writing students when he made grade deductions for typographical errors. "I knew how to spell that," the typical student would say, "and, besides, I'll have a secretary to check these things." To this protest Mr. Watson would invariably reply, "Son, I've taught her too, and she can't spell either!" No matter whether it's the writer or the typist who has the better eye for catching spelling, grammar, or typographical errors, the signer takes the blame. If your letter will make the difference in a millions-of-dollars deal, you will be well advised to read it backward as well as forward, many times if necessary.

Once you and the typist are satisfied that the letter is ready for sending, one of you will prepare an envelope. As we noted earlier in reference to the letter's inside address block, business

Modified Block Format on Plain Paper

245 Fairlane Street
Danville, CA 94526
November 11, 1993

Mr. Rodney Banks
Young Talent Search, Inc.
72 Castro Street
San Francisco, CA 94226

Dear Mr. Banks:

 I am writing to protest the treatment that my daughter Junie received from your Talent Coordinator, Miss Hess, during the TV commercial tryouts at the Bayside Mall last week. The poor child has been in a funk for days and is unable to concentrate on her studies.

 Junie takes her dancing very seriously and for this occasion had worked up two numbers to show the range of her talents. She had intended to follow the tap routine, which she was grudgingly allowed to perform after some delay, with her slow dance to "The Tennessee Waltz," but after the first number Miss Hess only said "Thank you" and would not let her find the music for the second piece on her tape.

 If I had been able to be present, I would have demanded an explanation on the spot, but owing to difficulties in parking, I had to let Junie out of the car at the mall's front door and told her I would be back to pick her up there at 3:30. Because of Miss Hess's inefficiency in running the tryouts, Junie was 35 minutes late, I burned up half a tank of gas circling around and around the mall, and I was twice told to move my car from the taxi pickup zone.

 This whole experience has been highly frustrating, and I cannot understand why you would employ someone as unprofessional and as disorganized as Miss Hess. Junie's opportunity is wasted, and I can only express my disappointment.

Sincerely yours,

(Mrs.) Josephine Jewell

Full Block Format for Full-Page Letter

Young Talent Search, Inc.
72 Castro Street, San Francisco, CA 94226

Date

November 14, 1993

Inside
address
block

Mrs. Josephine Jewell
245 Fairlane Street
Danville, CA 94526

Greeting

Dear Mrs. Jewell:

Body

Gifted young people are in demand for television commercials today, and the turnout for our November auditions in the Community Room of the Bayside Mall was a clear indication that many talented youths are just waiting to be discovered. Our pleasant task at Young Talent Search is to match the appropriate talent with the currently listed opportunities.

Alicia Heseltine, who conducted our Bayside auditions, is one of our most skilled and experienced Talent Coordinators. On the day your daughter auditioned, the crush of five- to thirteen-year-old aspirants, many of them not accompanied by parents, challenged (but did not defeat) Miss Heseltine's legendary calm. She had only a short time to explain to Junie that the November 5th Call for Talent was limited to brief speaking parts, as indicated in our announcement's request for "a brief recitation of a poem or a dramatic monologue, not exceeding three minutes." Miss Heseltine was there to judge general poise and speaking voice quality rather than dance or music performances.

Seeing your daughter's disappointment and thinking of possible future talent needs, Miss Heseltine agreed to have Junie perform one dance number within the same time limits allowed others who were eagerly awaiting their chances, and she helped Junie find the extension cord for her tape player. Miss Heseltine's "Thank you" is simply a conventional way of indicating that the fixed audition time is over.

Although tap and ballroom dancers are less often sought for commercials today than they were a decade ago, we will be looking for terpsichoreans in our December 5–6 auditions at the Downtown Oakland Mall. The official mall opening time is 10 a.m., but we have arranged for participants to be admitted at the South Entrance beginning at 9:15. This should enable you to park near the door and to accompany your daughter. We much prefer to have parents present at all auditions, as our newspaper announcements suggest. "First in line is the first to shine," we like to remind our guests. Miss Heseltine will look forward to meeting you and to seeing Junie again.

Complimentary
close

Yours truly,

Signature
Typed name
Title

Rodney Banks
General Manager

Typist's initials

ms

Enclosure

Encl.: Auditions schedule

Modified Block Format for Shorter Letter

Young Talent Search, Inc.

72 Castro Street, San Francisco, CA 94226

variable spacing

November 15, 1993

variable spacing

Mrs. Josephine Jewell
245 Fairlane Street
Danville, CA 24526

one blank line

Dear Mrs. Jewell:

one blank line

single-spaced body

Our greater pleasure at Young Talent Search is to match school-age performers with the active needs of advertising and promotional agencies throughout the Greater Bay Area. The newspaper announcements of our monthly auditions always specify the desired ages, performance skills, and other requirements for television commercials, fashion shows, and other promotions that are moving from planning to production. In other words, our focus is on specific one-time work assignments.

one blank line

When your daughter appeared in dance costume at our November 5th auditions, she was apparently unaware that our listings for the month were limited to speaking parts in television spots, aside from one call for a freckled male yo-yo virtuoso. When our Talent Coordinator, Alicia Heseltine, called your daughter to the front of the auditorium, she expected to a hear a brief recitation by which she could judge voice quality and body carriage. Sensing Junie's disappointment, Miss Heseltine allowed her to use the same amount of time given each hopeful performer, but she tried to make it clear that this was only for the sake of auditioning experience and a little free coaching.

Since then, however, I have received requests for tap and ballroom dancers to be used in two major department store centennial promotions, so I invite you to accompany Junie to our next auditions, to be held on December 5th and 6th in the recently vacated Vanity Fair site at the Downtown Oakland Mall. We have arranged early admittance for participants at the South Entrance, beginning at 9:15. I hope to meet you and your daughter there.

one blank line

Yours truly,

variable spacing

Rodney Banks
General Manager

variable spacing

margin of at least one inch   ms

Simplified

Compass Television Productions
4590 Palomar Parkway
San Francisco, CA 94237-1405
(415) 423-2589

variable spacing

November 1, 1993

variable spacing

Rodney Banks, General Manager
Young Talent Search, Inc.
72 Castro Street
San Francisco, CA 94226

one blank line

YO-YO ARTIST NEEDED

one blank line

You have sent us a number of appealing young-
sters for earlier commercial projects, and I hope
you can help us this time.

one blank line

We are developing the storyboard for a 30-sec-
ond Meadowbrook Ice Cream Shops spot on a
nostalgia theme. For a turn-of-the-century soda
fountain scene we need a red-haired, freckle-
faced boy, 8 to 10 years old, who is well skilled
with a yo-yo—i.e., can do "walking the dog" and
" 'round the world" with great panache and confidence. He will wear a straw boater hat, so a bit
of fullness in the face (a young Arthur Godfrey
look) will be ideal. Clean-cut freshness is a must.

Hope we aren't being too particular here, but we
have a very definite concept going with the
client. Please call right away if you can fill this
need.

variable spacing

Harley Deaver
Producer

variable spacing

sjb

writing tradition says that the line divisions, punctuation, capital-ization, and other features of the envelope address should exactly duplicate the presentation in the inside address. However, the annually revised preface pages of the U.S. Postal Service's *National Five Digit ZIP Code and Post Office Directory* seem increasingly insistent that the all-capitals, minimum-punctuation style recommended there (with minor year-to-year changes) is necessary for the efficiency of human and automatic mechanical mail sorters. Many business writers will continue to use the tradi-tional addressing style inside the letter and yield to the Postal Service's wishes in preparing the envelope:

inside address	*envelope*
(traditional)	(U.S. Postal Service)
Mr. Bernard Coke	MR BERNARD COKE
P. O. Box 129	PO BOX 129
Parker, Colo. 80134	PARKER CO 80134

For the seven types of "basic address formats" defined by the Postal Service, see "Section 2. Proper Addressing" in the latest available *ZIP Code and Post Office Directory,* available at large Post Offices and by mail from

> Superintendent of Documents
> U.S. Government Printing Office
> Washington, DC 20402

You will place your return address in the upper left corner of the envelope, about one-quarter inch from the left edge and one-quarter inch below the top edge of the envelope's face. The send-ing (addressee's) address should begin at the vertical middle of the envelope or postcard (or one line above the middle, if more than three lines are used). On a standard (No. 10) business enve-lope, the address should begin four inches from the left edge. For a No. 6¾ envelope or a USPS postcard, begin the address two inches from the left edge.

Now that the letter and its envelope are ready, you have come to the final step, folding the letter for insertion into the envelope or, from the recipient's perspective, for easy removal. While this folding does not require the degree of dexterity needed for origa-mi or even a fancy paper airplane, you should know the correct method of folding the 8½ by 11-inch sheet to fit the standard (also called the "long" or "legal size") envelope. The letter should be folded and creased in thirds from the bottom up, so that the lower third faces (upside-down) the middle third, and these are in turn covered by the downward-pressed top third. When the recipient pulls the letter from the envelope, the upper third of the sheet will appear first, and subsequent unfolding will reveal the middle and lower thirds.

The smaller No. 6³/₄ envelope, often used for personal letters and sometimes for business correspondence, calls for a different folding pattern. To leave a thumbhold of about one quarter of an inch at the top of the sheet, crease the page just below its horizontal middle and place it on a flat surface. Bring the right third of the folded sheet toward the left until your eye determines the mid-way point of the remaining two-thirds. Place the right edge at that point and press down the right side, forming a creased panel which now covers the middle third of the page. Now bring the left third over to the right edge of the partially folded page and press down. Insert the paper into the envelope so that the recipient's fingers will first touch the edges, not the center creases, of the folded sheet. Seal the letter, add a stamp or run the envelope through the postage meter, and send your message on its way.

CHAPTER PERSPECTIVE
In this chapter we have been concerned with the mechanics of the business letter and its envelope. Some of this material is simple and routine, but we have also considered choices that determine the kind of welcome your letter might receive. Sloppy, indifferent, incorrect, or inappropriate handling of the format will make the reader wary or distrustful of your message. As we begin to look at the standard types and purposes of business letters, we will continue to see reciprocal relationships between format and content, medium and message.

Direct-Approach Letters

INTRODUCTION AND MAIN POINTS

In the three preceding chapters we have been primarily concerned with external correctness and standard form: Is this the right word? Is it spelled correctly? Is the memo acceptably formatted? Is the letter page well balanced? If you have read these chapters one after another, you have probably noticed a gradual shift away from the absolutes or near-absolutes of spelling, grammar, and accurate definition (detailed in Chapter 4) toward emphasis on your options within letter and memo formats (described in Chapters 5 and 6). Chapter 7 and its immediate successors move still further from specific "do" and "don't" advice and toward greater reliance on your understanding of what happens on that sheet of paper where your interests and your reader's meet—and either clash or reach a productive accord. Now we focus on a very important concept: that careful placement of ideas can strongly influence the reader's perception of your letter's message.

At one time or another each of us is inclined to read between the lines, and the successful business writer will remember that letters carry covert as well as overt messages. Like an ill-chosen word, a too-short paragraph might be read as a brush-off. A cliché-ridden letter, or one where all the sentences are the same length, producing a monotone, droning effect, might translate into a bored, indifferent consideration of the customer's problems. Readers are sensitive not only to the meanings and implications of individual words and phrases, but also to the pacing and the patterning of statements. If you must send your reader bad news, you will want to build toward your basic negative answer in ways that will be detailed in Chapter 8. The primary emphasis of Chapter 7, however, will be on the direct approach, the preferable pattern for three large groups of business letters: (1) good-news messages, sometimes called "yes" letters, (2) routine inquiries and responses, and (3) complaint and adjustment letters.

After studying the material in this chapter:

━ You will know where to place your basic idea and how to use follow-up details.

━ You will consider where and how to express reservations and conditions that apply to an essentially positive message.

━ You will see how careful control of sentence patterns and paragraph lengths can reinforce your words and ideas.

A GOOD START

Beginnings in business often depend on appearances or first impressions. An experienced job recruiter will say, "I know whether or not I'm going to hire an applicant when the person walks into the room." Well-fitting and fashionable, correct clothing, a pleasant smile, and a firm handshake create the positive first impression that gives you a chance at the real work of selling—confirming an interviewer's initial judgment of your qualifications, selling your product to your customer, or convincing a potential investor that your idea has great profit possibilities. You arrive at your meeting prepared for just the right moment to initiate your selling strategy. You leave little or nothing to chance. You plan.

The same principle that works for people in business works for documents too. Starting with a blank sheet of paper, you create a page that seems unified but not cramped, relatively open and inviting without seeming to waste space. Your attractively arranged memo, letter, or report, confidently correct in grammar, spelling, and word choice, earns you a hearing. Ideally, every business message "arrives" through its appropriate page presentation, measurable in margin inches and in single and double spacings. These features create a first impression for the reader's eye, while parallel strategies establish a clear direction for the reader's *understanding*.

Let's face it: most business messages finally amount to "yes," "no," or "Let's talk about it." But you would no more reduce your memo or letter to just those words than you would arrive at a board meeting clothed only in your underwear. Just as your page arrangement gives your message an appropriate physical presence, so your opening sentences create the psychological space the reader needs to accept your offer or your explanation. Just as you would not rush into a stranger's room without knocking, your letter would not blurt out "No, thanks," to a job applicant, or "Sorry, no refunds" to a loyal customer who has requested a reasonable adjustment. Routine letters carry little emotional freight, but in bad-news letters it is often difficult to say "no" without seeming to reject the person along with the request. Although "yes" letters are usually easier to write than "no" responses, you will often need to say "yes, but" or "yes, if"; you may be granting the request but not giving away the store. "Yes," "no," or "maybe"—each type of message works best when you combine polished outer form with the appropriate pattern of ideas.

THE DIRECT APPROACH

The direct approach is almost always best for good-news, complaint, and adjustment letters as well as a wide range of routine correspondence, including inquiries, invitations, orders, and acknowledgments. In a good-news or an adjustment letter, you want to showcase the news that the reader has hoped for, and your opening sentence establishes your generosity, or, in a contested situation, your reasonableness. The customer *will* receive the refund or exchange. The company interviewers were impressed, and the applicant *will* get the job offer. A teenager's contest essay has been chosen, and she *has* won a date with her favorite rock star. The medical lab sends a definitive "all clear" from the biopsy. The vacation home loan is approved at a favorable repayment rate. The budding entrepreneur has beaten out his rivals for a coveted "hot" franchise. The cost-is-no-barrier collector has submitted the winning bid for the rare stamp from British Guiana. Why hold back such welcome messages as these?

Although a complaint letter has a less pleasant purpose than the good-news one, the claim will get most favorable attention if the writer offers his basic case clearly at the outset, coupling his description of the problem with calmness and the certainty that understandable confusion has complicated the alteration of his suit, the repair of his car, or the seating designation of his season tickets. Gruff, aggressive, accusatory opening sentences in a claim letter might lead the reader to conclude that the writer's business is not worth keeping. The writer who begins with a tempered, rational summary of the transaction and the consequent difficulty is more likely to receive the benefit of the doubt than the hothead proclaiming rampant incompetence.

Routine and pleasant letters, although far less emotionally involving than good-news announcements, usually begin in the same direct way. The writer declares a need for information about a product line's color, size, model, and price choices; about a credit applicant's job performance; about transportation, dining, and lodging rates for a couple or a tour group; and about countless other "information, please" situations. Likewise, the "We want you to know" letter might open by informing a regular customer of a firm's new product, service, or relocation. The same direct beginning works well for a brief letter of invitation: "Please circle Monday, April 2, 1996, on your calendar and reserve that day for our preview fashion showing in the Magnolia Room promptly at noon," or "Our company celebrates its seventy-fifth anniversary this fall, and we very much hope that you will agree to give an after-dinner speech at our employee banquet on October 21 at the Carleton Hotel." The letter of thanks is still another form of pleasant-letter communication best handled in the direct order. After staging a very successful conference at a local hotel, you might write the manager to express your thanks for the careful attention that the staff gave to everyone's equipment and comfort needs. When the city police and fire departments have averted a disaster at your production plant, your letter to each department's chief (with copies to the mayor and to the city council chairman) will begin with a warm statement of gratitude for tireless and heroic efforts during a long, tense night. You might conjure up any number of similar situations where a direct (but not blunt) beginning is effective.

If your letter begins with its essential message, what is left to say? Usually, plenty. You can follow your positive announcement with appropriate amplification ("But wait! There's more! This offer gets better and better"), qualification ("Certain restrictions apply to all winners"), or both. Not every blue sky is entirely cloudless; often you must qualify your opening good-news message with a clearly phrased, nontechnical specification of any conditions, reservations, exceptions, or other legally binding requirements that the recipient must meet before the loan or franchise contract can be signed or before the contest winner can collect the winnings.

In accepting merchandise for exchange, you might begin your adjustment response with a confirmation of your fair-minded policy, and your second paragraph might list your packing and shipping requirements for the return of goods. Firmly but unmenacingly you will remind the customer that returned nondefective merchandise must be received in resalable condition. Alternately, your line of business, dealing with high-end merchandise offered to impulse buyers with plenty of cash, might require an extremely flexible policy on returns. When an audio enthusiast complains that his 150-watts-per-channel amplifier caught fire three weeks after he brought it home from your store, you decide that you have no way of proving that the wiring was not, as he asserts, defective. Under your "benefit of the doubt" policy you agree to replace the unit, but, assuming a neutrally informing tone in your second paragraph, you can also mention that pages 21 and 22 of the owner's manual offer useful warnings about ventilation space needed for the safe operation and prolonged life span of electronic devices. "Yes, we'll keep our word," you are saying, but you subtly make the point that you will very closely scrutinize the return of a second heat-damaged component from the same customer.

When no such restrictions or reservations apply to your good news, you can supplement your brief first-paragraph announcement with pleasant details and happy images. Congratulating the successful applicant for an executive position in your firm, you can review the benefits open to the new jobholder. Notifying the winner of your store-opening prize drawing, you can tie the customer's happiness to appealing qualities of your product or service. As a company physician writing the required letter-report about a manager's annual physical examination, you can congratulate him on his general good health and reassure him that the recent pins-and-needles sensations in his legs are the body's temporary protests that naturally follow a usually desk-bound person's sudden burst of physical activity—a golf tournament or a weekend of strenuously raking leaves. You can suggest ways of avoiding pain peaks by maintaining a moderate fitness regimen. You can persuade him that his continued good health will benefit the company as well as himself and his family. In such good-news situations, the direct-order letter reveals its full message like a flower opening its bud in a time-lapse film.

In writing a routine information request, you will obviously begin by stating your needs and purposes, but you will not want to overwhelm the addressee with an open-ended query. You will narrow your request through a series of specifications or limits ("You need not include any data from years prior to 1986" or "Our genealogy is concerned only with descendants of H. Malmgren and Anna Broughton Smith"), and you will end with the mention of a reasonable reply deadline, cushioned by thanks for anticipated efforts on your behalf. If you are requesting data or document duplication from a public or university library, you might ask whether or not a researcher's fee will be charged. As more and more public institutions must function on pinched budgets, formerly free services are now operated on a pay-as-you-go basis.

Sometimes clarifying your purpose is no less important than stating what you want to know. Obviously Gerber Products would not cheerfully respond to questions about its baby food formulas, bottling techniques, or promotion efforts if those queries were posed by Beechnut, H.J. Heinz, another competitor, or a newspaper or a television program known for its muckraking investigative methods. On the other hand, the chief nutritionist at a children's hospital might have a quite legitimate concern about preservatives or other ingredients used in an infant formula that could be fed to very young patients with dietary or chemical intolerances. If the nutritionist, writing on hospital letterhead, expresses her need for information in terms of patient health and safety, the manufacturer will be morally bound to help the health professional determine the conditions in which an allergic or chemical reaction might be anticipated. The formula maker will not release its trade secrets to anyone, but self-interest and safety concerns will prompt the company to help avert a crisis involving its products.

Perhaps your information request opens the possibility of great benefit to the addressee as well as to you. In searching for a new regional distribution center site, you have noted the geographical advantages of Kentucky, a state whose television commercials declare it "Open for Business." Writing the Office of Economic Development or the Kentucky State Chamber of Commerce, you will first indicate your need for cleared acreage suitable for a large warehouse (described in square footage) and a smaller administration building. The middle portion of your letter will list your requirements for utilities and transportation access, and you will mention employee housing needs and other factors that might influence the choice of one city or another. You will probably ask about tax advantages and industrial park incentives, and you might ask for a ranking, with justifying details, of four or five attractive sites. In the closing paragraph you will indicate that you would welcome, by January 15, the agency's recommendations. Although your letter asks someone to go to some trouble on your behalf, it also appeals to the recipient's interests, so you need not be too apologetic about requesting genuinely needed details. Your closing paragraph will declare your anticipation of a useful response, this expectation being pegged to the date by which your must begin the final phase of your site selection. If you have allowed sufficient leadtime for representatives of a business-hungry state to furnish information, and if you have limited your request to the kinds of material really needed, you can expect a timely, well-packaged response.

For relatively brief and uncomplicated good-news announcements and routine requests, then, a three-paragraph arrangement will work well:

	good-news letter	**routine request**
first paragraph:	key good news, with related basic details	basic request, defined by scope and purpose
second paragraph:	still further good news and/or qualifying statements (time limits, legal obligations or restrictions, exceptions, other reservations) applying to your offer	detailed requirements, perhaps listed in priority order; limits of time span, cost range, or any other coverage specification
third paragraph:	empathetic reinforcement of the good news, expressed in a congratulatory tone, often incorporating a deadline date for reply or other required action	thanks for the recipient's anticipated efforts; indication of the date by which you need the reply

You can easily expand this three-paragraph pattern into four paragraphs if your message includes a burgeoning list of job responsibilities, an intricate explanation of a legality, or a long catalog of prizes won. Since the second paragraph will be the most detail-heavy, you can look there for subgroups of details that you will recast into separate paragraphs. In welcoming a new member to your country club, for instance, you might devote a paragraph to the benefits that approved membership will bring to the paying member (new business contacts, social entree, facilities available by reservation for meetings), while the following paragraph will outline the privileges and social and recreational opportunities extended to his family. In the same way, a national park superintendent might divide the middle of his job-assignment letter into descriptions of the newly appointed resident ranger's duties in the heavy tourist season and the ostensibly quieter off-season months when the ranger must be alert to winter weather emergencies and repair needs. Whether you use three paragraphs or four, the outer paragraphs are likely to be brief (but not abruptly short), while the middle of the letter carries the greater proportion of details.

Further Shaping the Good News

Held to a single page if possible, the three- (or four-) paragraph good-news or request letter is a highly workable form. The briefer opening and closing paragraphs have much to do with setting the letter's dominant tone, while the more detailed middle portion offers enough contrast in length, texture, and pacing to avoid any sense of monotony. The last paragraph, reinforcing and broadening the tone of the opening one, gives a sense of completeness, of coming full circle. Notice how each paragraph contributes to the cumulative effect in the following letter from a medical school's Director of Admissions to a prospective student.

In the opening sentences the basic news needs little or no cushioning. A student with solid credentials would expect to be admitted, and this one has the benefit of family connections, too.

On behalf of the faculty at the DeMarr Medical University, I congratulate you upon your acceptance into the first-year program. Your transcripts and test scores show outstanding promise, and your recommenders are most persuasive advocates of your intellectual and personal qualities.

The formal touches in the phrasing ("upon" rather than the plainer "on," for instance, and "most persuasive" in place of "very convincing") are not mere affectations or verbal badges of office. As we will see, these word choices prepare for the final paragraph's appeal to tradition.

In the meantime, the Director of Admissions will use the middle paragraph to exert a little pressure for a prompt decision. His job is to fill all spaces, and he knows that for every applicant who stands near the admissions door, someone further back in line hopes for a chance. The letter's warm opening leads to a reasonably subtle appeal:

You are probably aware that we receive 500 to 600 applications for the thirty-five places available each year. While some applicants have higher test scores or more prominent recommendations than others, nearly all can make a compelling argument for admission on one basis or another. Some are representatives of Third World countries; others have committed themselves to rural or inner city settings in the United States, places where well-trained medical professionals are scarce. Because the admissions board has the enormous responsibility of opening medical study to a variety of qualified applicants, I ask that you accept or decline your place in the entering class by May 15. Naturally, I hope that you will accept.

The paragraph's last sentence is also the shortest, and its brevity and placement make it the most emphatic. Aside from politely suggesting that the reader must cast his lot with DeMarr or yield his opportunity to someone else, the paragraph also obliquely recognizes the likelihood that the pre-med student has been accepted by other schools and might have a difficult choice to make, especially if urged toward an early decision. The writer must find a "difference" factor that competing schools cannot offer.

To enhance DeMarr's special appeal, the Director of Admissions closes his letter by returning to the positive mode of the opening paragraph, but here the emphasis is on an added personal element. The reply deadline (which might otherwise appear here) has already been stated, so this paragraph further nudges the recipient toward a positive response by that date.

Your father is a highly valued alumnus of our program, and your brother John's reputation for surgical skill has grown steadily since his days with us. Please convey our greetings to them, and please give your strongest consideration to sustaining your family's ties to the DeMarr Medical University. I look forward to your response.

The compact closing sentence is the quietly effective climax not only of its paragraph but also of a letter that both offers and asks. This letter has arched from the personal as well as the institutional "On behalf...I congratulate" through "I hope that...." to the stronger wish implied in "I look forward to...." Coming to rest on the prompting word "response," the final sentence seems to say, "The ball is in your court; you'd better make a shrewd return." In its firm brevity, the last sentence also subtly challenges the reader, as if to suggest, "With these persuasive factors placed before

you, how could you answer other than 'Yes'?" The family connections, the direct first-person appeal of the second paragraph's
closing sentence ("Naturally, I hope that you will accept"), the
general argument for accepting the earned opportunity at
DeMarr, and the implicit reminder of the looming May 15 deadline all fuse into an understated but confident expectation.

The three-paragraph direct order pattern allows the writer of
this carefully crafted, rather compact letter to layer his rational
and his personal appeals. Not every letter will be so closely
gauged, but the same basic pattern (key statement, elaboration
through detail, prompt to action) will work well for many purposes.

Further Shaping the Routine Letter

Even when it follows a standard pattern, the routine letter need
not seem routine. "Neutral" correspondence does not have to be
coldly impersonal. When a customer goes to the trouble of writing a letter to spell out exactly how he or she wants an order
filled—a wedding cake described to the last detail of flavoring
and decoration, a chair of exactly the right wood and fabric color
and finish to be placed in a newly renovated room—that customer is investing some hopes in the request, and the wise
respondent will take those expectations into account. Even correspondence between a manufacturer and a supplier can benefit
from the occasional "human touch" of thanks for the honesty in
grading, for the consistent quality of supplied materials, or for the
reliable promptness of payment over the years.

A home decorator might begin a request to a rare book dealer:

> In renovating a formal library for a very particular client, I
> need a large set of volumes bound in Persian blue, dull finish,
> preferably with silver stamping on the spines. You have often
> met my requirements for other customers, and I hope that your
> generous stock will contain something suitable this time.

The second paragraph will likely suggest the cost range and mention the expected professional discount for this transaction, and
the brief closing paragraph will offer thanks for the book search,
coupled with a deadline for notification of the result of that
search. With surprising quickness the bookseller might respond:

> I believe that I have exactly the right leather-bound set for your client. Your timing is fortunate, because only last week I received shipment of seventeenth and eighteenth century books from a Connecticut estate. Among these is an excellently bound 1688 set of the plays, histories, and novels of Aphra Behn, printed in London on fine vellum.

In the following paragraph the bookseller will detail the well-preserved condition of the volumes, noting the crispness of the title stamping and the absence of cracking in the morocco bindings. He will also mention a very slight water stain, detectable only by the most careful examination, on the bottom edges of half a dozen pages in one volume, a regrettable minor imperfection that is reflected in the stated net price. The closing paragraph will describe the rich, deep blue of the bindings and will offer to hold the set in reserve for ten days. Each of the correspondents in this exchange has followed the direct order, first stating his essential business, continuing with particulars, and closing with a pleasant statement of confidence in the capability or satisfaction of the reader.

Usually a buyer knows exactly what he wants and can state his order with efficient brevity:

> Please ship and bill us for 24 INvision television receivers, model 3542-Y, with remote handsets. I understand that this shipment will qualify for a 15% volume discount on the wholesale price.

Other customers are not so sure. When a mother must make arrangements for her daughter's wedding in a distant city, for instance, her initial dealings with a formal wear rental agency will take place by mail, and she might ask about the availabilty of a particular cut and the one-day rate for a dozen dinner jackets. Perhaps she will give a brief description of the heirloom wedding dress and ask for suggestions for the outfitting of the bridesmaids, the groomsmen, and the ring-bearer in related styles. The manager will begin his reply by assuring the prospective customer that he has just the right outfits to achieve a judicious blend of traditional and contemporary touches, and the middle part of his letter will explain that his stock of well-maintained rental garments includes a wide range of sizes and accessory choices at quite reasonable rates. His next step is to urge the mother to send him a list of sizes required, and he will close by offering flexible hours for pickup and return as well as necessary fitting adjustments.

Most inquiry and order letters, then, begin with brief identifications of the needed merchandise or service, often detailed in product names and model numbers and sometimes tied to a delivery deadline or anticipated use date. The second paragraph will further define the writer's needs and expectations, and the closing paragraph will confirm the wish for a helpful reply.

An acknowledgment of a large order will take a similar shape. A commercial printer might write the editor of a high school yearbook,

---

Thank you for selecting Printcraft to produce the 1993 edition of The Yearling. Valley High School's graphic arts department always produces outstanding photographs and page decorations, and with your school's usual promptness in meeting copy and engraving deadlines, I can promise delivery of a yearbook you'll be proud of. You will have 728 copies by April 15.

Recently we have published a number of yearbooks featuring heavy-stock colored pages as section dividers. Have you considered this low-cost option for bringing added distinction to your book? I'm sure you will be convinced of its effectiveness when you see the volume that we printed last year for an Iowa school, winner of its regional student publication award. You should receive a sample copy in three or four days.

Your own school has an excellent publication record, and I know that the current staff will sustain that achievement. At your early convenience please return the printing contract signed by you, Miss Arnett, and Dr. Harrison. Thanks for trusting Printcraft with your efforts.

While the basic purpose of that letter is to confirm an agreement, the writer also quietly urges attention to submission deadlines, and he uses the middle paragraph to introduce a new sales factor.

Sometimes you must couple an acknowledgment with an apology, one balancing the other in the opening paragraph. For example, the advertising director of a pharmaceutical company will deal with a sudden change in product promotion by writing the head of an agency,

> Thanks for sending the broadcast storyboards so quickly. Everyone here agrees that the animated characters are ideal for our children's vitamin line. However, we have decided to put the campaign on hold for several weeks. In the face of another package-tampering incident involving our gelatin capsules, we cannot jump into a promotion emphasizing jollity and brightness.
>
> For the time being we will concentrate on informational advertising that points out signs of product tampering. As we remove all capsules from the market, we want to assure the public of the safety of our products packaged in a variety of other ways. Please let us have your ideas on these sober themes, and please continue refining the vitamin characters for use at a more opportune time.

If the pharmaceutical manufacturer were canceling its advertising entirely, this would be a bad-news letter, written in another pattern. Instead, this episode illustrates the roll-with-the-punches adaptations that businesses must make, and the advertising agency is apt to gain rather than lose through this change of plans.

Often a well-conceived complaint letter will also begin by balancing positive and negative factors. A disappointed customer writes an importer of Swiss watches,

> Until now I have always found Greenwich quartz watches to be ideal high school and college graduation gifts for my many nieces and nephews, but the most recent order is a sad exception. Although the box that I received this morning lists the number of the catalog item that I paid for on my Visa card, the watch bears little resemblance to the one in your illustration, and the oversized dial simply will not do for little Annette.
>
> Your watches are attractive and reasonably priced, and your shipping is prompt. In hopes of continuing this little gift-

continues on next page

giving tradition, I have carefully repacked the watch and will return it to you when I mail this letter. Since Annette's graduation is still three weeks away, you should have time to send me model number SA 92 (and no other). I cannot accept a late arrival, however. If this model is unavailable, please credit this return to my Visa card and cancel the order.

Surely some honest mistake has occurred, and surely you will correct it in plenty of time.

This credit card-wielding aunt is not to be taken for granted. She writes a cunning letter, hinting that the seller will lose her long-standing patronage if he and his staff don't watch themselves. She knows what she wants, and the only convincing reply will be a straightforward one, written, like her own letter, in the direct format:

My firm has sold over 80,000 watches in the United States since I began importing them seven years ago, and would you believe that I have never before seen a return of an incorrectly boxed item? A Greenwich SA 92 is on its way to you with a check to cover your shipping expenses.

I like to think that my retail business is as orderly as the shops of our Swiss craftsmen. However, we experienced an electrical emergency in our storeroom last week, and in the rush several storage shelves were overturned. Clearly the watch you received had evaded our efforts to reunite every timepiece with its proper box. I ask your understanding and assure you that all future orders will be double-checked.

The SA 92 is supplied with a genuine leather band. In your package you will also find a complimentary durable cloth band, which your niece might enjoy as a fashion change. As a further sign of my gratitude for your patience, please return this letter with your next order and receive a 20% discount.

The three-paragraph direct pattern is ideal for this letter. The first paragraph promises a quick adjustment, the second offers a credible explanation for the shipping error, and the third appropriately rounds off the letter by offering unexpected bonuses.

The Long and the Short of It

Much of this chapter has focused on how you can use the three- or four-paragraph direct presentation for many good-news and routine messages, including invitations, inquiries, product or service orders, cancellations, complaints and adjustments. Our primary attention has been directed toward the broad clustering of ideas into paragraph patterns—the basic message in the opening paragraph; explanation, amplification, or qualification in the middle paragraph(s); and a verbal handshake at the end. Scattered through the examples and the explanatory material in this chapter are illustrations of still another means of shaping your message: controlling sentence and paragraph lengths. It is time to bring that element into the foreground.

Every paragraph and every sentence within it has its task. If it did not, it would be redundant, and you would edit it out of your final draft. Beginning paragraphs concentrate on establishing common ground between the writer and the reader: here's what we are concerned with, in essence. At first the writer should mark off the boundaries of his subject territory, succinctly touching on key names, dates, model numbers, and so on. Two to four sentences, of short to moderate lengths, will accomplish the letter's first task. In the middle paragraph, the writer points out specific features of the landscape, often clustering them into parallel words or phrases. Here the sentences are apt to grow longer, and the writer needs to be especially watchful that his statements maintain clear, unambiguous direction. The last paragraph, balancing the first one, is also likely to be briefer than the middle one, but you should avoid closing with a paragraph containing only a single standard statement such as "Thanks for your time" or "Thank you for your attention to this matter." The rubber-stamp effect will seem glib and in some contexts a little callous. (You also don't want to commit the opposite fault of false effusiveness that resembles the nervous chatter of someone who doesn't know how to end a phone conversation.) Rather, the last paragraph is your opportunity, in two, three, or four sentences, to add a personal touch to an otherwise cut-and-dried transaction or to put a misunderstanding into perspective.

Letters have formal formats, and the paragraphs within those formats set up a measured rhythm. Likewise, the sentences within your paragraphs can sustain a confident tone or dramatize an appeal. Consider this personal plea for understanding:

> I have served your firm for many years, working nights, weekends, holidays, any days and hours that the deadline required. Your father and your uncle praised my work, and you have given me raises, bonuses, and awards, for which I am ever grateful. Unfortunately my wife's illness and long hospitalization tempted me to reach into the till, thinking that I could repay the cash later. Having been detected and having no means now of replacing the money, I can only offer my resignation. I am sorry.

Whether this letter strikes you as heartfelt or weepily melodramatic, its ending is undeniably forceful. The shortest possible statement of regret puts a period to the longer, more complex statements of justification and confession. The sudden change of sentence length, especially at the end of a paragraph, is a device that can be overworked, but when used wisely, it is very powerful.

Reviewing the letter examples in this chapter, you might notice the confirming effects of the closing short sentences in the second and third paragraphs of the medical school admissions notification. Not only are the sentences themselves emphatic— "Naturally, I hope that you will accept" and "I look forward to your response"— but they also end on prompting words that summarize the writer's hope: "accept" and (positive) "response." In the sentence that ends the complaint letter about the watch model, the writer uses parallel phrasing and similar clause lengths to yoke her basic complaint with her basic demand: "Surely some honest mistake has occurred, and surely you will correct it in plenty of time." To say anything more would spoil the crisp effect achieved in this emphatic compound sentence.

A shift in the lengths and patterns of a paragraph's sentences can lend force to the sentence that breaks the pattern, particularly if it is the concluding sentence. Last sentences in internal paragraphs are springboards to the next phases of your message, and a carefully chosen last word or phrase can have a powerful impact on the reader's perception of tone and idea.

CHAPTER PERSPECTIVE

While the direct order is by no means mandatory for good news and routine letters, this pattern suggests an honest, businesslike directness that allows most writers to organize their messages into three or four paragraphs, usually of moderate length. Nearly all brief business letters except the bad news letter will fit this order of presentation.

Within the direct letter's pyramid-like broadening into details, you will discover other opportunities to control your tone and to urge attention to this or that idea. Your message will be clear enough if you express your thoughts in well-phrased, grammatically correct statements presented in coherent order. However, using the power inherent in sentence and paragraph patterns can make the difference between an indifferent or a sharply attentive reading of your message. The more you are aware of how your sentences strike the reader's inner ear and how they build into paragraphs and ultimately whole letters, the better you will become at putting your thoughts on paper.

Indirect-Approach Letters

CHAPTER

8

INTRODUCTION AND MAIN POINTS

In Chapter 7 you saw the advantages of beginning a good-news letter with the "yes" message, followed by details of any conditions, directions, requirements, or reservations tied to your offer or acceptance. You will use a very different strategy, however, when you must reject a request or decline an offer. Although your basic message will be "no," you will phrase and place the negative response so that your reader will accept your judgment as fair, reasonable, and appropriate. Your word choices, sentence patterns, and tone will persuade the recipient that you have reached your firm decision after sufficiently considering his or her point of view as well as your own capabilities (or your company's).

A well-planned bad-news letter will cushion its message both literally and psychologically: it will use positive or neutral opening and closing statements to "contain" the negative message and to buffer its potential effects. The goal is to establish a mutually acceptable context for conveying the bad news while simultaneously protecting, as fully as possible, the longer-term positive relationship between the company and its customer, a supervisor and subordinates, a government official and a voter, or any other two or more people.

While the larger part of this chapter deals with bad-news situations, a later section will show how the same inductive pattern is useful for answering the correspondent who wants nothing more than a credible explanation or a recognition of his or her point of view.

After studying the material in this chapter:

■ You will understand how a correspondent's psychological needs (for fulfillment, for security, for recognition) might be tied, consciously or not, to a request or a demand made of you.

■ You will know how to place and buffer the basic "no" reply so that it is least likely to surprise, alienate, or unwittingly insult your reader.

▬ You will realize how to avoid negative wording, especially in the naturally emphatic positions in sentences and paragraphs.

▬ You will see how the lengths of your paragraphs and the arrangement of your sentences can influence the recipient's perception of your message.

THE DECISION TO SAY "NO"

You have saved and borrowed to start your business, you have hired employees and built an inventory, and you like to think that you are making a well-earned profit on reasonably priced goods or services that meet your customers' needs. As your business grows, however, you find that you must fire as well as hire, that you must prefer one job candidate to another, and that you cannot maintain an adequate profit margin if you invariably yield to the dictum "The customer is always right." A large department store chain might be willing to write off costly returns, no questions asked, for the sake of justifying its slogan "With us, the sale is never final," but unless you have very deep pockets, you will sometimes reach the point of having to say "no" to a customer, a supplier, or a charity appeal. You cannot hire both leading applicants for one position, so you must send congratulations to Ms. Holliday and regrets to Ms. Sayers or vice versa. You can replace a jacket once or twice if the customer finds that the seams were not sewn with utmost precision, but you cannot forever indulge the shopper who finds fault, large or minuscule, with every item bought from you.

Before deciding to say "no" to a potential supplier, to an eager but inexperienced job candidate, or to a steady but choosy customer, you will anticipate both the immediate and the long-term effects of your choice. In refusing to pay huge fees for exclusive area distribution rights to a wildly popular product, you might miss a surge of sales at the peak of the fad, but you will not be stuck with unsellable inventory when the public enthusiasm wanes. Will you say "yes" or "no"? If you try to end the spiraling cycle of Mr. Turner's refund and exchange demands, will he cut up his store credit card in a fit of anger and toss a twenty year retailer-customer relationship into the wastebasket? How long can you afford to continue saying "yes"? Can you package a "no" so that it does not seem to shout "NO!"? Of two job applicants, Nina Holliday has years of selling experience with a leading firm in another city, but she has begun to project a superior air, while

Alma Sayers lacks polish but brings a pleasing openness and freshness to every sales opportunity. Which one gets the job, and which receives the regretful "no" letter? Tough, tough decisions.

Before firmly closing the door with an unqualified bad-news message, consider whether or not you can turn a "No, we can't" response into a moderating, "Instead, we will...." Here you will judge whether the complaint is trivial or serious, whether precisely satisfying the demand is within or beyond your control, and whether or not the purchaser's incorrect and damaging operation of the device stems from your failure to caution him about its proper installation and use. In gray areas of responsibility, it is often worthwhile to replace the merchandise cheerfully, especially if the item is not expensive. If the cost of the item, the terms of the manufacturer's warranty, or any other factor blocks a full exchange or refund, you can offer to repair the device free of charge, you can extend the store warranty, or you can arrange a mutually convenient time for your service technician to check the product installation in the buyer's home or office and guide him through the correct operating procedure. Similarly, you can hire one applicant for the previously listed sales position while advising the other job-seeker to redirect her application toward a new opening that you expect to advertise soon. Offering relatively easy options such as these will allow you to keep friends rather than losing customers and alienating potential employees who might later achieve phenomenal sales records—for the competitor across the street.

YOUR CORRESPONDENT'S POINT OF VIEW

Generally, your "yes" responses will be easy to write, while your "no" and alternate-offer letters will challenge your diplomatic and strategic skills. As a businessperson you are not responsible for maintaining every customer's overall sense of well-being or smoothing each wrinkled brow. However, you would be remiss if you did not consider that an impossible or unreasonable request often originates in factors quite apart from the true worth of the product, the service, or the offer that triggered the demand.

A person making what he sees as a very simple request—for a loan, a job, a promotion, an exchange, a refund—will often tie that request to the satisfaction of some need or desire that is larger than he consciously realizes. What this person has asked of you, reasonably or not, is entwined with his or her view of the world. Usually this linking occurs subconsciously, but whatever its source, it can exert a powerful effect on the person's reception of your response. If a man's life experience has conditioned him to feel bullied, he might make unreasonable demands on your company to show that he "won't be pushed around anymore." He attempts to mask his insecurity by bravado, and he will dare you to disappoint his hopes and expectations. A widow made nervous by not promptly receiving her monthly Social Security check might feel compelled to insist that you make special arrangements about her bill payments—concessions that you will readily grant a longtime customer if you are approached in a reasonable way. (Without triggering yet another set of demands, you can allay her fears and outline an option: no lawyers or bill collectors will pound on her door, you can assure her, and your office will be pleased to negotiate a workable minimum payment plan.)

A customer who has felt cheated in his dealings with another firm might try to right that perceived wrong by insisting that your company grant him a greater discount, a closer delivery date, or a higher beginning salary than your capacity, company policy, or profitability can allow. How can you deny the request, if necessary, without "turning off" the person? The security of your position and even the health of your company might well depend on your ability to do so. Angry customers and disappointed jobseekers are often eager to shift blame toward the company and proclaim their hurt sensibilities widely.

In preparing to answer a hostile or an insistent letter, you will consider whether or not an empathetic, reasonable reply might neutralize the writer's feelings and keep him or her among your satisfied customers. Often an angry or disappointed consumer will have vented much of his negative feeling in the process of writing and mailing the letter. By the time your considered response arrives, he will probably have settled into a more accepting, rational, and even conciliatory mood. Your opportunity lies in encouraging that change of feeling.

Your first step, then, is to estimate whether a demand comes from an angry impulse or from a sustained disagreeableness. With luck, you will seldom have to deal with a letter as thoroughly hostile as the verbal attack on a men's clothing shop in Greenville, South Carolina, shown on page 117.

The exaggerated language, the unwarranted insults, and the transparently empty threats only prompted the store owner to return the letter, torn into four pieces, with a copy of his newspaper advertisement on which he had circled the printed phrases "No Returns, No Refunds While the Sale Lasts, Please" in red and added the marginal note "Go to Hell!" Although neither side

Gentlemen (if I may call you that):

At your recent, highly over-advertised sale of bargain suits, I bought a tan suit marked down from $159.95 to $110.00. The salesman, obviously drunk with power, kept assuring me it fit beautifully, it was just my style and brought out the "real" me, and it would be gone if I waited to make up my mind. (I think he meant it would be whisked back to the storeroom to be turned into dishrags, since I was his last hope of making a sale).

Yielding to that con artist's blandishments, I bought the suit and had it measured for alteration. Today when I brought it home and tried it on again, I realized that the so-called "beautiful fit" was a snare and a delusion; the damn thing bags in the seat as though I were hiding a covey of quail in the hip pockets. The sleeves are an excellent length for a man of 5' 3" height; I am 5' 11" in my thinnest nylon socks. The width of the coat's back would accommodate me and my brother together, with room left over for a very thin blond (fun, but impractical at best).

In addition, that great "bargain" had faultily sewn seams that puckered like the girl's mouth in the TV mouthwash commercials; one lapel was a half-inch wider than the other (intriguing, but not this year's fashion, to say the least); and your tailor—you know, the alcoholic with the crossed eyes?—made one leg two inches shorter than the other.

I am bringing this abomination back to you, and I expect a full rebate on the purchase price. No more, no less. Let me assure you that if you can't see your way clear to being reasonable, I have an excellent lawyer who can explain it to you in court so that you *can* find it in your flinty hearts to give me my money back. In any event, if you make trouble about this shoddy piece of chicanery, I am fully prepared to buy a half-page ad in the comic section of the Sunday newspaper to state my case to the public. (I choose the comic section because I feel certain that it is the only part of the paper where *you* are sure to see it).

> Yours in the spirit of loathing
> and justifiable hostility,...

won in this skirmish, most disagreements allow at least a little room for movement. Making (or enlarging) such space is a large part of succeeding in a bad-news letter.

You decide to deny a request, but you also trust that your correspondent will respond to a reasonable explanation or a fair counteroffer. Once you have gauged your reader's attitude, your next task is to organize your letter so that you have an opportunity to present your case before you announce the bad news. The indirect order is ideal for this purpose, because it allows you to surround the disappointing core message with good-will or neutralizing statements as well as convincing details.

WRITING THE LETTER

A bad-news letter written in indirect order (leading toward and then away from the core bad-news statement) will typically fall into this pattern:

opening paragraph:

> buffer (good-will or neutral statements)

middle paragraph(s):

> explanatory details, then bad news, then
> positive alternative

closing paragraph:

> perspective-giving goodwill comments

Before examining and illustrating the specific contribution of each paragraph to the letter, we might note the general advantages of this plan. First, by placing the bad news at the center of the middle paragraph, you provide a double layer of protection against suddenly seeming to dismiss the reader and the request. By the time the reader reaches your "no" statement, she should feel that it is justified and fair, given the factors you have outlined. Second, since the last paragraph echoes the warm or conciliatory tone of the letter's beginning, your closing lines will assume a sense of completeness, subtly (never dismissively) suggesting that you have carefully reviewed the request and said what needs to be said about it.

The opening and closing paragraphs will be relatively brief, but not so short as to seem blunt or indifferent. They will set a positive tone by focusing on broad areas of agreement, and they will only distantly (if at all) touch on the specifics of any current anxiety or disagreement. In these outer paragraphs you should be especially watchful for the clichéd phrases that tend to creep into openings and closings and suggest a routine, impersonal handling of the subject.

For the opening paragraph you can choose among several approaches, depending on the length and nature of the writer-reader relationship and the degree of potential disappointment that the bad-news message will bring. You might express appreciation for the customer's longtime patronage, and you might mention one or two especially advantageous purchases he has made from you. Before telling him that you cannot allow a "like-new" trade-in valuation of a much-used lawnmower, you might begin, "I am grateful for your relying on Carswell's Lawn and Garden since we began serving our Centreville customers seventeen years ago. When I drive past your house each morning, I am proud to know that your impressive lawn is maintained with the THP-30 riding mower that I sold you back in 1982." Establishing the purchase date in the first paragraph, you can then devote the beginning of the next paragraph to an outline of the manufacturer's trade-in allowances.

Often an opening compliment will cast both the reader and the writer in the ruddy glow of mutual admiration— "Congratulations on your choice of Westwood Silver Sylph for your fine china. We are proud to be the exclusive agents for this imported tableware line, which you will use with undiminished pleasure for years to come"—and this beginning will prepare the way for your reluctant announcement that recent shipping difficulties have reduced your stock, so that you can send only a partial order to the eager bride. You can couple your assurances of the customer's good taste with an appeal to practicality ("You may rest assured that the silver rim is dishwasher safe"), and you can add your promise that the bride will soon set her table with "the china that is worth a short wait."

If your letter contains only one bad-news element and if that element is unlikely to be crucial, you can simply begin with the good-news part of your message: "Thank you for ordering Haycroft Farm Deluxe Mixed Fruits and Nuts packages for your Christmas giving again this year. Your gifts will be on their way to your friends by December 7." The word "again" in the opening sentence subtly reminds the customer of her reliance on Haycroft Farms for her annual gift-giving, and the second sentence indicates that the order is being handled in timely fashion. You have reserved the unfortunate detail for the second paragraph, where you will explain that a late freeze has reduced your Bosc pear crop this year and that you will ship another variety. You will immediately follow this detail with an offer of a refund or an alternate package, but your opening and closing assurances of the general quality of your products should persuade her to accept your promise that the substituted item will be just as appealing as the original one.

Your first paragraph might include neutral details about the transaction at issue (dates, places, model numbers), but you should avoid groveling or shrill apologies, negative words, and other word choices that confirm the reader's disappointment. If an antiques dealer's letter begins, "I am terribly distressed by your May 22nd letter, which tells me that one of those splendid Belgian lamps was crushed in shipment," he has certainly not relieved the buyer's anguish by adding his own. Rather, he has confirmed and enlarged the negative situation that prompted the letter, and this is scarcely an appropriate beginning to a letter explaining that the customer must file her claim with the shipping agency, which bears sole responsibility now.

If an apology seems warranted, make it quietly sincere rather than effusive, and preface it by acknowledging the customer's value to your company: "Thank you for directing my attention to the situation you encountered on June 16 at the Ballard Department Store. As a regular and valued shopper with us, you know that we only recently installed a new magnetic sensor security system in our dressing rooms, and I regret that a faulty circuit triggered the device and alarmed the sales associate." This appeal for understanding and continued store loyalty might be followed by an offer of a Preferred Customer Card, entitling the holder to fashion preview showings and special discounts. The apology is plainly made, but not before the writer has confirmed a positive relationship between the store and its frequent customer.

Since the opening paragraph establishes the letter's tone, you should be especially careful that hard, blunt, negatively categorizing words do not cluster there. Avoid confirming words such as "loss," "incident," "difficult," "emergency," and "forced" wherever you can, and measure your use of "sorry" and "regret" so that your opening lines do not seem to cue a disappointing key statement in the next paragraph. Ideally you should be able to avoid "no," "not," "cannot," "never," and other negative words throughout the letter, but they would be particularly bothersome in the first paragraph, where they would contribute a sense of closed-minded unhelpfulness. Guard, too, against using words that begin with negative prefixes such as "non-" ("nonapplicable," "nonrefundable"), "un-" ("unimpressive," "unreasonable"), "in-" ("incapable"), and "im-" ("impractical"). These early warning signals would be counterproductive to your aim of having the reader take in your whole explanation, not just the opening lines.

In the first paragraph, then, you should resist rushing into stating the bad news and following it with a defensively phrased rationale. Edit from your opening lines any word or statement that does not contribute to a company image of professional competence, fairness, and desire for customer satisfaction. The tone of the opening paragraph should be confident but not smug.

The middle paragraph (or two) will be the heart of the letter and will include the explanation for the answer, the negative message itself, and, if possible, a positive alternative. Your goal is to present your explanation in such a way that the reader understands how and why you arrived at your choice, knows that it was purely a business decision (nothing personal), and feels that you would have preferred to give a positive response to the request. He will understand what you can or cannot do under your company's guidelines or within the limits of the time, stock, or other resources open to you.

You can begin your explanation with concrete details that seem to lead logically to the judgment that follows. Avoid finger-pointing accusations here. Instead of saying, "You operated the television at much higher temperatures than it was engineered for," you might soften this key detail by shifting to the passive voice: "The television was subjected to higher temperatures than it is intended to operate under." Or you can express the problem as a detached rule of thumb: "Only television monitors housed in specially ventilated cabinets can run safely in open-air tropical conditions like the sun deck of your bar in Guadalajara." Similarly, if an employee questions the amount reimbursed for college tuition, you might demonstrate your reliance on objective standards by paraphrasing from the company manual: "Eastland encourages employees to take additional training and reimburses for credit courses on the following schedule: A = 100%, B = 75%, C = 50%." Through these details you imply, without bluntly saying so, that the same reward system applies equally to all participants, and you suggest, without condescending chastisement, that a player should know the rules before he enters the game.

The refusal statement should immediately follow the explanation and require only a sentence or two, but it should not be couched in a short, abrupt sentence that emphasizes the news. Ironically, your "no" statement should use the least negative phrasing possible. Avoiding words like "reject," "refuse," "unfortunately," "cannot," "claim," "policy," "shocked," "wrong," and "unable," you should try to incorporate the bad news statement into a longer sentence that also contains a softening or a balancing element: "Although every position is filled now, we will keep your application on file for six months." Instead of emphasizing the negative element—"Because you made only a C, we cannot give you the full reimbursement; we can give you only half"—, you can underscore the positive factor: "Because you made a C in the course, we are pleased to help with half of your tuition costs. You will receive your check for $250 within two weeks."

Do not end the paragraph on the sentence containing your refusal statement, no matter how smoothly you have phrased it. The bad-news message should not stand exposed at the naturally emphatic end of your paragraph, where it would suggest a "like it or not" stance. Instead, immediately after you have given the "no" statement, try to offer any feasible alternative to soften the effect. In lieu of a replacement or a refund, you might give a free repair of the appliance or component, a discount on a new appliance or piece of equipment, or referral to another person who might be able to help. If you are able to offer an alternative, do so gracefully. A grudging gift will destroy all the good will you have tried to develop. Your reasonable counteroffer will show your reader that you understand his or her needs and will work within your capacity to meet them. You have not been dismissive, and the reader should now see how his or her request fits into the range of possibilities open to you.

In the closing paragraph, return to the larger picture in the expectation of restoring or sustaining a positive relationship between you and your correspondent. Avoid any reference to the "problem" or "incident" or "refusal," and do not apologize for your negative response, because an apology would imply that your decision is not firm or completely thought through. Don't try to placate the reader by saying, "Please let me know if this is not satisfactory," an invitation that would undo all you have done to present your reasonable position. If your clearly defined counteroffer requires any response from the reader, such as choice of color or style for a substitution, make the response easy by listing a toll-free telephone number or enclosing a reply postcard.

The tone of your closing paragraph will reflect your reasonable assumption that you have handled the issue as clearly and painlessly as possible in the middle paragraph(s) and that you can now look forward to continuing your business relationship. Close your letter with any congenial comments appropriate to the situation, picking up a positive detail or two that promise a positive future association. Refrain from parroting such trite closings as "Please call on us again soon" or "I look forward to serving you." Mention an upcoming sale or an anticipated new job opening that might interest the reader, or simply close with amicable, freshly phrased "good faith" comments, but end your letter strongly and positively.

PUTTING PRINCIPLES INTO PRACTICE

To review the principles of placement and wording in a bad-news letter, first consider the mistakes illustrated in an Indiana firm's rejection of a construction bidding invitation from a neighboring state:

HiWay/BiWay Transporters, Inc.
P. O. Box 17002
East Akron, OH 44309

ATTN: Mr. Geoffrey Tanner

RE: RT-6-68-122
      Terminal Renovation

Dear Geoff:

We are disappointed to have to tell you that we will be unable to quote on the referenced inquiry. We hope that we will be able to accommodate such projects in the future and that you will keep us on your bidding list.

Our trouble is that we do not presently hold a valid Ohio Contractor's License. In a letter from the Licensing Board for Contractors, we learn that we cannot offer any bid in your state until we are fully licensed there. We used to be licensed in Ohio but dropped it for lack of business. We are preparing for the next round of tests, but they will not be offered until after your bidding deadline. Although we will be unable to bid this job, we should be able to undertake your proposals after July 1.

Sorry for this fowl up. Thanks for calling on us, and please write us again.

This writer is eager and honest, but his letter lacks polish not only in such specifics as the misspelling of "foul-up" and in the piling up of self-condemning phrases ("our trouble," "unable to quote") but also in the formatting and in the general impression of not keeping current on professional responsibilities. Moreover, the writer tips his hand in the opening sentence, where the negative words "disappointed" and "unable" leap to the reader's eye and discourage further reading. Although an attention line is a conventional option for routine correspondence, this formal treatment of the recipient's name is inconsistent with the greeting "Dear Geoff." (The manager's name and specific title should begin the inside address, too, for he, not the incorporated firm, will make the guiding decisions.) The letter is also an unfortunate recital of rubber-stamped clauses and phrases: "We are very disappointed to have to tell you that...," "the referenced inquiry," "Thanks for calling on us, and please write us again." The writer seems content to string together these conventional utterances on behalf of a vague company identity ("we," "our").

An alternate version of this letter makes many improvements. It pictures a hands-on approach to business:

Mr. Geoffrey Tanner, General Manager
HiWay/BiWay Transporters, Inc.
P. O. Box 17002
East Akron, OH 44309

Dear Mr. Tanner:

Thank you for sending your specifications for the major terminal renovation in Cleveland. Your expansion project is yet another sign of your success, and I am pleased that my company has won several of your construction contracts.

In the recent recession I decided to concentrate on the business available in Indiana and Illinois. The necessity of sending a dozen men to take the revised qualifying tests in Ohio seemed unwarranted at a time when we were fully occupied with projects closer to home. However, in a few days I will announce the acquisition of Armstrong Construction Co. in your state, to be run by its excellent staff as a wholly owned subsidiary of this company. Once the sale is completed, we will have fully licensed coverage of the Midwest, and we will be eager to meet your needs anywhere in the region.

Again, congratulations on your expansion, and please let me know how I can assist you on your next project.

Here the writer portrays his company as both careful and forward-looking in the use of its resources. Although he is unable to bid at the moment, he offers concrete reasons to support his promise of being ready to supply high-quality work next time. Not relying on vague hopes, the manager cushions his "no" with credible assurances that the answer won't be "no" next time.

INDIRECT REPLIES TO COMPLAINTS

The indirect pattern, which we have heretofore applied to the bad-news letter, is also ideal for answering the general complaint letter, where the customer wants nothing more than an explanation or an apology. For instance, Mrs. Fenimore was pleased to find her new carpet in your store, but she felt that the clerk was slow or rude. She doesn't want to return the carpet, but she does want better service next time. She challenges you to provide it, and through the indirect pattern you can send her assurances that she will receive it. You can follow your opening compliments on her judgment in fabric color and texture with an explanation of a neighborhood emergency that upset the clerk on the day Mrs. Fenimore visited your store, and you can close with a personal invitation to a special preview and sale of Italian lighting fixtures at your showroom next week.

Rather than directly challenging a correspondent's view of an incident involving your company, you can use the indirect pattern to frame a different perspective, one that corrects misunderstandings without seeming to quarrel with the reader. Consider the correspondence between Josephine Jewell, the anxious stage mother, and Rodney Banks, the talent agency manager, who had very different perceptions of what happened when Mrs. Jewell's daughter entered an audition for television commercial performers. (The full text of Mrs. Jewell's complaint letter and two versions of Mr. Banks's reply are given in Chapter 6, where they illustrate letter formats. The exchange is treated in summary here). Mrs. Jewell writes "to protest the treatment that [her] daughter Junie received from [the agency's] Talent Coordinator, Miss Hess, during the TV commercial tryouts at the Bayside Mall last week," and she charges that Miss Hess was both abrupt and indifferent in handling the child's opportunity for stardom. Mrs. Jewell's disappointment was aggravated by her difficulties in parking, a factor that kept her from accompanying Junie and witnessing the audition herself. Thus the mother's view of the episode depends heavily on the child's account, supplemented by her own distant observation.

She cannot expect Mr. Banks to turn back the clock, but she remains angry and accusing.

Mr. Banks's indirect-pattern reply skillfully defuses Mrs. Jewell's charges, corrects a number of misunderstood details, gently reminds her that a parent is expected to accompany the young performer, and invites both parent and child to the next auditions offered by his agency, Young Talent Search, Inc. Beginning his response with a buffer description of his service's purpose, Mr. Banks uses the middle portion of his letter to set the record straight through a factual account. He does not rebuke Mrs. Jewell or her daughter for a careless reading of the audition call-list (which did not include work for dancers like Junie) or for incorrectly identifying the agency's coordinator (who is Alicia Heseltine, not "Miss Hess"). The nondefensive, straightforward tone of Mr. Banks's explanation contrasts with Mrs. Jewell's huffy, excited accusations. He shows that rather than being indifferent to the child's disappointment, Miss Heseltine generously took several minutes from a pressing schedule to offer Junie suggestions for polishing her performances. In the closing sentence of his letter, Mr. Banks underscores his agency's strong preference that a parent be present at the professionally conducted auditions. Rather than casting (or accepting) blame for the misunderstandings of a past occasion, he emphasizes the more appropriate opportunity listed for the next auditions. Mr. Banks's letter cannot be called a "put down" in any way, yet it subtly reminds Mrs. Jewell that she is responsible for understanding and acting correctly. Throughout the letter Mr. Banks maintains a courteous, positive tone that neutralizes the complaint without fawning and without being indifferent or dismissive.

CHAPTER PERSPECTIVE

The indirect pattern is useful in letters that offer explanations to anxious, overly optimistic, potentially resistant, actively hostile, or merely curious readers. Your goal is to have the reader know and accept the conditions that have led to your choices, and the indirect pattern allows you to delay your basic response until you have given the relevant details behind your reasoning. The relatively brief opening and closing paragraphs act as buffers, the first paragraph establishing a plane of mutual interest and the last one pointing beyond the immediate situation and looking toward a restoration of positive feeling. In the middle paragraph(s), the bad news is further surrounded by justifying detail and, where appropriate, a counteroffer. The closing paragraph should reflect the writer's confidence that the reader will accept a reasonable explanation or a fair alternative in the spirit in which it is made. You should avoid ending with clichéd, dismissive phrases ("Thanks for your understanding") or with invitations to further discussion ("Let me know if this is not satisfactory").

Rather than directly asserting that the writer of a complaint letter is wrong, you will put the complaint into perspective through a calm review of the facts or guidelines leading to your decision. Here you might emphasize factors previously ignored by or unknown to the inquirer.

Remembering that each paragraph's first and last sentences are exposed, emphatic places, you should particularly avoid using negative or bald details at these points. Not only in these naturally strong positions but, as much as possible, in all of your phrasing, you should avoid negative words and prefixes that leap to the reader's scanning eye and telegraph your answer, deflecting attention from your legitimate explanation.

Persuasive Letters

INTRODUCTION AND MAIN POINTS

No matter what its announced purpose, almost any business document is finally meant to *persuade*. The experienced writer of an "objective" report knows how to select and place details to convince the reader that the subject has received full, accurate coverage. The relevant details must be there, of course, but the writer's confident handling of content, style, and organization will encourage the reader to trust the writer's analysis. In this way, a job applicant argues that her credentials make an ideal match for an advertised position, and later in her career she will submit an updated resume reflecting increased experience and responsibilities to support her contention that she has earned a promotion. A tenant's letter to a landlord might argue that improvements are needed if the property is to remain livable, while the owner might reply that he will be happy, with a reasonable rent increase, to invest in landscaping or security improvements. While some documents are more explicitly persuasive than others, every wish, hope, design, or expectation offers the basis of a persuasive appeal. This chapter centers on three major types of directly persuasive writing.

Although expensive multimedia campaigns are best left to professional agencies armed with demographic charts and creative consultants, you should be able to write a persuasive letter to one reader or several hundred. Choosing from the approaches outlined in this chapter, you can invite former customers to return to a revitalized downtown store, urge a delinquent free-spender to pay his bills, or ask someone to invest time, money, or talent in a civic endeavor, a charitable campaign, or an anniversary celebration. The better you know your audience, the better results you will see from your sales letter, private collection letter, or altruistic appeal.

After reading this chapter:
▬ You should be able to select a leading quality or primary focus of attention.
▬ You should capture your reader's interest and relate it to your product, service, or need.
▬ You will adapt your letter's format to the purpose and tone of your message.

ATTENTION, PLEASE

You have chosen to persuade one or more readers through the letter format because you do not need an expensive television campaign or full-page newspaper ad. You have relinquished the cinematic splash of the TV spot and the page-dominating photographs of the print ad. You prefer to "narrowcast" your message, to tailor it to one reader or a relative few. Your design firm, gallery, specialty store, or antiques business depends on the patronage of clients whose tastes you know and try to please. One busy person is the ideal after-dinner speaker for your school's year-end banquet or your company's fiftieth anniversary celebration, and you must persuade that individual to set aside other responsibilities to prepare for your event. You want to announce a private sale or a special discount to a select list of loyal customers. In each situation, the persuasive letter, readily adaptable to circumstances, is likely to be the most convincing form of invitation. It is the medium that allows you to shape a specific image or supply a motive that will gratify the individual reader or the closely defined group.

Casting your reader in a role that appeals to him, a role believably within reach, is often a highly persuasive tactic. The man who now delays paying his bills will, with your service, become a man of stable finances, free from the threats of Accounts Receivable or the firm of Bilson, Mote, Stanley & Gunning. The avid shopper will be the first to learn where to find designer clothes at discount prices—at your shop. The reluctant public speaker will see himself enthralling your group through his knowledge and genial wisdom. You can choose among infinite numbers of images that will please your correspondents and customers.

According to commentator Alistair Cooke, a young British boy wisely told a BBC survey that he preferred radio to television because with radio "'the pictures are better.'" Why? Because the radio audience has a larger part in creating its own images from the suggestions given by the medium. Your persuasive letters can achieve a similar effect. Think of pleasing images that incorporate or suggest your product or service, and place your reader prominently in the picture. Before considering how you might adapt such images to three kinds of persuasive appeals, we will review some elements of phrasing that will help you fine-tune your message.

Some Aids to Persuasion

Emphasizing "you" and "your" rather than "my product" and "my company," especially in the letter's opening sentences, is a natural way to gain your reader's interest. "Picture yourself in the sweeping lines of a fine Italian gown on your next evening out" is a far more effective opener than "I have some nice imports I'll be pleased to show you when you stop by The Leisure Lady." You might honestly claim "Our golf ball is engineered for maximum distance," but what manufacturer or distributor would not say much the same thing? Besides, that generalization involves the reader only very distantly. The reader, not the golf ball, becomes the center of attention in a revised version: "'How did you develop that power stroke?' your partners will ask after you switch to the PowerPac II ball." The admired-golfer role is underscored by the "you...your...you" pronoun pattern, and "develop" and "switch" describe decisive actions that will gratify the reader while linking his imagined success to the PowerPac II.

As you have just seen, carefully choosing your verbs (and their most emphatic forms) will also heighten your letter's impact. The general preference for using the *active voice* ("Buy it here") rather than the passive construction ("This product may be purchased at our three locations") clearly suits the purposes of most persuasive letters. Especially in opening and closing paragraphs, the measured use of *command forms*—though not so many that you seem overeager or pushy—will also sustain your emphasis on the action you want your reader to take. Since "you" is the understood subject of any command-form verb, you are reinforcing one persuasive element with another when you begin your sentences with such invitations as "Imagine...," "Choose your...," "Buy now and get an additional...," "Start ...," "Send...," and "Listen!" Use *shorter verbs* ("Buy") at emphasis points, reserving longer synonyms ("Purchase") for variety. Both for variety and for a polished, well mannered effect, remember to occasionally preface a verb with "Please (try)" or "Won't you (try)...?"

Try to picture a specific action rather than a general one, selecting verbs that bring your product, service, or request into sharp focus. For example, say you distribute a safe but bitter-tasting liquid that can be painted on a child's fingers to discourage thumb-sucking. You might make the claim "Thumb-sucking is annoying and unhealthy," but the linking verb has led into a flat and obvious statement. The anxious mother is much more likely to respond to the warning "Prolonged thumb-sucking hinders proper gum formation and opens a ready pathway to infection and disease." "Is" is static; "hinders" and "opens" describe conditions that no parent would want for her child, and these verbs encourage visualizing. Similarly, a toy company does not simply say that its products "are" entertaining. Rather, they "involve a child" in play, "help him accomplish," "encourage (growth, creativity, or confidence)," "develop (motor skills, sense of direction)," and finally "bring happiness"—a gratifying number of promises for metal and plastic playthings. What toddler's parent or grandparent could resist products with such persuasive attributes? The verbs seem to invest inherent powers in the products they describe.

Human beings revel in the capacity to initiate, to heighten, to redirect. Try, then, to choose verbs that associate your message with the power to change some<u>one</u> or some<u>thing</u>. True, people do not like the changes brought by advancing age, declining health, or loss of accustomed power, and, in fact, they often try to mask or compensate for those changes by initiating counter-transformations. Home renovations, facelifts, vacation plans, and new book club memberships bear witness to people's continuing desire to grow and strive for fulfillment. Letters announcing health spa programs, furniture store promotions, and continuing education seminars often carry the language of "becoming." A freshly outfitted family room or new carpeting will, so the building supplier or home decorator promises, "enhance" the home or make it "blossom." The loan department at the bank will invite a depositor to "realize a dream" by financing a world tour or vacation home. For several years the United States Army has urged potential recruits, through the radio, television, and print media, to "Be all that you can be," a slogan that bears powerful witness to the desire for growth and change.

The chrysalis-to-butterfly transformation appeals very strongly to the human psyche, yet too many promises clustered together will draw suspicion and distrust. Selecting the verb, the dominant image, or any other element to catch the reader's attention is a part of the persuasive writer's task. Placing these elements effectively within the whole message is equally as important as choosing them carefully.

Organizing the Sales Letter

What do a handmade goose-down quilt, a Colorado time-share condominium, a well-cared-for 1956 Thunderbird, and a rustic building lot have in common? On the surface very little, except that each might be highly desirable to one person or another. But why? As investments? As objects for practical, everyday use? Any one of these items could appeal to the physical senses, to one's aesthetic appreciation, or to the desire to own something individual or out-of-the-ordinary. A quilt pieced together by an Appalachian folk artist might sell for an astonishing price because of its museum-quality design and workmanship. A similar quilt might be bought by an economy-minded person as a hedge against high heating bills, especially in transitional seasons. To someone else, a genuine folk quilt might define personal values of earthiness and simplicity.

Most sales and other persuasive letters are organized by the indirect method. They first create or encourage a desire and then offer a means of satisfying it. The writer who knows his customer(s) will also know whether an appeal to good sense, to aesthetic values, to investment priorities, or the acquisitive instinct is likely to make the most effective beginning. The quilt might be offered for its beauty: "Imagine waking to the sight of a richly varied field of color spread across your bed each morning." For a collector of folk art, the same item might be prized as an example of a vanishing craft to be purchased while still available. From the first sentence forward, your letter will strive to induce a "must have" wish.

The marketer of time-share houses and condominiums will have a similar range of possible beginning points. In a recessionary period he might guess that his clients want to trim vacation expenses here and there, so he might underscore the cost advantages of a time-sharing plan. For the traveler always eager for "something different," the agent can point out the variety of ski, beach, Southwestern desert, and island locations open to the time-sharing participant. Each year can bring a new vacation adventure in a different place, yet the standard of property maintenance will be assured at any of hundreds of locations. The letter will be rich in images of sunrises, sunsets, ski lifts, and nearby theme parks.

Whatever you want to promote or sell, then, you will want to initiate or heighten interest by offering an appeal to the senses, to practicality, to convenience, or to value. To sell a gas barbecue grill, let the steak sizzle in your opening sentences. Promote mail-order Polish or Italian sausage by evoking the sights and flavors of the "old country." Inviting your customer to consider a new stain-resistant carpet, start with an "Oops" and a spill of wine or catsup, followed by a sense of relief as the potential disaster wipes away easily and completely. For selling home insurance, an opening picture of rising smoke, storm-snapped trees, and downed power lines can be very persuasive. The promotion director of a retirement center might open with images suggesting a homelike, active environment to younger retirees, while for older inquirers he will emphasize barrier-free accessibility, convenient arrangements of living quarters and service areas, and freedom from worry about food preparation or health care. The opening of a sales letter, then, establishes interest through the product's or service's most promising appeal.

The sales letter's middle section will direct the reader's thoughts from the opening point of attraction toward the purchase (or further inquiry) decision. In the middle paragraphs you might use testimonial evidence to support the opening claims, or you might list backup points of interest: "not only beautiful but also easy to care for," "maintains high trade-in value," "will age gracefully," "will bloom year after year." The letter's second phase should confirm and expand the initial interest and handle any likely resistance.

In a letter offering a subscription plan for fine silverware, for instance, the first paragraph will be filled with images of gleaming table settings, elegant occasions, and admiring guests. The potential buyer is tempted, but she has nagging doubts about cost, usefulness, and practicality. The middle part of the letter can assure her that an easy payment plan will help her complete the table service after the wedding guests have made their contributions. Is table silver impractical? "I've used mine every day for years," the jewelry shop owner might assure the bride-to-be in a warm and chatty letter. Doesn't it need tiresome polishing? Not if stored properly in the bonus silver chest supplied to every member of the pattern completion plan.

For any expensive purchase, whether of insurance, art objects, or a car, price will be a concern. If your major selling point is a bargain price or highly favorable rate, you have probably mentioned that in your opening. If your charge is the same as or little different from others', you might omit mention of the price entirely and simply offer a toll-free number or a convenient reply card for "further information." Alternately, the middle section is an appropriate place to suggest that your superior service and generous store warranty make the item an unbeatable value. Or you might emphasize that skilled installation is included in the quoted price. Writing to graduating seniors at a local college, a car dealer might mention "our low monthly rate for first-time new car buyers" rather than listing the full purchase price.

The beginning and middle sections of your sales letter might require one or two solid paragraphs each, depending on the amount of detail you want to supply. The final phase will prompt the reader to act, and you will need only a brief paragraph for this further nudging toward the purchase decision. "You have nothing to lose and much to gain by calling our toll-free number now," you might say, or "If you reply within the next fifteen days, you will receive a bonus of...." If your offer has an expiration date, be sure to mention it as a further inducement of prompt action.

With its opening appeal, its middle-paragraph confirmation, and its last-paragraph urging to action, your sales letter, organized via the indirect approach, should fit into the conventional format—return address, inside address, greeting, body, signature block. However, you might choose to establish an instant mood of friendly casualness or create a news-bulletin-like urgency by omitting the inside address and (optionally) the "Dear Friend" greeting. Further, you might draw your reader quickly into your offer's excitement by turning your opening sentence or two into single-sentence paragraphs:

> Never say we didn't give you a chance at this never-to-be-repeated offer!

> or

> YOU'LL HAVE INSTANT CREDIT AND NO DOWN PAYMENT...

> or

> Here it is—the one you've been waiting for!

In some types of business letters a postscript (P.S.) provides for a previously forgotten detail, a last-minute development affecting the letter's subject, or a casual afterthought. In a very formal letter, a P.S. might seem a slightly embarrassing sign of the writer's disorganized frame of mind, but in a sales letter you might make very deliberate use of a brief add-on sentence or short paragraph.

> P.S. Pick up the phone and call us before you put this letter down. You won't regret it.

or

P.S. Watch the newspaper for big news about our store next week.

or

P.S. When you phone in your order, bill it to your Maxey's Preferred Customer Card and get another 10% off.

A clearly phrased postscript will often add a final nudge toward the purchase decision.

Even the most skillfully written sales letter is a wasted effort if the recipient fails to open it. However, a tastefully written appeal will seem pale and out of place if sent in an envelope splashed with the colors and exclamation points that proclaim "junk mail." In recent years more and more sales letter writers have chosen the middle ground between the address-and-stamp-only envelope and the circus poster effect. The phrase "your once-a-year opportunity" or "investment news," placed near the lower left corner of the envelope, will offer a tantalizing clue to the letter's content. For some recipients, the envelope's proclamation "The favor of a reply is requested" sets up an intriguing obligation and leads to attentive reading of the letter.

Writing Collection Letters

While no business person would make the effort of sending sales letters without reasonable hope of a return, the expectations are different with the collection letter, often part of the "collection series" of two to five letters, a progressive set of reminders that payment is overdue. Some kinds of businesses show more patience with debts than others. The large company, backed by collection specialists and, if necessary, lawyers, might send an initial no-nonsense request for prompt payment, followed by an "immediate payment required" warning with suggestions of the difficulties that might result from further failure to send a check or money order. Of necessity, the smaller business, often dealing with longtime or influential customers, will likely show greater patience. The following illustration of a collection series will be more readily adaptable to the needs of a locally managed firm than a large, impersonal, distant creditor.

If the shop owner knows the customer well, he might put the emphasis in the first letter on the customer's loyal patronage or pleasure in the recent purchase, and any mention of the delinquent payment might be postponed until a cordial, unaccusing tone is established:

Dear Mr. Ballenger:

With this spring's unusually frequent downpours, you must be especially pleased to have the exercise bicycle that you purchased from us in March, so that you can keep up your fitness routine in the dry comfort of your recreation room. The Safe Pace 5000 is an excellent machine that will last a long time.

In looking over our accounts this week, Jim, I noted that your bill has not yet been paid. Since you have always been prompt in sending us checks, this is probably an oversight. Can you send us the $595.63 payment soon?

Please stop in and let me know how you're doing with the exercise program.

If neither Mr. Ballenger nor his check appears, a second letter, with greater emphasis on the oddness of the nonpayment, will be necessary. This might be couched in terms of concern—as much for the customer's welfare as the company's cash flow:

Dear Mr. Ballenger:

On June 8 I sent you a reminder of the unpaid bill for your exercise bicycle, and I am surprised that I have not heard from you. Is there a problem here?

If there are difficulties related to your medical expenses last year, please call or visit the store so we can work something out. I'm sure we can set up a mutually agreeable payment schedule.

Should this letter elicit no response, the third letter in the series will focus less specifically on individual circumstances and will shift the emphasis to principles. The customer has incurred a debt and offered no explanation for nonpayment; the business depends on its customers' prompt payments so that the firm, in turn, can pay its suppliers. The tone here should be reasonable and objective ("You will understand that we have creditors too"), not cold or accusing.

Even after three or four tries, your final letter should be neither condemning nor funereal, but you will likely suggest a wistful regret that a business relationship has come to this pass. Brief but not so short as to seem dismissive, this letter will carry two further messages:

Dear Mr. Ballenger:

On June 8 I sent you the first in a series of reminders of your overdue $595.63 payment for one Safe Pace 5000 exercise bicycle, charged at our Freeland Mall store on March 18. Before you let this last reminder from me go unheeded, please think of the effects on your credit rating and perhaps your community standing if a collection agency becomes involved.

I urge you to reply by September 12. If you send at least a partial payment by then, we will work out the remainder. Should I not hear from you, I must regretfully place the matter in other hands.

Throughout the series, you should leave the door open to restoring good seller-customer relations. While the reader might be reminded of the nature and terms of the purchase, references to the nonpayment itself should be neutrally phrased ("Payment has not arrived") rather than accusing ("You have failed to send....") Even the unsmiling final letter would not be written if there were no last hope of prompting payment, and hostile language will not fit this purpose. Rather, you might end the last appeal with the suggestion that good faith can be restored and the matter settled quietly and privately through at least partial payment, with the balance to be arranged.

Writing Requests for Favors

You are in charge of your company's or your city's hundredth anniversary celebrations, and you must persuade an excellent speaker—doubtless a busy person with a full calendar—to prepare and deliver the keynote address. You are the company representative for the United Fund, World Hunger Day, the Community Chest, the Larson Family Emergency Fund, or another worthy appeal. You find little pleasure in pleading and cajoling. How can you ask someone you don't know to prepare a speech, travel to your city, and speak to an audience of potentially indifferent strangers? And, not incidentally, you must add that while you will pay all travel expenses, the civic club or business league's funds allow for only a token speaker's fee, if any. At best, you are asking a favor.

Rather than apologizing at the outset for possible inconvenience or for your limited capacity to repay the reader's contribution, you can emphasize the prospect of sharing ideas, spreading influence, joining a pleasurable celebration, contributing to a clearly defined goal. You will be pleasantly surprised at how often and how much people *like* to be asked:

Mr. Claire, when I heard you speak at the Forum Club in Charleston last January, I knew that you would be the perfect speaker for the Fullerton High School commencement this spring. Can I persuade you to make some appropriate remarks, of eight to twelve minutes' duration, for our brightest class yet? The audience will include 255 graduates, their parents, and friends, and I'm sure all will be entertained by anecdotes from your business career and travels.

As a school board member yourself, you know that educational institutions are pinched for funds, so you won't expect a large fee. Of course we will pay all travel expenses for you and your wife, and you may choose to stay free of charge at Janice Bradley's popular bed-and-breakfast or to accept the hospitality of Mayor and Mrs. Partridge, who are sending their own invitation. Be sure to bring your golf clubs, since you will have guest privileges at Forest River Country Club for the duration of your visit here.

Please share your humor and wisdom with us. We will do our best to show you a comfortable, enjoyable time, and we will be ever grateful for your contribution to our commencement.

For a retired businessman, a confident public speaker, and an avid golfer, this should be a welcome invitation, a promise of two or three days' change of scene among pleasant, enthusiastic people who sincerely welcome him and his message.

Finding the right positive tone will also ease the task of asking for monetary contributions or other material gifts—an author's papers to a library, for instance. Soberly considered tax advantages will appeal to some, while others readily respond to the "fair share" or "do your part" persuasion. A timid request is no more effective on the one side, however, than an insistent demand would be on the other. As vividly as the nature of your request warrants, *picture* what a "yes" response will do: feed starving children, bring smiles to listeners' faces, open windows to refresh closed minds, or simply celebrate the values of a firm or a professional organization, a public institution, or a locality.

CHAPTER PERSPECTIVE

Persuasive letters are occasioned by serious problems (long overdue bills) and by highly positive prospects (an offer to chair a prestigious panel or to lead a celebration). Sales letters hold out the promise of small satisfactions or major changes in people's lives. Sensing the appropriate tone for phrasing your offer to a single person or a group, you should also seek the persuasive *image*. Let the reader see herself or himself in the situation that most vividly shows your product, service, plans, or needs. If well thought out and carefully executed, your letter will initiate a process of imagining that the reader will take up and act upon.

Report Characteristics and Types

INTRODUCTION AND MAIN POINTS

Reports are a mainstay of corporate life, and as companies expand, so does the demand for well-written, substantive reports. Reports give managers and other employees many different kinds of information about company operations. Reports may come from sales representatives noting the week's calls on distributors, from regulatory officers monitoring drugstore prescription sales, or from construction supervisors updating the progress on a new apartment complex. The vast majority of reports are assigned, but some are offered voluntarily by perceptive employees who see specific problems and wish to propose solutions. Reports are so important that a person's advancement within the corporate structure depends in part upon his or her ability to write clear, substantive, accurate reports.

After reading this chapter:

■ You can recognize the options in approach, style, and format available for presenting report material.

■ You can shape your report to fit your purpose and audience.

■ You can judge the amount of detail needed to verify and persuade.

REPORT CHARACTERISTICS

Business reports are difficult to describe since they have such a wide variety of characteristics. They are unified by their emphasis on factual information. They differ, however, in whether they are circulated inside or outside the company, in frequency of submission, in degree of formality, in organization of segments, and in format.

Factual Orientation

Verifiable data is essential to business reports. No matter how far reports go into interpretation and analysis, they begin by presenting and summarizing facts. A report usually offers statistics, analysis, and illustrations in the form of graphs. Reports share the journalist's interest in the fundamentals of who, what, when, where, why, and how. Many reports, such as product test evaluations or reports of accidental injury to an employee, require enough depth and scope of detail to serve as evidence in a court of law, if necessary.

Circulation

Reports may be circulated either inside or outside the company. External reports may be sent to regulatory agencies, sponsors of a project, or stockholders. Internal reports may be sent in any direction within the company—laterally, upward, or downward. Reports sent upward may simply present information, as with production figures for the week, or may discuss situations in some detail, as with recommendations on opening a plant in Des Moines. A report sent laterally may inform all employees of the salary comparison findings from a recent study. Reports sent downward may announce procedures for direct deposit of payroll checks or detail the expanded responsibilities of the assistant manager.

Frequency of Submission

Many reports are submitted routinely and periodically—weekly, monthly, quarterly, semiannually, or annually. Such recurring reports as expense accounts, product testing results, sales figures, and product distribution data frequently use preprinted forms for reporting operations.

Reports may be singular and nonrecurring, however. The salary comparison study may require only one report, while a building renovation project will generate a series of reports—project proposal, progress reports, and final report. These nonrecurrent reports usually include more analysis of the data than do the periodic reports, and often include recommendations.

Formality

Audience and subject matter, more than length, influence the formality of a report. Reports sent upward in a company or intended for wide distribution use fairly restrained language and precise format. In a report to your president on employees' attitudes toward instituting flex-time, you will probably try to maintain a more professional style and a more structured format than you would for a memo to the computer coordination chair outlining your computer needs. Here you might adopt a more casual approach, addressing the chairperson by first name and using contractions, parenthetical comments, acronyms, and abbreviations. Obviously, the relationship between the writer and the reader of the report—as well as the sense of the report's importance—influences the degree of formality.

Direct or Indirect Approach

Just as you did with letters and memos, you will choose between direct or indirect order for arranging the material in your report. If you anticipate a neutral or positive reaction, direct order is best. Readers want to know early—in the first or second paragraph—the purpose of the report. In fact, some writers begin by stating "The purpose of this report is...." The body of the report then proceeds with discussion that relays factual information, and the conclusion recaps the major findings and makes recommendations substantiated by the data. Direct order presents information in the layout easiest for people to read and assimilate.

On the other hand, if you expect a less-than-enthusiastic response to a request for a major expense or change, such as the proposed purchase of another computer for your office or a move to payroll deductions for employees' contributions to the Good Health Appeal, you may find it advisable to use the more subtle indirect order. To begin your discussion, you can make positive comments that represent mutual agreement—the importance of maintaining a high level of productivity in your department, or the desirability of employees' contributing to a worthwhile program. Once you have buffered the opening, you can establish the focus of your report by outlining the difficulties resulting from the current situation. Your reader may not be aware that a problem exists, or may believe that the situation is not serious enough to warrant action. Your role is to discuss the inequities or ineffectiveness associated with present methods or policies in a very objective and factual manner, omitting any hint of personal criticism. Once you establish that the change is justified, you can present the details of your proposal and describe the benefits to your organization—increased efficiency or additional employee participation in the charity program.

After you have discussed the advantages, of course, you have to estimate the related costs: equipment purchase, service agreements, increase in staff support, major or minor construction work, or computer time. You can compare these costs to projected benefits, but you should keep in focus the overall desirability of your proposal. By establishing justification for the change before advancing your plan, you increase your chances for having it approved. Use indirect order only if you believe that the more subtle arrangement will enhance your reader's receptiveness.

Arrangement of Points

In contrast to preprinted reports, which allow little flexibility in arrangement of material, discussion reports offer a great deal of freedom. But this freedom brings with it a challenge. Certainly every writer intends to arrange report material in the most logical manner possible, but achieving that goal is not easy.

You have many options when it comes to putting these various segments of your report in some kind of order: chronological, spatial, strongest-to-weakest, subject-by-subject, point-by-point, general-to-specific, specific-to-general, causes-of-effects, effects-of-causes, and others. Chronological order is suitable for schedule- or time-oriented documents such as accident reports, summaries of meetings, trip reports, and test reports. Spatial order is appropriate for showing the layout of a building and marking inspection or installation points or sketching a proposed protective suit designed for asbestos removal crews. Ranked order, from strongest to weakest, is best for discussing the strengths of the top candidates for a position or your recommendations on word-processing software programs.

When you compare items, you have a choice between proceeding subject by subject or point by point. If you are gathering figures before purchasing a new copier for your department, you may want to discuss the copiers in ranked order, giving information on costs, features, warranty, and service agreement for each. You may decide, however, to arrange your report by the comparison criteria—cost, features, warranties, and service agreements—focusing on strengths and weaknesses of the copiers in relation to each category. You may not find a best-in-all-categories copier. If you don't, in the last section you will need to weigh the importance of the various criteria in order to substantiate your recommendation of one copier, perhaps mentioning your second and third choices and reasons for each choice.

The optimal arrangement of points varies, of course, according to the subject material and treatment. In organizing your material, you should attempt to select the order most advantageous to your report content and your reader's ease of understanding.

Format

Reports may utilize either preprinted forms or different discussion formats—memorandum, letter, or formal report, brochure, and booklet. Periodic reports are often sent by means of standardized forms, which streamline the writing and reading processes and, thus, decrease the time and cost involved. Such forms signal to report-writers precisely which details are needed and allow readers to scan the data quickly. The following examples illustrate the informational nature of reports submitted on preprinted forms.

PROJECT BUDGET PROPOSAL	
Date: Department: Employee ID #:	_____Required Work _____Elective Work
Project/Program:	
Project Description:	
Proposed Budget:	

WEEKLY SALES REPORT	
Name:	Territory:
Week:	
Summary of Calls:	
Dealers	
Distributors	
Other	
Products Sold:	Amount:
1.	
2.	
3.	
4.	
Concerns of Customers:	
Sales Suggestions:	
Comments:	

TO: William Blankenship   FROM: Bryant Boswell
      Training Director   Systems Analyst

DATE: October 24, 19__

SUBJECT: ISTD Fall Training Meeting

On October 18–19, 19__, Barry Crenshaw, Jim Bayer, and I
attended the Indiana Society for Training and Development
(ISTD) Fall Training Conference at the Indiana Inn in
Muncie. The following is a summary of the meeting.

9:00–10:30 a.m. Harold Webb of the Midwestern Industrial
Training Center, Peoria, Illinois, began the conference with
the speech "Productivity: Where America Stands." Webb
discussed America's declining productivity and focused on
the way improved training programs could play a major role
in raising this low productivity level.

Melvin Haynes of Haynes and Associates, Columbus, Ohio,
followed Webb with the presentation "Selling Training to
Management." Haynes' discussion centered on the following
points:

1. The advisability of using the problem-solving
    approach to training.
2. The need to identify problems and needs in a compa-
    ny's training program.
3. The advisability of "selling" training programs to
    management.
4. Methods of influencing management without creating
    resentment.

This information is particularly important to personnel
involved with training as management seeks to cut costs by
eliminating some of the training, especially during recessionary periods....

If you are not restricted to the use of a printed form, you have the opportunity to design your own report format, determining the length, style, and order of points. An account of a two-day conference with several speakers and topics uses chronological order for the three-page report. The first page is illustrated on page 146.

You may select the more frequently used memorandum lay-out suitable for reports of ten or fewer pages, or the formal report format appropriate to longer reports. You will observe that the two formats display a considerable difference in length, amount of detail, and treatment of the preliminary sections. The formal report (which is the focus of Chapter 12) includes several preliminary pages: transmittal letter or memo, title page, abstract, and table of contents. In memorandum or letter reports, the "To," "From," "Date," and "Subject" lines replace the formal report's title page. The memorandum report's introduction condenses the information found in the formal report's synopsis and table of contents: background, purpose, scope, conclusions, and points to be discussed. The supplementary pages consisting of sources, appendices, glossary (and other sections considered necessary) vary little between the two report formats, except in number of entries.

ESSENTIAL TYPES OF REPORTS

Although reports are infinite in their variety, they may be broadly categorized into four essential types: periodic reports detailing routine company activities, annual review and policy reports, assigned or commissioned reports, and proposals and other self-initiated reports.

Periodic Reports on Routine Company Activities

Periodic reports may consist of internal accounts of company activities or external reports to regulatory agencies. They may be weekly call reports, monthly car expense reports, semiannual employee evaluations, project or program budget reports, demonstration or test reports, injury or accident reports, and countless others. The samples shown on pages 148–149 illustrate the nature of this type of report.

This credit report form might be used internally in processing a credit application:

REASONS FOR CREDIT DENIAL OR TERMINATION

Credit File:
 ___Incomplete credit application
 ___Insufficient number of credit references
 ___Inability to verify credit references
 ___No credit file

Employment:
 ___Temporary or irregular employment
 ___Inability to verify employment
 ___Inadequate length of employment

Income:
 ___Insufficient income for amount of credit requested
 ___Excessive obligations in relation to income
 ___Inability to verify income

Residence:
 ___Insufficient length of residence
 ___Inability to verify residence

Credit History:
 ___Poor credit performance with us
 ___Garnishment, attachment, foreclosure, repossession, collection action, or judgment in progress
 ___Bankruptcy

This monthly car expense report simply asks for information.

Car Expense Report	
Name:	**Date:**
Department:	**Region:**
Gasoline (Total number of gallons)	$
Maintenance	$
Mechanical Repairs	$
Accident Repairs	$
Car Rental (during repair of company car)	$
Tax & License	$
Other Expenses	$
Total	$

REPORT CHARACTERISTICS AND TYPES

This accident report segment includes some discussion and analysis.

Accident 1			
Date:	February 15, 1990	**Estimated Damages**	
Time:	12:10 p.m.	Truck	$15,000
Location:	I-85, mile marker 178	Cargo	$ 500
Cargo:	Frozen food items	Total	$15,500

Accident Description: Driver Robert Blassingame was traveling at 55 m.p.h. in clear weather, transporting a shipment to Young's Grocery in Belton, Virginia, when the front left tire ruptured. As a result, the vehicle struck a guardrail and partially overturned, causing substantial damage to the right side of the truck. Approximately half the cargo was declared undeliverable. The driver sustained cuts and bruises but required no hospitalization and missed no work. Damages totaled $15,500.

Reports to regulatory agencies might include quarterly or annual income tax reports to the Internal Revenue Service, product testing results submitted to the Food and Drug Administration, safety testing results submitted to the Occupational Safety and Health Administration, and affirmative

---

EMPLOYER'S FIRST REPORT OF INJURY

Company: _____   File # _____

Address: _____   Employer Code # _____

_____   Carrier Code # _____

_____   Carrier File # _____

Nature of Business: _____

Location of Accident: _____

                              (City)   (County)   (State)

Date of Accident: _____   Hour: ____ A.M. ____ P.M.

                (Month)   (Day)   (Year)

Name: _____

          (Last)   (First)   (Middle Initial)   (S.S. Number)

Address: _____

       (Street or Apt. #)   (City)   (State) (Zip Code)

Age: _____ Length of Employment: _____ Dept.: _____

No. of Hours of Work/Day: _____ No. of Hours/Week: _____

Wages: $ ___ per hour ___ $ ___ per week ___ $ ___ per month

action reports submitted to the Equal Employment Opportunity Commission. Many of these are submitted by means of the agency's preprinted form, although those such as annual reports to stockholders, required by the Securities and Exchange Commission, may take the form of a brochure. The segment from the first report of injury required by a state industrial commission (shown on page 149) illustrates the factual nature of such reports.

Annual Review and Policy Reports

Among the most frequently written review and policy reports are performance reviews and policies and procedures manuals.

When supervisors annually or semiannually review the performance of employees, they may use complex forms with numerical ratings, or those with ratings and discussion, or those with a purely discussion format. At any time that you write performance reviews, you should clearly focus on facts rather than impressions or assumptions. You may mention the number of committees a person has chaired, the number of projects completed, national offices held, and specific work in progress. Any negative comments you make should revolve around concrete data—deadlines missed, number of sick days taken, or requests by employees not to work with a person on a project. Because performance reviews become a part of a person's permanent record, and negative evaluations may open a writer to charges of libel, you as a manager or supervisor should carefully phrase and substantiate evaluation comments.

The following extract from a performance review uses a printed form for evaluation and gives room for both numerical ratings and comments:

SKILLS DEVELOPMENT				
	Poor	Fair	Good	Excellent
1. TECHNICAL QUALIFICATIONS	1	2	3	4
Comments:				
2. MANUAL SKILLS	1	2	3	4
Comments:				
3. COMMUNICATION SKILLS	1	2	3	4
Comments:				
4. WORK METHODS	1	2	3	4
Comments:				

Managers are responsible, too, for providing employees with detailed statements on company structure, on administrators' duties, and on company policies concerning sick leave, job termination, grievance procedures, submission of travel vouchers, and other matters. Writing a policies and procedures booklet demands thoughtful phrasing as you attempt to consider all the circumstances that might arise in employee-employee or employee-manager relations. Although it is necessarily complex, this document requires only periodic (usually annual) updating. Each employee should have a copy of this brochure and be able to understand its contents.

The following are excerpts from typical policies manuals. The first is tabulated because of the brevity of each entry and variety of details covered.

Office Maintenance

1. Lock your office when you leave for any substantial period of time, and secure all laboratory doors when you have finished your work there.

2. Do not move furniture from one room to another. If you have special needs, contact the main office.

3. Smoke only in closed offices. No smoking is allowed in hallways, public areas, or cafeteria and snack areas.

4. Report to the main office any problems involving the air-conditioning or heating systems, lighting, or similar office conditions.

The following information on computer room materials involves discussion rather than a simple listing:

Computer Room Construction Materials

The room containing the computer system shall be built of noncombustible material. All materials including walls, floors, partitions, finish, acoustical treatment, raised floors and floor supports, suspended ceilings, and other construction involved in the computer room shall have a flame spread rating of 25 or less. Exposed floors should be covered with materials such as asphalt, rubber, or vinyl floor tiles, linoleum, high pressure plastic laminant or fire retardant carpeting.

Assigned Reports

Managers often assign reports to gather data for confident decision-making. These reports may require surveys of select groups, laboratory testing, contacts with company representatives, or plans for construction work. Some will need only a single report; others will involve several.

If you have undertaken a complex study that will span weeks or months, you will probably submit one or more progress reports, either voluntary or required, to assure your superior or client that you are moving ahead on the work. The frequency with which you report your progress will be agreed upon by both the sponsor and your company or department. Progress reports are usually short and present detailed information on work completed, work to be done, problems encountered, and projections on meeting the scheduled deadline. For an uncomplicated project, one paragraph on work accomplished and one on work remaining will suffice.

Open your progress report by identifying your subject and detail what has been accomplished. Even if you have had difficulty in gathering information or contacting sources, emphasize your successes and positive expectations.

TO: Jim Boles   DATE: October 1, 19__
FROM: Bob McMillan
RE: Progress on the Study of 123 Traffic Congestion

In my study of the design problems at the intersection of US 123 and Highway 96, I have located the highway department records of accidents that have occurred there within the last five years. I have also completed my interviews with members of the local police and sheriff's departments.

The State Highway Department engineer, Jim McConnell, has been on medical leave for two weeks but is expected to return to his office on October 15. After my discussion with him the following day, I will have collected all the data that you require, and I expect to have the finished report on your desk by noon on October 19.

If you have any suggestions, please let me know by the 17th, when I will begin writing the final draft. I believe that you will be pleased with the definitive results of the study.

Once the project or study is completed, the sponsor will expect a final report that includes the kind of concreteness shown in Marc Fisher's report, which follows.

To: Ms. Janis Falstaff, Human Resources Director
From: Marc Fisher, Systems Analyst
Date: October 15, 19__

Subject: Recommendation of Computerized Absentee Control System for Use at Beta Corporation

Introduction

Beta Corporation employs approximately 1500 hourly employees at its Wilmington plant. Due to the labor-intensive nature of the multi-layer ceramic capacitor manufacturing process, the corporation needs a system to lessen the high cost of employee absenteeism.

The current manual system is obviously inadequate to handle the volume of data control necessary to the efficient operation of the company. Developing a computer-based information system is an option that is essential to maintaining the records important to Beta Corporation.

Uses for an Absentee Control System

A fundamental requirement for this system is a reliable method for tracking absences of hourly employees for disciplinary reasons. The ACS tracks unexcused absences for other purposes, however. It maintains accurate records of employee vacation time and sick pay, and at the end of the fiscal year, hourly employees are reimbursed for unused sick pay and vacation time. Additionally, the ACS maintains data on each employee's date of hire, supervisor, division, and job classification. All of this information is vital to calculating accurate vacation and sick pay time accrued. Employees may at any time request information on their current status: number of vacation days used, number of vacation days left, sick pay hours accumulated, unexcused absences charged, and other information kept on file.

The Current System

The ACS presently used is a manual one. One system administrator is assigned to maintaining the ACS. Each employee's absences are recorded on a 4" x 6" index card designed specifically for that purpose. The cards are kept on file in the personnel department, and absences are recorded on the cards daily.

With a work force ranging from 1500 to 2000 employees, the administrator finds the task of maintaining these absentee records formidable. Each employee accumulates approximately 30 transactions (excused absences, unexcused absences, reprimands, and other actions) per year, for a total of 45,000 to 60,000 transactions per year. An employee's request for status check requires the system administrator to locate the employee's absence card and manually perform the requested calculations, a time-consuming process.

Recommended Action

A microcomputer-based version of the ACS is recommended for implementation at Beta Corporation. This option would have several advantages. The system administrator should be able to enter the daily transactions in approximately half of each work day, as compared to the full day presently required. Savings estimated to be realized, based on the $29,000 annual salary, would be $14,500.

The personnel department already owns a DYAD File Management System, so no additional expenditure would be required for data storage. Software development is estimated to require three months of programmer time at a cost of $10,000. Training and ACS administrator consultant time is estimated at $600. Purchase of an IBM PC with monitor and printer is estimated at $3200. The projected costs for implementing a microcomputer-based system would total $13,800, $700 less than the projected savings in system administrator time.

Adopting this system offers several distinct advantages. It would allow the system administrator to compile the required management reports in a matter of minutes, as well as heighten our ability to track absenteeism, increasing the effectiveness of our disciplinary system and decreasing absenteeism. Its major benefit, however, would be the expansion in our information-generating capabilities and the potential for extended use in the future. In view of these perceived advantages, I recommend that we implement this system.

Proposals

Whether initiated by the writer or assigned by a supervisor, proposals are designed to provide solutions to problems. One proposal may suggest a change in the paycheck distribution procedure to increase security. Another may outline research for testing a new product. Others may offer bids on a university's telephone system. Three kinds of proposals follow.

April 29, 19___

TO: Mr. Ryan McGraw   FROM: James Cothran
        President   Operations Manager

SUBJECT: Purchase of a New Rock Washer for the Sand Plant

Over the past two years demand for washed stone has increased significantly. Within the last six months orders have doubled from 1000 to 2000
tons per month. We are the only suppliers of washed stone in Rockport,
and customers have requested that we produce more. We have paid a
price for not being able to meet our customers' needs.

Current Production Levels
Following is the data for the last six months:

Tons requested:	12,540	@ $15/ton	$188,100
Tons sold:	6,200	@ $15/ton	93,000
		Money lost	$95,100

For two reasons we are unable to produce the washed stone requested. One
is downtime. During the past six months, the downtime has averaged two
days per week, costing us $8,500 in lost revenue. Another factor is size.
The present rock washer, when running, averages five tons of washed stone
per hour. The Caterpillar X-7, which I propose buying, will wash seven
tons of rock per hour, more than doubling our present production with its
greater reliability and increased capacity, as the following figures show.

	Tons/ hour	Hours/ day	Days/ week	Tons/ week	Tons/ month
Present washer	5	10	4	200	800
Caterpillar X-7	7	10	6	420	1680

Proposed Purchase of Caterpillar X-7
The cost of the Caterpillar X-7 is $135,000, plus setup costs of $12,000.
The setup costs include Caterpillar's coming in with its own crew and setting up the machine from start to finish. The cost of the machine should be
recovered within six months with the projected rock sales of 1680 tons per
month. This figure does not take into account the repair costs saved.

Caterpillar X-7		$135,000
Set-up costs		12,000
	Total	$147,000
Six (6) months @ 1680 tons/month		$151,200

On the basis of these figures, I recommend that we purchase the
Caterpillar X-7 rock washer for the sand plant. I am enclosing a brochure
on the Caterpillar X-7 and will be glad to provide any additional information you request.

November 15, 19__

To: Robert J. Freeman   From: Thomas Bryant
    Snow Ski Club President   Membership Chair

Subject: Proposed Study to Improve Member Participation in Club
           Activities

Introduction
The Longmont Snow Ski Club currently has over 100 members. Each fall the club has strong attendance (50–75), but after four or so meetings, the members' attendance begins to drop steadily until only 20–25 members attend each meeting.

Purpose of Study
The purpose of this study is to gain insight into the problems associated with members' low participation in club activities. Concentration areas for the study will be members' reasons for joining the club, their opinions on club effectiveness, and their evaluation of club leadership. This information will provide organization leaders with recommendations for altering meeting strategy, advertising, and agenda for activities. The findings may also suggest direction for the club's future needs.

Sources and Methods of Data Collection
Thirty members of the Longmont Snow Ski Club will be questioned by means of a randomly distributed questionnaire about skiing background, reasons for joining the organization, club participation, and suggestions for improvement.

Study Outline
    I. Introduction
   II. Reasons for Joining the Organization
  III. Evaluation of the Club's Effectiveness
      A. Activities
      B. Advertisement
      C. Meetings
   V. Evaluation of the Leadership's Effectiveness
  VI. Suggestions for Improvement
 VII. Conclusions and Recommendations

Schedule
Distribution of Questionnaire — November 20
Collection of Questionnaires — December 1
Completion of Study — December 8

PROPOSAL

Date:
Proposal Number:

Proposal Submitted To:	**Work To Be Performed At:**
Name _____	Street _____
Street_____	City _____
City_____	State_____
State _____	Date of Plans _____
Telephone Number_____	Architect _____

Work To Be Completed:

Costs:

Method of Payment:

All material is guaranteed to be as specified. Any alteration from the above specifications, including additional costs, will be directed by written orders and will become an extra charge. All agreements are contingent upon strikes, accidents, or delays beyond our control. Owner will carry fire, flood, and other necessary insurance. Workers' Compensation will be carried by _____

_____ .

Submitted by:

Signature_____
Date_____

This proposal will be withdrawn if not accepted within _____ days.

Acceptance of Proposal:

Signature_____
Date_____
Conditions of acceptance:

Proposals begin with a statement of the problem. As you develop this section of the proposal, you will comment mainly on that which is verifiable and objective. Your discussion of the current policy or procedure should remain detached and professional. The greater the change proposed, the greater the need for your diplomacy and persuasiveness. The second section of the report advances the proposal itself, incorporating statistics on projected benefits and costs. The advantages must outweigh the costs, and your role is to focus on the feasibility of your suggested change or action. Your reader is convinced both by the facts of the proposal and your persuasiveness as a writer.

You may originate an internal proposal when you see a problem with your organization that you believe can be eliminated or lessened. The proposal on page 155 uses indirect order to request a piece of equipment.

When you initiate a study or are assigned one, you will submit an outline of the plan for the projected work. That proposal may be only one page or considerably longer, depending upon the complexity of the study, but you will include the details pertinent to the study: background, purpose, methods, sources, scope, areas to be studied, time frame, and any costs involved. Discussion on each of these sections should be concise and precise. The report on page 156 proposes distributing a survey to find the causes of poor attendance at organization meetings.

A sales proposal is designed to project the costs and benefits of the proposed activity offered as a response to the stated problem. Such a proposal will specify details of work to be done, costs involved with the project, time frame for completion of the work, financial arrangements for payment, and frequently, credentials of personnel handling the work. A construction company might offer a sales proposal such as the one that appears on page 157, which has the effect of being a definitive estimate or a binding contract.

CHAPTER PERSPECTIVE

Competence in report writing is a valuable commodity in the corporate environment. Every writer can achieve this, but its development depends on careful, logical thinking and organization. The intelligent writer takes the time to think through the elements of a report and select the order, treatment, and format that projects the information in the most effective way possible. Writing clear, strong, coherent reports will gain you appreciation from clients, coworkers, and supervisors.

If you discover the need to design a form for reports in your department or division, you should consider these points:

1. Carefully determine all the information needed.

2. Present points in the order that makes it most convenient for the reporter to respond and most logical for the report reader to process.

3. Use simple-to-complex order for report entries. Begin with factual information such as name, division, and date. This section will both cover the basics and lead the report writer to the completion of the report.

4. For the interior of the report, define precisely the pieces of information desired. Make specific rather than general requests.

5. Use emphasizing techniques and white space to increase the readability of the form: headings, bold-faced and underlined words, numbers for items in a series, and distinct separations between sections.

6. Provide sufficient space for people to answer questions or give required information. You may leave open space, lines or boxes for answers, or you may provide responses in a check-list format. If you think there may be longer replies, make note that additional comments may be written on the back.

7. Field test your form before duplicating it. Make sure all questions and required information are clearly stated so that valid responses are received. Avoid duplicating questions.

8. Keep entries focused. If you have an entry of a dual nature, separate it into two entries.

9. Keep the form as short and simple as possible while providing all the information needed. The easier the report is to complete, the more quickly and dependably report writers will complete and return it.

10. Identify and define all sections so that the form is self-explanatory, without reference to any other document.

Survey Reports

INTRODUCTION AND MAIN POINTS

Surveys are useful in furnishing statistical data for making business decisions. A company can assess the marketability of a proposed product, obtain feedback from clientele on the success of its advertising campaign, or solicit opinions from employees on means to improve working conditions. Whatever its use, it should be designed to gather information quickly and reliably. All facets of the survey—the design and distribution of the questionnaire, analysis of the data, and writing of the report—must be logical, substantive, and objective. The value of the report hinges on the credibility of the researcher and the research methods.

After reading this chapter:

▬ You will be able to design an unbiased questionnaire that produces reliable and valid data.

▬ You will be able to distribute questionnaires in a systematic manner to assure accurate, representative sampling.

▬ You will be able to analyze the results of a survey to reach convincing conclusions and recommendations.

▬ You will be able to organize the report into a coherent presentation.

DESIGNING THE QUESTIONNAIRE

To obtain credible data for a study, you must begin with a well-thought-out questionnaire. Little of value can come from a questionnaire that is incomplete, confusing, or intrusive in nature. For the survey to be valid, respondents should be asked specific, unbiased questions that they are able—and willing—to answer. They should not have to ponder answers, do research, or falsify responses to protect themselves.

Explanatory Section

Respondents need to know at the outset the purpose of the study and the group of respondents being surveyed. Either in a cover letter or an explanatory section at the top of the questionnaire, you should provide information on both these topics. If the questionnaire is being sent outside your company, use a cover letter; if it is being distributed internally, you may include the explanation on the questionnaire itself.

In addition to establishing the purpose and identifying the survey group, your cover letter should state the purpose of the survey, note the deadline for return of the questionnaire, and thank the participants for responding. If the topic is sensitive or controversial, assure those being surveyed of the confidentiality of their responses.

Demographic Questions

Either at the beginning or end of the questionnaire, you need to ask respondents questions on the aspects of their background that you consider influential to the study—occupation, age range, educational level, home ownership. These questions seem to work best at the beginning of the questionnaire to lead the respondent from easy questions to substantive ones, but some questionnaires locate them at the end.

For sensitive topics such as age and salary, the answers need to be expressed in ranges wide enough to give some feeling of anonymity to the respondent. Use ten- to fifteen-year increments for age and $10,000 or $15,000 increments for salary. Be wary of asking questions on salary range. Ask only if the information is absolutely necessary to your study and leave a "prefer not to answer" option.

Check-Response vs. Open-Ended Questions

Respondents should be able to answer a questionnaire in five or ten minutes. Few people are willing to spend much longer than that on a questionnaire, unless they see real benefit to themselves. Almost all the questions in the survey will provide check responses. Respondents will be given a range of answers from which to choose rather than being asked open-ended questions that require more thought and effort. Check-response questions have two distinct advantages. They allow the respondent to answer quickly and spontaneously, provided that you have listed all the feasible answers and they facilitate later tabulation and analysis of the data. Analyzing the responses to open-ended questions takes more time and yields less precise data because results are difficult to present as percentages. Thus, most of the questionnaire should use check-response questions, with perhaps only one to three open-ended questions. You can add "Comments" at the end of the questionnaire to allow respondents to express any opinions not asked for by the questions.

Open-ended questions are appropriate, however, for interviewing a small number of people. With interviews you prefer depth to breadth—in-depth replies to a few questions rather than the quick-response answers from the large group that you expect in a survey. The guidelines presented in the following section, since they encourage check responses, apply more particularly to designing a questionnaire than to phrasing questions for an interview. Aside from that facet of devising questions, however, the information applies to both surveys and interviews.

As you begin work, your initial step is to list all the questions that might reasonably relate to the topic. Your list will obviously include some questions that are only indirectly or peripherally related to your subject, and when you start sorting questions, you will drop some of them. Attempt to group the questions so you come up with a reasonable number of sections, none of them awkwardly long or short. Obviously, the number of sections and length of the report depend on the number of questions you ask in the questionnaire.

The length of your questionnaire, in turn, depends on the kind of questions you ask. The major questions have *yes/no* or *strongly agree/strongly disagree* options, or multiple choice responses. The simpler your questions, the more of them you will need to provide sufficient data.

Yes/No Responses

The simplest kinds of questions are those with *yes/no* answers and you may add follow-up questions such as "Why or why not?" or "If yes, what brand?" Use such questions only for gathering factual information:

> Do you subscribe to a newspaper? ____yes ____no
>
> If so, which one? _____

Yes-and-no answers are not adequate for responding to questions on moral issues and may not yield credible results because of people's wide ranges of opinion on such issues.

Lists

Survey designers frequently include a listing of features, options, or qualities—desired options on a sports car, countries visited, reasons for exercising—then ask respondents to *rank* their preferences or rate their response to each entry. With a question of this nature, you may request that respondents rank their choices—first, second, third, forth. (Beyond fourth, fifth, or sixth, distinctions tend to blur.) If you want responses to all the entries in the list rather than simply an indication of participants' top choices, you should direct respondents to *rate* the entries on scales such as these:

- High, medium, low
- 1 (low) to 10 (high)
- 1 (high) to 5 (low)
- Excellent, good, fair, poor
- Very important—not important

For the listing, you may ask respondents to "Check all that apply." The responses, then, will produce data that exceeds 100 percent, a point that you would note when presenting data on that question in the report. Examples of ranking and rating questions follow.

How important to you are the following characteristics of grocery stores?						
	Important				Unimportant	
Convenience:	1	2	3	4	5	6
Parking						
Location						
Roomy aisles						
Automation						
Speedy checkout						

Which of the following outdoor activities have you tried? (Please check all that apply.)	
_____Biking	_____Kayaking
_____Mountain climbing	_____Canoeing
_____White-water rafting	_____Skydiving
_____Tubing	_____Horseback riding
_____Other:	

Please rank your *top five* choices for vacation sites:		
_____Miami	_____Atlantic City	_____Bahamas
_____Orlando	_____Denver	_____Mexico
_____New Orleans	_____San Diego	_____England
_____Atlanta	_____San Francisco	_____Germany
_____Washington, DC	_____Canada	_____France
_____New York City	_____Hawaii	_____Spain

Likert Scale

The Likert Scale, with its *Strongly Agree–Strongly Disagree* range of responses, is a question-and-answer technique that makes it possible to obtain responses on sensitive topics. This approach gives much objectivity to answers that are difficult to phrase without using emotionally-charged words:

> Please respond on the Strongly Agree–Strongly Disagree scale to the following statements concerning college students and the distribution of contraceptives:

1. Contraceptives should be distributed free of charge to college students.

   SA   A   No Opinion   D   SD

2. Contraceptives should be made available to students for a nominal fee.

   SA   A   No Opinion   D   SD

3. Students should receive information on sexually-transmitted diseases but not be given contraceptives.

   SA   A   No Opinion   D   SD

The multiple-choice answer format is frequently used for questionnaires—the number of times per week respondents exercise, the month they prefer to vacation, the car they drive. For this type of question, you need to offer all the answers that seem likely;

however, you usually need to add "Other:_____ (Please specify.)" to allow responses you have omitted:

What was the reason for your visit?
___Family reunion   ___Attractions
___Relaxation   ___Business
___Vacation   ___Other: _____

As you design your questionnaire, consider how you will analyze your data once you have collected the surveys. Ask questions in a format that will facilitate analysis and presentation in the report. Numerical responses such as "1 (low) to 10 (high)" allow you easier analysis than do word responses like *excellent*, *good*, *fair*, and *poor*. Using the "*Important* (1) to *Unimportant* (6)" rating scale, you may produce results similar to the following figures on characteristics influencing customer satisfaction with grocery stores:

- Parking = 1.1
- Location = 1.5
- Roomy aisles = 2.5
- Automation = 3.4
- Speedy checkout = 4.0

With the word responses, you will indicate the significant responses: "A majority of the respondents (58 percent) rated the service as *good*, followed by a sizable number (31 percent) who rated it *fair*. Only five percent rated the service *excellent*."

As you phrase the questionnaire entries, you need to guard against including leading questions. Respondents should feel free to answer all questions honestly without having to give ego-damaging responses. A question like "How often do you exercise?" with the answers "Frequently," "Occasionally," "Never" may cause a person who never exercises to answer "Occasionally" to avoid the suggestion of laziness or poor self-discipline. You might, instead, focus the question on the frequency of exercise:

- __ 0–2 times/week
- __ 3–4 times/week
- __ 5–7 times/week

The numbers avoid the value-laden words, and the ranges offer the respondent some sense of privacy.

Another kind of leading question is one that encourages a person's rebellious spirit. A question such as "Do you think a person should have to…?" usually provokes a "No" because the child in us does not like being required to do things (although we live with requirements daily). More objective phrasing might be "What is your response to the requirement that…?" with answers on the *Strongly Agree–Strongly Disagree* scale.

Coordinating the Questionnaire and Report Sections

To facilitate writing the report, you should plan your questionnaire so that it coordinates closely with the sections you intend for the report. In the introduction to the report, you will declare your purpose, scope, methods, and sources. For your sources, you will note the demographic data—number or percentage of males and females, age ranges, the number who own VCRs—that you asked for in the questionnaire.

The body of the report is divided into its respective sections, each containing discussion of questionnaire data. Each question in the questionnaire should fit into a section of your report plan. An sample arrangement might be similar to this:

Introduction:	purpose, scope, methods, and sources, questions 1–3
Convenience:	questions 4–7
Quality of Service:	questions 8–11
Atmosphere:	questions 12–14
Suggestions for Improvement:	question 15
Conclusions	

If a question does not readily fit into the plan, consider whether to omit it or to add several more questions on the topic, thus developing it into an entire section.

All questions need to fit logically into your planned outline because in your report you will discuss the significant data on every question you ask. Once you have decided to include a question, do not withhold the results simply because you do not like or had not anticipated the responses. You are justified in editing out responses or results only if you believe the respondents falsified information or misunderstood the question. In either case, you would not delete, say, item eight in a ten-question survey without explanation. A silent omission would open you to the charge of manipulating or slanting data.

Objectivity in both wording and approach is of utmost importance to the reliability of study. Your credibility as a researcher and the worth of the results rest upon your ability to design an objective questionnaire, then distribute it in such a way that you will achieve a trustworthy and representative set of data.

DISTRIBUTING THE QUESTIONNAIRE

To obtain valuable data, you need to distribute the questionnaire using accepted sampling techniques. In surveying a limited number of people and considering them spokespersons for a larger population, you must carefully plan and execute the circulation of the questionnaire. Your methods must assure accurate representation as much as possible. Exhaustive discussion of sampling techniques is beyond the scope of this chapter, but three of the most commonly used approaches are a systematic random sampling, quota sampling, and probability sampling.

Systematic Random Sampling

To utilize a systematic random sampling, you need a complete list of the population being surveyed—voters in the school district, members in an organization, employees in a company. After deciding how many respondents you need for the study, you will determine the pattern of selection. For example, if you want to survey fifty of your 300 members, you will begin at the top of the list and select every sixth member, keeping the pattern of selection consistent.

Quota Sampling

For quota sampling, you need the percentages on gender, race, age, and other statistical information pertinent to your population. Your sampling then attempts to mirror these demographic categories. You first distribute the questionnaire, which contains relevant background questions randomly. The next step is to gather the returned questionnaires and determine how far your sampling is from the ratios of women, African-Americans, over sixties, etc., you need. You may have to distribute a second sampling among a select group in order to obtain the ratios you want. This kind of follow-up sampling does make the sampling less random, but will achieve the desired quotas.

Probability Sampling

Probability sampling is less systematic than the other two methods and, unless handled carefully, may produce less reliable results. For sampling to be realistic, you should distribute the questionnaires in a location where all segments of the group gather: a departmental meeting, the company cafeteria, the break room, or the shopping mall. The probability sampling is best used as an indicator of trends rather than as a set of data on which major financial decisions are based. The more significant the decisions, the more systematic and precise the sampling methods should be.

ANALYZING SURVEY DATA

After collecting your data, you will tabulate responses and convert them to percentages for easier handling and presentation in the report.

A very important initial action is dividing the questionnaires according to the demographic classifications of your population—gender, age, ownership of a VCR, for example, to determine differences in their responses. You will probably have asked three or four demographic questions, and you must consider them one at a time. This may seem like a time-consuming process, but it provides data that is extremely valuable to most studies. If, after you have sorted and studied the questionnaires in this manner, you see no significant differences between the respective groups' answers, you can present the responses from the group as a whole.

In your report you should choose one demographic factor for differentiation. Even though you may have seen some difference between males' and females' responses, you may see a sharper distinction between salaried and hourly employees' responses. Because you will not be able to discuss more than one, you should select the predominant distinction for focus in the report.

Once you have figured percentages and determined the important demographic distinctions, look at the questionnaire to focus the responses. Consider combining similar responses, such as "Strongly Agree" and "Agree," "Strongly Disagree" and "Disagree," for simplifying presentation of the data, but be careful not to oversimplify. Look at the respondents' answers perceptively to determine how their answers to one question relate to responses on other questions. Record your observations for use later in writing your report.

You will want to present all your data in the context of its meaning to the study. You force your reader to analyze the data if you use statements such as, "When asked how frequently they eat out, 5 percent said less than once a month, 20 percent said once a month, 50 percent said once a week, 10 percent said two or three times per week, and 15 percent said daily." You might express this finding as, "A large majority of the respondents (75 percent) eat out at least once a week. Of those, 15 percent eat out daily. This statistic correlates clearly to respondents' relatively high figures on food expenses."

Even though you will mention every question you asked in your questionnaire, you need not cite every response. Instead, you will report only the meaningful data. In most cases, you will focus on the majority responses in order of their strength: "The students overwhelmingly chose better food (77 percent) as their major reason for being off the meal plan. Other reasons they cited were convenience (13 percent) and lower cost (10 percent)." In some situations, you may also choose to mention the minority responses: "None of the participants exercise for the purpose of building muscle mass or counteracting an injury to the body."

If you asked for rankings or ratings, you will find data analysis time-consuming but satisfying. You will average the numbers on each response: add the numbers cited and divide the total by the number of respondents to the question. For a ranking of the top five choices, you will probably generate numbers like 1.3, 2.5, 3.1, 4.5. You will rarely have whole numbers—1.0, 2.0, 3.0, or 4.0—because people will not unanimously agree on the rankings. You will note the actual numbers (with decimals) in the report. Readers like to know, for instance, how close to 1.0 the first choice was or how close to each other the third and fourth choices were.

For ratings, you will analyze the figures in the same averaging process, provided that you have given numbers to the rating:

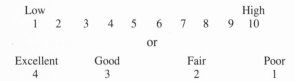

Once you define the scale, you can introduce your conclusions: "On the scale of 1 (low) to 10 (high), respondents rated service at 8.2," or "Using an Excellent (4) to Poor (1) scale, tenants gave a high 3.8 rating to the apartment facilities." You may find it advisable to reiterate the evaluation scale periodically if you think the reader may have forgotten the meanings of the numbers: "Still using the 1 (low) to 10 (high) scale, readers gave a 7.8 rating to the layout of the newspaper."

In examining the data, you have the obligation to determine which responses deserve focus and what interrelationships between responses are important to your study and the reader. You will rely on your logic and judgment and will shape the report—in content and form.

WRITING THE REPORT

To do justice to your research efforts, your report must present your findings in a coherent fashion. If, in reading or scanning your report, the reader does not comprehend the significance and subtleties of your study, your valuable research work may be wasted. The value of a study to the reader rests with your ability to clearly express your findings. The report is your major or sole medium for presenting the data to the reader.

Logical ordering of the various sections of the report does much to assure your reader's understanding. The standard sections are introduction, body, conclusions and recommendations, sources, and appendix.

Introduction

The introductory section of this report should present an overview on the background of the problem, purpose of the report, scope and limitations, methods and sources, and in some cases conclusions. (Whether or not to include conclusions depends on the length of the report. If it is as short as four pages, you will probably omit the conclusions, but if it is as long as ten pages, you may want to include them. Reading through the report will usually show you whether it is helpful or necessary to present the conclusions of the study at the beginning of the report.)

The sections of the introduction may have headings if each is several paragraphs long, but since these are frequently short sections, you may present them merely as paragraphs with no headings. For each section, state your information specifically: background of the problem, purpose for the study, details on survey methods, and information on the sources—the number of randomly selected respondents, their demographic data, and names and titles of any authoritative sources surveyed.

Somewhere in the introduction, either in the purpose statement or in the last paragraph, you should also indicate the sections contained in the report, identifying these sections with the same wording that will be used later in the body of the report. These directional signals are extremely helpful to your reader. Your introduction may read like this:

INTRODUCTION

Employees of the Belknap Department Store have recently expressed their increasing concern about the inordinate amount of stress present in the work atmosphere of the store and in the performance of their duties.

Purpose: The purpose of this study was to determine the sources and levels of stress that sales associates experience in their working environment, as well as their primary methods of reducing the stress.

Methods and Sources: To obtain the information and opinions used for this study, I randomly distributed twenty-five questionnaires to sales associates in the Belknap Department Store in Bryant, Colorado. Of the twenty-five questionnaires distributed, twenty were returned and considered usable. The ratio of male-to-female respondents was nearly equal (45 percent males, 55 percent females). Most employees (90 percent) have worked at the store for at least one year. Because of the small number of sales associates in the store, respondents were not asked to indicate their department.

Body of the Report

As you begin writing the text of your report proper, you will need to consider (or reconsider) the order in which you present your points, headings you will utilize, presentation form for numbers, and style.

The actual order in which you raise each point may remain relatively consistent with your initial plan; at some point in writing, however, you may find that logic demands your changing the arrangement. If, for instance, you are gathering opinions on the best word-processing software for your office, or information on the major users of your company's cleaning services, you would start with the highest-ranked group, then present the remaining groups in descending order. Before you begin writing the report, then, you need to look closely at your findings to determine what is the most logical order.

Each section of the report should be introduced with a heading. You will certainly use first-level headings, probably second-level, and perhaps even third- and fourth-level. First-level headings will be *Introduction*, section headings for the body (using phrasing for the sections parallel to the listing in the introduction), *Conclusions*, *Recommendations* (or a combination of the two), *Sources*, and *Appendix*. You may need other preliminary or supplementary sections. If so, introduce them in the same manner with a first-level heading.

Heading positions vary. Many arrangements are acceptable, as long as they show major-to-minor relationship and parallel sections use the same format. Some of your options include the following:

First-level	Centered or left justified, all capitals or all upper and lower case, bold-face or underlined, if desired.
Second-level	Centered or left justified, upper and lower case, bold-face or underlined, if desired. Should be less emphatic in presentation than first-level heading.
Third-level	Integrated into first sentence of section, bold-face or underlined, period after heading and paragraph following.

As you take up each section of your report, you will want to introduce the topic early in the first paragraph, cite the relevant statistics and their significance (integrating necessary graphic aids), and end with comments concluding that report segment. Each section should be complete in itself yet clearly relate to the overall plan.

You will need to cite precise data in the report, either in visual aids or in the text. If you use a table or graph which gives full data, you may use general terms in the text—*most, majority, a few*. If you are presenting the statistics entirely in the text, you will use very specific language:

> Fifteen (64 percent) of the respondents indicated...
> Twenty-five of the thirty people surveyed...
> The majority (85 percent) of the commuters said...

As you begin writing the report, you may find it helpful to refresh your memory on some of the major rules for using numbers:

1. Make a decision as to whether you will write out numbers greater than ten or greater than one hundred. Most business

documents use numerals rather than spelled-out numbers—because most involve large numbers and because numerals are easier to read and assimilate than numbers expressed in words.

2. Spell out numbers at the beginning of sentences, but try to rephrase any sentence that begins with a number. Place the number later in the sentence so you can use a numeral for greater clarity. Change "Three hundred twenty accountants attended the meeting" to something like "The meeting drew 320 accountants."

3. Use numerals for the following: money, ratios, temperatures, page numbers, measurements, percentages, and dates.

4. Maintain consistency in the use of numbers for the same items. If most are under the number you have chosen for your cut-off, use worded numbers for all. If most are over, use figures.

In styling your report, use active voice whenever possible: "The respondents indicated...." or "The study shows...." Avoid such passive constructions as "It was indicated by the respondents that...." and "It was shown by the study that...." Passive voice is appropriate when focusing on the action rather than the actor: "Fifty teachers were included in the survey." However, you will condense and strengthen your report phrasing by maintaining active voice unless the situation specifically calls for passive voice.

As you present your data, you will cite by name any authoritative sources you have consulted for the study: "Dr. Frank Lee, Director of the Outreach Program in Nashville, Tennessee, indicates...." Unless the name is so widely known that everyone will recognize it, add the title identification.

Conclusions and Recommendations

In this section, you will recap—in general terms—the major conclusions you have drawn from the study and draw overall conclusions. You may offer your recommendations with the conclusions or as a separate section, but present them specifically, tabulating them if feasible:

CONCLUSIONS AND RECOMMENDATIONS

Since performance at work is actually enhanced under moderate amounts of stress, managers must take care to maintain a healthy balance between beneficial and counterproductive amounts of stress in the work place. Since the employee stress level at Belknap is normally distributed around moderate, the level seems reasonable and perhaps beneficial. However, various departments are involved in the study, and this rating represents the average of the responses.

Recommendations based on the study are as follows:

1. Commission should remain the store's method of payment and incentive for employees. However, the number of employees working for commission in a single department should be kept to a minimum in order to keep conflict to a reasonable level while maintaining the positive effects on productivity.

2. More group activities and social events outside of work should be coordinated. The result would be increased communication among employees in all departments, as well as, it is hoped, higher work satisfaction levels among employees.

These two suggestions, if implemented, may lower undesirable stress levels and, at the same time, increase overall productivity and satisfaction. Because stress levels at Belknap are not unusually high, as indicated by the survey, any improvement would serve to complement an already satisfactory work environment.

Sources

The reference section may use the headings Sources, Sources Cited, Interviews, References, or any comparable word and should include a list of interviewees and bibliographical citations to any secondary sources used. Cite name, title, company and location, and date for each interview included. Alphabetize entries, either as a whole or separated into Secondary Sources, Interviews, or other category designations that you consider appropriate. Chapter 12 discusses documentation in greater detail.

Appendices

In the Appendices section, include a copy of the questionnaire or interview form you used and any supplementary material important to the study but not suitable for including in the report. Examples might be related reports, complex visual aids from which you extracted data, brochures, receipts, projections, or copies of pertinent records. You should label and title each entry: *Appendix A. Sample Questionnaire.*

The report shown on pages 177–181 on backpack preferences and use incorporates most of the recommendations pertinent to short reports.

CHAPTER PERSPECTIVE

The emphasis throughout this chapter has been on the precise and unbiased handling of data. The focus of the report is the data and its relevance to your particular purpose. If you have rationally and painstakingly completed the multifaceted process discussed in this chapter, you should be confident concerning the validity of your statistics and conclusions. Such a report can provide a secure basis for any manager, president, or owner who makes major decisions.

To: Mr. J. Black, President, Appalachian Trail Outfitters
From: Eric Rodgers, Store Manager
Date: October 17, 19___
Subject: Recommendations on Backpack Purchase and
             Merchandising

INTRODUCTION

The purpose of this study is to survey the backpack demands of
Appalachian Trail Outfitters customers in order to more effectively
select merchandise for sale and to develop a strategy to draw catalog
business into our store. The survey was designed to discover what factors influence a backpack purchase and to determine whether a significant number of people shop through catalogs.

A total of fifty randomly selected backpacking customers of
Appalachian Trail Outfitters completed the questionnaire (included in
the appendix). The questionnaire was distributed to those clients who
had purchased a backpack and had at least some backpacking experience. The conclusions to this study are based on the responses to the
questionnaire, as well as my nine years' experience in three different
backpacking shops, extensive backpacking experience, and ownership
and use of a number of packs of different types and construction.

Topics to be discussed in this report are preference of internal-frame or
external-frame packs, patterns of pack usage, and competition from catalogs.

PREFERENCE OF INTERNAL-FRAME OR
EXTERNAL-FRAME PACKS

Of the fifty customers surveyed, 65 percent chose external-frame packs
and 35 percent internal-frame packs. One reason for this imbalance is
that external-frame packs have been in use for a much longer time than
the relatively new internal-frame packs. In addition, external-frame
packs are less expensive. Each has distinctive advantages and disadvantages.

External-Frame Packs. External-frame packs enable the hiker to carry
large, bulky items because of the ability to strap them directly to the aluminum frame. Sharp-pointed items can be carried more comfortably
because the pack does not come in contact with the user's back.
External-frame packs are cooler than the internal-frame packs because
the pack is set away from the user's back by a breathable mesh back-
band. External-frame packs are also easier to fit to the hiker's body or
adjust to another user. In addition, they are generally less expensive, an
important consideration for most buyers.

Internal-Frame Packs. Internal-frame packs lie against the hiker's back, placing the pack's center of gravity much closer to the hiker's own. All of the hikers who own these packs use them when backpacking. Less than a third (29 percent) use the packs for ski touring or climbing, although internal-frame packs provide the balance that is crucial to such activities as cross-country skiing and rock-climbing. Only 14 percent chose them for traveling or canoe camping. Internal-frame packs are less bulky because of their internal aluminum supports, making them easier to load and unload from small spaces, and a majority of users (86 percent each) cited volume/capacity and carrying of heavy loads as primary reasons for selecting this style.

Because the pack comes into direct contact with the user's back, however, it is much hotter than the external-frame pack. Only 56 percent of the internal-frame pack owners use them in the summer, although all use them during the spring, fall, and winter.

PATTERNS OF PACK USAGE

Determining patterns of pack usage, both lengths of time spent on the trips and the seasons of use, as well as features that influence pack purchase, will help us in stocking the different kinds of packs.

Weekend vs. Long-distance Hikes. According to the survey, all of the pack owners use their packs for weekend trips, and 75 percent use them for long-distance hikes. Thus, large-capacity packs that carry well and hold enough supplies for a lengthy hike will be desirable to most people, as will those with the sophisticated suspension system that distributes the weight of the large pack evenly, allowing more comfortable walking. For weekend-trip users, a smaller capacity pack with a simple suspension system will suffice. Weekend campers generally take a more casual approach to hiking and do not require the higher volume and quality backpack that long-distance hikers demand, nor are they willing to pay for it.

These simple facts indicate that the backpack stock at Appalachian Trail Outfitters should be distributed in a ratio of 75 percent large-capacity, more sophisticated packs to 25 percent smaller, simpler packs.

Seasons of Pack Usage. Seasonality is another important consideration in stocking merchandise for a retail store. Retailers need to know when a large supply of packs is needed so they do not tie up capital with unbought packs during an off season. This survey shows top pack usage in the spring and fall (100 percent each season). The lull in winter (75 percent usage) is expected because of the number of campers who do not have the extra equipment or the incentive necessary for winter camping.

The decrease in internal-frame pack use in summer (90 percent usage) contributes to a general selling slowdown at that time. Thus, summer inventory should contain fewer internal-frame packs. Inventory should be highest in spring and fall, lowest in winter. The ratio of internal-frame packs to external should be 35 percent to 65 percent, following the ratios of people who own and use each type of pack.

Features Important to Pack Choice. After deciding when to stock packs and what ratio of internal-to-external packs to stock, we should decide what features customers look for in buying a pack. Figure 1 shows the relative importance of the various pack features to this group of respondents.

Figure 1. Criteria for Pack Purchase.

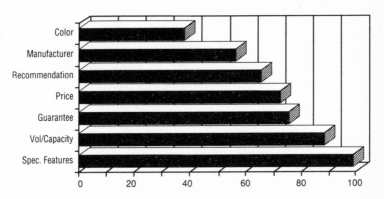

Special features such as pockets and suspension and volume/ capacity are the two most important criteria considerations for these consumers when purchasing a pack. Guarantee and price are also important, but color is of little significance. We should consider all these criteria and their relative scoring when determining pack inventory.

COMPETITION FROM CATALOGS

Even with careful buying, the retailer may have difficulty providing customers with adequate stock at sufficiently low prices. As a result, many customers order from sporting goods catalogs. Of the respondents to this study, 75 percent compare prices in different stores, and 95 percent shop through catalogs. In spite of the disadvantages of not being able to see and feel the merchandise and experiencing some delay between ordering and receiving the goods, price plays a major role in the purchase. The major advantage of catalog shopping is lower prices for the customer, and it is difficult for stores to attract catalog shoppers without lowering retail prices and reducing profit margin. A knowledgeable and effective sales person whose recommendations are respected, however, often can make the sale.

CONCLUSIONS AND RECOMMENDATIONS

The responses to this survey suggest the following conclusions that will affect our inventory selection:

a. External-frame packs are more popular than internal-frame packs by a 65:35 ratio.

b. Buyers consider special features such as pockets and suspension and volume/capacity the two most important criteria in backpack selection.

c. Spring and fall are the top seasons for pack usage, and winter is the lowest. In addition, internal-frame pack owners camp less in summer.

Finally, the fact that almost all backpackers (95 percent) shop through recreational equipment catalogs suggests that we at Appalachian Trail Outfitters should strengthen our advertising and customer service in an attempt to counteract this catalog-shopping trend.

APPENDIX: SAMPLE QUESTIONNAIRE

This survey centers on the considerations of backpack users when buying a pack and the uses made of the pack. Your answers to these questions will help us at Appalachian Trail Outfitters as we select the packs most desired by you, our customer. Thank you for your comments.

1. Do you have an ___internal or ___external frame pack?

2. If internal, why did you choose the internal frame? (Check all that apply.)

   For: ___Its ability to handle heavy loads
           ___Its volume or capacity

   For: ___Traveling   ___Climbing
           ___Backpacking   ___Ski touring
                                 ___Other: _____

3. For what activities do you use your pack? (Check all that apply.)

   ___Weekend trips   ___Canoe camping
   ___Long-distance hikes   ___Traveling
                              ___Other: _____

4. When do you use your pack? (Check all that apply.)

   ___Spring   ___Summer   ___Fall   ___Winter

5. How important are the following are to you in purchasing a backpack?

	Very important	Moderately important	Unimportant
Special features— pockets, suspension	____	____	____
Volume/Capacity	____	____	____
Brand	____	____	____
Guarantee	____	____	____
Color	____	____	____
Price	____	____	____

6. Do you compare prices in different stores? ___yes ___no

7. Do you shop through catalogs? ___yes ___no

8. Do you look at merchandise in stores, then order items from a catalog? ___yes ___no

9. If you order from catalogs, what is your major incentive?

   ___Convenience   ___Lower cost   ___Higher quality

Formal Reports

INTRODUCTION AND MAIN POINTS

A formal report is almost always a long report, but it is not simply an overgrown short report burgeoning with details. While formal reports and short ones share many of the writing devices considered in Chapters 10 and 11, these kinds of documents are conceived differently: they have different purposes and, very often, different audiences. If an employee has a fender-bender in a company truck, a supervisor files a brief accident report, insurance claims are settled, and the matter is soon relegated to the files. On the other hand, a large organization's Director of Transportation, seeing an alarming three-year trend in accident frequency, will ask for a comprehensive report to assess fleet reliability and maintenance needs, employee driver training, and insurance cost containment. The short accident report will pass through only two or three employees' hands, but the lengthy investigative report will be printed (perhaps in dozens of bound copies) and circulated to all interested parties. Many such formal reports are planned for both internal and external distribution.

A business firm or a public entity will tend to use formal reports either very often or seldom. Some organizations handle their writing functions almost entirely through short reports, often formatted as letters or memos. By contrast, many companies have special units devoted to finding and packaging data. If your duties include regularly writing formal reports, you will probably receive a company manual that details the preferred (that is, mandatory) format, documentation style, and distribution procedures. If you write a formal report only occasionally, however, and if your company or your professional field has no established format, you may take this chapter (which is a synthesis of formal report styles in several business and academic areas) to be a general guide. The aim here is to illustrate the principles that should produce polished results in the absence of an imposed format.

After studying the material in this chapter:

▬ You will know how to divide your report into front matter, body, and end matter.

▬ You will consider your options for placing and labeling graphic elements.

▬ You should be aware of your obligations for documenting borrowed material.

FORMAT AND CONTENT

What makes a formal report "formal"? Like many other types of business documents, the long report omits contractions and collo-quialisms, thus assuming a degree of formality in its wording. A formal report's title page, transmittal letter, or preface might take an almost ceremonious tone in directing the report to the attention of the person or the group requesting it. The true hallmark of a formal report, however, is the writer's careful use of the docu-ment's *form*—its format—to make its content accessible. Usually the formal report is highly structured, and its sections are gener-ously labeled.

You can adapt the standard format to your review of the effectiveness of a product, a subsidiary, or a program. The *front matter-body-end matter* progression is equally useful for assess-ing merger possibilities, studying a proposed investment, or pro-jecting a new market. Using this format, you can review the development of a problem, assess current operating procedures, forecast profits or other benefits, and consider the advantages and disadvantages of realigning resources.

The body of your report will contain the details and interpre-tive points that justify your conclusions. You can organize that middle section in the indirect pattern (building through details and preliminary conclusions toward an overview or a set of rec-ommendations) or the direct one (making an assertion and then supplying the details that will support it). With either pattern, you will not keep your reader in suspense: the front matter will include a summary of your conclusions and the basic rationale supporting them. The end matter will give further justifying detail, often in graphic form.

Each section and subsection has its own relationship to the full document, and within the three main sections you will have several options for the inclusion and placement of subsections. Although you will probably compose the body of your report first, next flesh out the end matter, and then shape the front matter, we will exam-ine those sections in the order in which the reader will see them.

Our discussion will be illustrated by excerpts from "Packaging in America in the 1990s," a forecasting investigation conducted by two specialists in food science writing under a grant administered by the Institute of Packaging Professionals.[1] Although most excerpts from this report are presented here in their original form, a few have been altered slightly, by the authors' permission, to illustrate the differences in style and format in various fields.

Front Matter

The front matter of your report will contain a title page, a table of contents, and a list of illustrations or appendices. Relatively brief front sections will also address the intended readers of your report, give credit for any assistance you received in preparing it, and provide a convenient digest of your study's main points. To achieve these purposes you may choose among the transmittal letter or memo, the executive summary, the abstract, the preface, and the introduction. Using all of these would create considerable redundancy. You will select the combination of front elements that fits your needs.

The *title page* will have four elements defined by spacing (see page 186).

Main titles are given in all-capitals. The initial letter in any subtitle will be capitalized, as will the first letter in each significant word.[2]

The second group of lines directs the paper to its primary audience—a person or a group. If the food packaging report had been commissioned by one executive rather than an industry group, this cluster might read:

Prepared for:
James Gossett, Chairman
Royal Banquet Foods, Inc.

Here the inclusion of the company name indicates that the report was prepared by researchers outside the company.

If two or three authors have contributed relatively equal shares, their names are listed alphabetically in the third cluster. If one person is to be seen as the principal author, that writer's name will be listed first and the remaining authors alphabetically arranged. (Other contributors may be acknowledged in the preface or the introduction). Report writers in scientific areas follow their names with the standard abbreviations of their highest academic degrees, but in other fields these degree designations are not included.

PACKAGING IN AMERICA IN THE 1990s

Packaging's Role in Contemporary American Society—The Benefits and Challenges

Prepared for:

The Institute of Packaging Professionals

Prepared by:

Robert F. Testin, Ph.D. and Peter J. Vergano, Sc.D.

Clemson, South Carolina

August 1990

The final cluster will indicate the place and date of the paper's release. This information will be useful for filing the report, and future readers will be able to determine by glancing at the title page whether or not the study might contain recent enough material for their purposes.

To follow the title page and to enlarge your recognition of the person or the group requesting the study, you will write a brief section that first expresses thanks for being entrusted with the assignment and then highlights features of the report that should appeal to the reader's interests (surprising data, shrewd observations, unforeseen directions):

1. The transmittal *memo* (for an internal reader) or single-page *letter* (for the reader or group outside the company) is the most personal of these approaches, directly linking the writer and the reader: "At your suggestion I have evaluated our XT-11 assembly process and have found two major and several smaller opportunities for streamlining." If your report is addressed to one of your peers, you might relax the prevailing formality here: "Clara, you have often talked about improving the XT-11 assembly process, and I have put together some data for your review."

2. The *abstract* is a straightforward digest of the report's central section reflecting key or representative details and inferences drawn from them. Normally, the abstract makes little or no mention of the study itself, and it avoids the "I" and "you" relationship of the memo-letter option. Rather, the abstract will focus on the subject from the same objective stance maintained in the body of the paper. This beginning summary simply gives the core ideas in shorter form to accommodate the busy executive's need to know the report's basic scope and thrust quickly. Scanning the one- to three-paragraph abstract on receipt of the paper, the reader can save the full text for the working weekend.

3. The *executive summary* blends some qualities of the earlier options. If you find the objective abstract a little too impersonal, you will prefer the executive summary's recognition of both the message and the medium. While an abstract might begin "Food packaging demands in the 1990s will entail...." the executive summary will more explicitly lay out the paper's aims. (See page 188)

EXECUTIVE SUMMARY

This paper reviews the benefits that packaging brings to modern society through an overview of the role of packaging in three areas: food packaging, distribution of goods, and quality of life. The paper includes a section on current issues, where various segments of packaging are examined from the perspective of packaging's impact on solid waste.

The paper concludes that packaging is essential to maintaining public health and economic well-being in a modern society. It further concludes that through product protection and waste reduction, packaging makes a significant positive economic and environmental contribution to the welfare of the United States.

The paper includes the following packaging facts:

1. By protecting against damage and spoilage, packaging *reduces* rather than adds to the solid waste stream.

2. Packaging is an essential component of the U.S. distribution system, which makes a wide variety of consumer goods conveniently available at reasonable prices.

3. Packaging enables Americans to enjoy their leisure time by cutting down the time required for shopping and food preparation.

4. Competition among packaging materials and suppliers results in continuous pressure to use less packaging, providing an automatic "source reduction" ethic in the packaging industry.

5. Single-use food packaging provides significant public health benefits by virtually eliminating the possibility of disease transmission.

6. Complete elimination of whole categories of packaging materials would make virtually no difference in the cost of waste disposal in the United States.

7. Environmental compatibility has become a very high priority for package designers in both North America and Western Europe.

Both industry and government efforts to respond to and correct packaging's alleged deficiencies, particularly in the environmental arena, are reviewed. Efforts from both sources often suffer from narrow approaches that may be counterproductive in the long run.

The role of packaging in a modern society is extremely complex and woven within the entire fabric of civilization. On balance, this role is positive. Care must be exercised by both the public and private sector to be certain that correction of real and perceived packaging deficiencies proceeds in a carefully planned manner to ensure that the net public result of any action is positive.

Begin each major or distinct section of your report on a new page, and center its heading in all-capitals.

You will notice that the lower-case Roman numeral ii appears at the bottom of the Executive Summary page. All preliminary pages should be numbered consecutively in this way. The title page will count as Roman numeral i, although by conventional procedure you will not place the number on that page. (Use Arabic numerals for pages in the main body of your report.)

You will also observe that this Executive Summary shifts the order of the material presented in the full paper. For the reader's convenience, the report's basic conclusions are drawn together into the two-sentence second paragraph, followed by a list of the considerations leading to those conclusions. In the last paragraph, secondary conclusions round off the Executive Summary.

Your title page and transmittal note or summary section will be followed by a *table of contents* (see page 190), dividing the remainder of the report into sections and subsections, their titles phrased in grammatically parallel forms. Spelling out the word "chapter" before each Roman numeral is optional, but you should follow the practice of using Roman numerals to indicate the largest divisions, capital letters for the next organizational level, and Arabic numerals for further subdivisions.

You will follow the table of contents with a *list of illustrations* for quick finding of the flow charts, maps, bar graphs, sketches of proposed logos, or other graphic matter. Identify each graphic item by figure number and title, and begin each title with an indication of the type of graphic element being shown:

Figure 5.
Map of Cherokee County, Showing Homestead Boundaries...6

Figure 6.
Bar Graph of Decline in Homesteading Family Population...8

You should use the illustrations list whether your graphic elements are placed at appropriate points in the text or gathered into a set of appendices in the end matter, although you will omit page numbers when your illustrations are gathered into the appendices.

Having moved from the title page through an acknowledgment of the reader to the table of contents and the list of illustrations, you probably feel that you need a bridge section to indicate your movement from front matter into the central section. Espe-

TABLE OF CONTENTS

cially if you need to acknowledge the help of research assistants, expert advisors, typists, or editors, you can express your thanks in a brief *preface* that can, in fact, pull together a variety of preliminary notes. A three- or four-paragraph preface might begin with a paragraph outlining landmark work done on the topic, a second paragraph might define terms or set the limits of the investigation, a third paragraph might comment on the methodology or rationale pursued, and the last paragraph can credit anyone whose aid contributed broadly to the study: "Cara Lyons, Director of Information at U.S. Fusion Corp., generously supplied data on...."

The Body of the Report

The purpose of your report and the nature of its subject will determine your precise placement of the introductory material, and your choice of the direct or the indirect approach will also influence the way you open the middle section. Some topics require a review of research, which you might prefer to list as the last front-matter section, offered for those who need the background information. In this arrangement, the body of your report can begin with a brief current-status overview of the subject, leading directly into your detailed analysis of components. The authors of the packaging study see no special needs in presenting background, and they have chosen to present their general *introduction* as the opening segment of the report's main body (see page 192). Note the use of headings and subheadings, phrased just as they are in the table of contents.

Since a long report calls for sustained attention, and since you will not want your reader to be uncertain of your direction, you should not underestimate the usefulness of conventional organizing and signaling devices. Strong, crisp topic sentences—"The packaging field remains open to innovations in materials and processes"—and closing sentences—"Thus the Kilmer model offers many advantages"—will suggest a clear direction. Organizing sentences listing a, b, and c elements are useful:

> Three disadvantages undercut this location choice: the cost, the remote site, and absence of housing for construction personnel.

Section headings and subheadings such as "The Nature of Packaging" and "The Importance of Packaging in the U.S. Economy," used in the introduction, will reinforce clarity of

CHAPTER I
Introduction

Packaging is somewhat like Mark Twain's comment on the weather—"Everybody talks about it, but nobody does anything about it." In the case of packaging, "Everybody talks about it, but nobody knows anything about it." This paper is intended to help correct that situation.

The Nature of Packaging

By strict definition, packaging is protective material used for preserving and shipping goods. While there are more detailed definitions available, this one will do for most purposes. The key point is that packaging is a protective unit for a commodity. As will be covered in more detail later, the cost of the packaging is usually minor, compared to the value of the commodity being protected. If the package allows the product to be delivered to the consumer in a usable form and not broken, damaged or spoiled along the way, the investment in the package is money well spent.

The Importance of Packaging in the U.S. Economy

Packaging is a major contributor of jobs and revenue to the U.S. economy. Over one-half million people earn their livelihood making packages and packaging materials and many more are responsible for packaging the vast array of consumer and industrials goods produced in this country. Virtually nothing is made that is not packaged at some point in the manufacturing cycle. Packaging is a $70 billion business in the United States, the third largest in terms of sales. [1]

In spite of the size of the packaging business, it contributes less than 2% to the $4 trillion U.S. gross national product. Packaging also makes up a relatively small percentage of the cost of goods sold. On average, packaging costs are about 7% of the price consumers pay for any given product.[2] Yet, for this relatively small cost, packaging's role is to protect and market almost all of the products produced by other sectors of the economy.

In the all-important area of food production and distribution, in underdeveloped countries where packaging is minimal to non-existent, losses of 30–50% between the producer and consumer are not uncommon. In the U.S., that figure is less than 3% for processed foods due primarily to protective packaging....

organization. Using a subheading before every paragraph would make your report seem cluttered, but grouping every few paragraphs under an appropriate subheading will remove any doubt about your direction. Ideally, your headings and subheadings will form a clear outline of your main ideas. A buried idea will be lost. Keep important ideas and key supporting data accessible.

Enumeration is another convenient way of grouping ideas. The following passages show a variety of ways in which you might list points that require differing degrees of explanation.

> The butcher shop was the final step in the distribution system. The distribution system for beef consisted of four prior steps: 1) the slaughterhouse; 2) refrigerated railcars; 3) local warehouse; and 4) refrigerated trucks. Once prepared at the slaughterhouse, the product was not cut, changed or packaged before reaching the local butcher shop.
>
> • • •
>
> Packaging is an essential ingredient in modern distribution systems that provide consumers with the products they want:
>
> 1. when they want them
> 2. at convenient shopping locations
> 3. in the quantity (large or small) desired
> 4. at reasonable prices
>
> • • •
>
> Obviously, the marketplace system of distribution has a great many deficiencies. It is worth reflecting on these in order to appreciate the advantages of a modern distribution system. Some of the obvious deficiencies include:
>
> 1. Limited storage life—Perishable meats, fruits and vegetables must be consumed within their natural quality time limits.
>
> 2. Limited availability—Only goods produced in a local region are available and only in the season of their harvest.
>
> 3. Quality limitations—If the region produces good potatoes, the potatoes are good; if not, the potatoes are bad.
>
> 4. Sanitation problems—No precautions are taken to protect foods from contamination by flies and human handling.

Consider, for example, the butcher shop that served the American consumer forty or fifty years ago:

1. Storage life—Refrigeration was the only means of extending shelf life in the small butcher shop. For red meats, which were cut to order, refrigeration was more than adequate. For poultry, however, purchases made on the day the poultry arrived from the wholesaler were preferred. Alternatively, the shop kept live fowl and slaughtered them as needed.

2. Availability—Although the typical proprietor worked a fifty or sixty hour week, consumers had to get to the store during limited hours, say between 8:00 a.m. and 5:00 p.m., Monday through Saturday. Often the shop would run out of a particular cut. Seats were often provided since it was not unusual for customers to have to wait in line.

3. Quality—Quality of meats offered for sale was dependent upon the skills of the individual proprietor butcher.

4. Spoilage—The proprietor butcher would receive meat in the form of a half or quarter carcass. Fat and bone were either thrown away or given away to customers; they were not available for secondary products such as soap, fertilizer, and animal feed.

Other Adaptations of Material

When you place graphic elements in the text (rather than in the appendices), you should take care to integrate them by referring to key data, but keep the major focus of your sentences on your subject, not on the fact that you have supplied a table, map, or graph. In the first sentence following Table V. 3, Drs. Testin and Vergano have used the structural words (the subject "vegetables" and the verb "are available") to hold topic interest, while the secondary phrase "listed in Table V. 3" ties the text to the graphic component. A sentence beginning "Table V. 3 shows . . ." would draw primary attention away from the subject itself and toward the means of presentation.

In the following passage, note also the economizing use of the abbreviation "MSW," defined as "municipal solid waste (MSW)" at its first mention in the paper. Observe also the underscoring through italics of a key fact.

TABLE V.3 VEGETABLE PRODUCTION AND WASTES (10)

Vegetable	Annual Prod. (mil. lbs.)	% Inedible Refuse	Total Refuse (mil. lbs.)
Lima Beans	172	60	103
Snap Beans	1775	12	213
Broccoli	376	39	147
Carrots	2309	41	967
Cauliflower	295	61	180
Sweet Corn	5411	64	3463
Green Peas	1145	62	710
Spinach	409	28	115
Brussels Sprouts	662	10	66
Totals	12,554		5944

The vegetables listed in Table V.3 are available to the consumer both as fresh and as packaged foods. Typically, 47% of purchases are in fresh form, 20% are canned, and 33% are frozen. If all of the annual production were listed in the fresh form, these vegetables would contribute three million tons of MSW per year (10).

In New York City alone, the use of packaging for just the nine vegetables in Table V.3 annually eliminates the need to dispose of over 100 thousand tons of MSW (11).

A recent study (12) compared the food wastes generated by households in Mexico City with those typical of U.S. households. Mexico City was chosen because little of the food consumed there is packaged/processed food. For example, a Mexican family is much more likely to squeeze orange juice from fresh oranges, rather than use reconstituted frozen orange juice.

The study found that the average household in Mexico City discards 40% more refuse each day than the average U.S. household. Food waste in U.S. household refuse is only about half that in Mexico City refuse.

Citing Sources

Unless you base your report entirely on your own on-site research, you will not proceed very far before you need to cite sources in the text. (The bibliography will be considered in the discussion of end matter.) You may handle these internal citations of sources in several ways, depending on the subject area and the established professional methods for that area. In the scientific community, each source is numbered when it is first referred to, and these references are fully presented in a Cited

References section immediately preceding the Bibliography. In the passage just reproduced from the Testin and Vergano report on packaging, you will see parenthetic references to sources 10, 11, and 12. Turning to the Cited References section, you will find these corresponding entries:

10. B. K. Watt, and A. L. Merrill, Composition of Foods, Agriculture Handbook No. 8, Consumer and Food Economics Research Division, Agricultural Research Service, U.S.D.A., Washington, DC, 1963.

11. H. G. Van der Eb, *The Paperboard Package: Something of Value*, Container Corporation of America, 1977.

12. W. L. Rathje, M.D. Reilly, and W. W. Hughes, *Household Garbage and the Role of Packaging—the United States/Mexico City Household Refuse Comparison*, Solid Waste Council of the Paper Industry, July, 1985.

If you attended high school or college more than a few years ago, you will be familiar with the traditional use of raised foot-note numbers at the ends of borrowings, numbered consecutively throughout the research paper:

…in the opinion of H. G. Van der Eb.[20]

Here the interested reader will check for further data in footnote (or endnote) number 20. The footnoted reference system is gradually passing out of favor as interdisciplinary studies encourage wide adoption of an even simpler uniform means of identifying sources. Leaving full description of each source to the bibliography, the writer lists only the writer's surname and the page number for each reference cited in the text. You may handle this in two ways. First, you can mention the writer's name in quoting or paraphrasing the idea, and then add the page number in parentheses:

Van der Eb notes that appropriate packaging could save 100 thousand tons of MSW each year in New York City (23)

Or second, you can state the idea and then add both the author's name and the page number:

…each year in New York City (Van der Eb 23).

The corresponding footnote is now eliminated, and the curious reader checks for "Van der Eb, H. G." in the Bibliography. For most fields today, the simplified method is preferred.

If your report draws solely on in-house files—typescripts, memos, meeting notes, annual reports, 10K statements—you can follow each citation with a set of parentheses containing a short-hand reference to the source and date: (Preface to Annual Report, 1991) or (10K Report, 1989). Alternately, you can incorporate these references into your text:

> President G. K. Jastrow promised in the Preface to the 1991 GKJ Industries Annual Report....

> or

> According to the 10K filing of December 1989, the company had achieved a net worth of....

You can cite in-house interviews in similar ways:

> Karlin Moss, inventory checker at the Bloomington plant, also noted difficulties caused by the poorly designed loading area (May 16, 1990 interview).

> or

> On May 16, 1990, Karlin Moss pointed out how the poorly designed loading area inhibited her systematic listing of materials received.

We have considered the citing process in connection with the body of the report because you will make most of your citations there, but you have an obligation to reference your source for any idea or illustration placed in any part of your paper. *A borrowing incurs an obligation to cite the source, whether you rephrase the idea or quote it exactly within quotation marks.* Failure to credit sources is plagiarism, which can have legal consequences.

End Matter

The body of your report will have its own opening, its detailed pursuit of the topic, and its concluding perspective or recommendations, as a glance at the Table of Contents for the packaging paper will show. In turn, the centrality of the body will be reinforced by the framing provided by the front matter and the end matter. While the front matter prepares for the body of the report, the end matter has two main functions: (1) it contains graphic and other supplementary material, which you might prepare according to the suggestions in Chapter 13, and (2) it completes the documentation of sources. If parenthetic internal references have been used in the current Modern Language Association or American Psychological Association style, no endnotes are needed. If you are a scientist or an engineer who has numbered sources in the order of their first citations in the text, your Cited References will appear before your Bibliography. Except for the paper making use only of interviews or in-house sources, any report that contains borrowed material will end with a bibliography.

The end matter will include lists, maps, charts, graphs, copies of questionnaires or other documents, and any other material you believe will be useful for the reader's quick reference. Place the most basic, the broadest, the simplest graphics or other material first, and place subsequent items so that your appendices show a progression from the general picture to smaller segments of it. For instance, if your report deals with the complex organization of a conglomerate, devote Appendix I to a page of labeled boxes naming only the key divisions. Appendix II can then take a typical division and show, through boxed legends and arrows, its chain of command. If your study discusses possible sites for a power plant within a seven-county area, you might begin with a map of the whole area, followed by a list of available properties within the area, then a graph of acreage in those sites, and finally a list, line graph, or pie chart showing comparative acquisition or clearing costs. Again, arrange your appendices from basic to complex or from broad to specific display of material.

If you have chosen to incorporate some graphic materials in the body of your report, you will have listed those graphic figures in the Table of Illustrations, already discussed. To list your appendices, you should extend the Table of Contents like this:

You may designate appendices by capital letters or by numbers. Phrase the heading on each appendix in the same way that you have listed it in the Table of Contents.

The bibliography, the last item in your report's end matter, may be headed Works Cited, Works Consulted, or simply Bibliography. The latter designation implies that only works used in the study are listed; "Works Cited" makes the same distinction in a more emphatic way. The Works Consulted type of bibliography would include not only the sources for which you have given internal references, footnotes, endnotes, or Cited References notation but also additional works that will give the interested reader a greater sense of the material. Sometimes a Works Consulted list suggests an attempt at padding, but at other times you want to demonstrate that you have made a thorough search of available sources.

A bibliography (1) credits your borrowings, and (2) enables your reader to find a copy of your source for a particular point and to see its original context. To assist your reader in finding a book, pamphlet, article, or other kind of source, you need to give the appropriate information. For a periodical, cite the volume number. For a book, you need to list any edition other than the first: 3rd edit., Phoenix Edition. If a large work is printed in two or three volumes, you should list the number of volumes comprising the full study. For most company and government publications, and standard reference works such as Moody's and Standard & Poor's business guides, you can use simplified bibliographic listings. Be especially careful, however, to note year dates and edition numbers, where applicable. Of course you will give the full title of each reference work to distinguish, for instance, between Standard & Poor's Corporation Records and the quarterly Standard & Poor's Industry Surveys.

Although some bibliographies are subdivided into book, periodical, and government document sources, most are continuously alphabetized lists of sources. Alphabetize by the first listed author's last name or, for an unsigned article or pamphlet, by the first word in the title (except A, An, or The). Place titles of short works (single essays, chapters, newspaper columns) in quotation marks, and underline or italicize titles of full-length works (books, encyclopedias), collections of essays or research papers, and periodical publications (newspapers, magazines, regularly published bulletins).

Your own reference shelf or your company's library probably contains fine examples of a wide range of cited sources. The following is a brief sampling of basic types of sources.

single-author book	Cray, Ed. <u>Levi's</u>. Boston: Houghton Mifflin, 1978.
coauthored book	Levering, Robert, Milton Moskowitz, and Michael Katz. <u>The 100 Best Companies to Work for in America</u>. Reading, Mass.: Addison-Wesley, 1984.
essay or chapter reprinted in a collection	Amber, Charles. "Shortcuts in Statistics." In <u>Statistics and Populations</u>. Ed. P.A. O'Shee. Chattanooga: Numbers Press, 1993.
signed article	Barnett, Constance. "Managing Licensed Government Testing." <u>Management Society Journal</u>, 55 (1990), 15-26.
unsigned encyclopedia article	"Computers." Encyclopedia Americana. 1988 ed.
unsigned company pamphlet	<u>Everyone Knows His First Name</u>. San Francisco: Levi Strauss, n.d. [twelve-page public relations pamphlet published by a company to describe its origins; year of publication not specified]
government agency publication	Federal Communications Commission. <u>Assigned Call-Letters of Broadcast Stations in the United States and Its Territories.</u> Washington: Government Printing Office, 1990.
interview	Broadhurst, L. B. Personal interview. 12 March 1994.
address or lecture	Palovsky, George A. "Old Wares Wearing Thin." American Retailers' Conference. Denver, Colo. 27 Oct. 1990.

CHAPTER PERSPECTIVE

Accessibility is as important as accuracy in the formal report, where well-chosen formatting devices can efficiently guide the reader through an amount and variety of detail that might otherwise be overwhelming. Summaries, introductory statements of purpose and method, tables of contents and of illustrations, text headings and subheadings, clearly readable graphics, and a variety of appendices are essential tools of the report writer who wants to be understood.

FOOTNOTES

Explanatory footnotes or endnotes like the following are useful for giving subsidiary information which, if presented in the main text, would create a diversion from the principal movement of ideas. You can use supplementary notes to define, to recognize exceptions to broadly stated ideas, or to list further examples.

1 *For information on obtaining individual or multiple copies of "Packaging in America in the 1990s," you may phone (703) 620-9380 or write; Institute of Packaging Professionals, 11800 Sunrise Valley Drive, Reston, VA 22091*

2 *Descriptive titles ("New Problems in Packaging Manufacture,"* Old Packaging for New Wine.*) and conventional section headings (Preface, Bibliography) are treated in different ways, depending on where they are placed and whether they cover whole works, main sections, or subsections.*

Do not use quotation marks or underlining when you refer to a generic section heading, such as an introduction or a discussion section. If you cite the Table of Contents in a particular book or report, capitalize the words as they appear in this sentence. If you refer to any table of contents as a conventional feature of a research document, use only lower case letters, as shown in this sentence.

Underline or italicize titles of full-length works and names of periodicals and place titles of articles, essays, chapters, unpublished short reports, and academic theses and dissertations in quotation marks.

Do not quote or underline your own descriptive titles (unless they contain borrowed phrasing) on copies of the document to which those titles apply. However, if your current report makes reference to your own earlier one, treat it in the conventional manner:

> Please refer to my book *New Packaging for New Times* (Ann Arbor, 1989)

> or

> Please refer to my article "New Packaging for New Times" in the *Packaging Industry Newsletter*, August 1992, 7–10.

Using Graphics

INTRODUCTION AND MAIN POINTS

Graphic elements play a major role in clarifying complex data, in illustrating trends and comparisons, in giving instructions for operating equipment, in directing work projects—in supplementing a wide range of explanations. Because they make information visual, they are particularly useful when readers need to understand complicated or unfamiliar material.

Visual aids may range from simple, ruler-drawn sketches to elaborately enhanced color computer graphics, but regardless of their sophistication, their purpose is always the same—to simplify, clarify, emphasize, and add interest.

After reading this chapter:

■ You will recognize when the content of a document can benefit from visual aids.

■ You will be able to design the major kinds of graphic aids—including tables, bar graphs, pie charts, line graphs, and illustrations.

■ You will be able to integrate graphics smoothly and logically into your text.

DECIDING TO INCLUDE GRAPHIC AIDS

Graphic illustrations are worthwhile additions to many documents, especially those that focus on data and give instructions. The primary purpose for using visual aids is to simplify complex material. A statement such as "The first half of the year recorded the following sales: January – $12,739, February – $15,892, March – $16,654, April – $21,662, May – $18,450, June – $18,781" comes close to reaching the limit of a person's willingness to handle a series of figures. You may choose to present the data as a tabulated entry:

Following are sales figures for the first six months of this year:

January	$12,739
February	$15,892
March	$16,654
April	$21,662
May	$18,450
June	$18,781

or in a table:

FIGURE 1. SIX MONTHS' SALES FIGURES			
January	$12,739	April	$21,662
February	$15,892	May	$18,450
March	$16,654	June	$18,781

You may also choose to emphasize April's higher sales figures in a graph—and this ability to show relationships is the second reason for using graphics. While tables offer exact figures, charts and graphs show trends, highs and lows, and comparisons. So, you may illustrate the data in a bar graph:

January–June Sales Figures

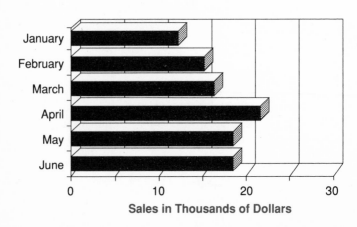

Sales in Thousands of Dollars

or a line graph:

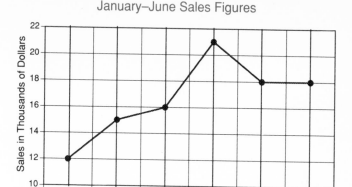

January–June Sales Figures

Another reason for using graphics is to add interest, especially to reports of several pages. Readers notice pictures and visual entries, and most people look at the tables and figures as they scan reports. Visual aids also break up long sections of paragraphed material. Certainly you should not include graphics solely to add interest, but graphs that you use to clarify or emphasize information do enhance the readability of longer documents.

USING VISUAL AIDS SUCCESSFULLY

As you incorporate graphics into your discussion, you will need to keep in mind several very important criteria.

Useful Purpose

Graphics serve to clarify report material—and before you add a graph or table, be sure that it does serve a purpose. Include it if your reader's understanding will be improved by the illustration.

Visual aids should always supplement, not substitute for, discussion of data. Use graphs to present data, but then go on to analyze or interpret the significant numbers.

Degree of Complexity

Visual aids should not overwhelm the reader with more information than is necessary or comprehensible. You may need to use two graphs to present the significant data, or you may omit some figures to keep the single graph readable, but your aim is to keep visual aids relatively simple and understandable at a glance.

Smooth Integration

Graphs and illustrations should be logically integrated into the text. The ideal pattern is to introduce the illustration, present it, then discuss its significance, preferably on one page. When you keep to one page, you encourage uninterrupted concentration on the report rather than asking the reader to flip back and forth from page to page to the coordinate graphic data and discussion. Some reports, however, locate the graphs in the appendix. However you arrange the sequence, the less complicated the pattern, the more readable your document will be.

Unobtrusive Reference to Figures

You will always point out a visual aid before you analyze it in the text. You can refer to the figure parenthetically with phrasing such as "The monthly costs associated with operating a tanning salon, *illustrated in Figure 2*, are...." or "Most of the respondents are unaware of the interest rate on their credit cards, *as shown in Figure 3*." In general, you should avoid beginning sentences by emphasizing the figure— "*Table 2 illustrates* data on new business ventures during the past five years"—because your content then receives secondary emphasis.

Self-Explanatory Nature

Graphic aids must be clear and simple enough to stand alone, to be understood when taken out of context. Each should have a consecutive number and label, with tables and figures numbered separately. If you have several chapters, you will add the chapter number to the graph number; "Figure 5.2" refers to Chapter 5, Figure 2. Following the number, describe the illustration with a short identifying label: "Figure 5.2. Television Ownership in the United States." You may position the number and label at either the top or the bottom of the figure or you may divide the two entries.

Label the horizontal and vertical axes for tables and all segments for bar and pie charts. When you lack the space for placing labels within the visual, you can attach an accompanying legend that identifies segments by color or shading. You may find it advisable to add clarifying notations such as "Figures in thousands of dollars," or "Revenues estimated for 1995," as well as citations giving the source: "Source: Securities Industry Association, 1988."

DESIGNING VISUAL AIDS

You may incorporate into reports a variety of tables, bar graphs, pie charts, line graphs, and illustrations, as well as pictographs, flow charts, and diagrams.

Tables

Tables are a useful for giving exact figures. They may present data on a single subject collected over a span of time—home sales this year, oil price fluctuations during the Gulf War, wheat production for the past five years. Or they may give data on several related subjects during one particular period—1990 population levels in Southeastern states, region-by-region voting percentages for the last election, May water levels for the five area lakes. The following table illustrates the format:

TABLE C-3. ANNUAL CHANGES IN ECONOMIC INDICATORS

Year	Real Gross Domestic Product			OECD Standardized Unemployment Rates			Consumer Price Index		
	Australia	Canada	United States	Australia	Canada	United States	Australia	Canada	United States
1979	4.2	3.9	2.0	6.2	7.4	5.8	9.1	9.3	11.3
1980	2.3	1.5	-0.1	6.0	7.4	7.0	10.2	12.3	13.5
1981	3.0	3.7	2.3	5.7	7.5	7.5	9.6	10.0	10.3
1982	-0.4	-3.2	-2.6	7.1	10.9	9.5	11.1	7.1	6.1
1983	0.5	3.2	3.9	9.9	11.8	9.5	10.1	4.4	3.2
1984	6.9	6.4	7.2	8.9	11.2	7.4	3.9	4.5	4.3
1985	4.9	4.6	3.8	8.2	10.4	7.1	6.8	3.8	3.5
1986	2.1	3.1	3.0	8.0	9.5	6.9	9.1	1.9	1.9
1987	4.1	4.0	3.6	8.1	8.8	6.1	8.5	2.8	3.7
Average annual rate*	2.9	3.1	2.4	8.0	10.0	7.6	8.0	5.5	6.1

* For period covered in LIS Data Base

Source: U.S. Department of Commerce, Bureau of the Census, *1990 Annual Research Conference Proceedings*, August, 1990, p. 493.

In addition to providing exact data in a table, you may, in the related discussion, highlight average, mean, median, highs and lows, contradictory figures, correlations between entries, conclusions supported by the data—and other significant information pertinent to your report.

Bar Graphs

While tables focus on precise numbers, charts and graphs illustrate trends and make comparisons. Bar graphs give information at a glance. They are frequently included in reports, newspapers and journal articles, and oral presentations.

With bar graphs, the "stub" (side identification) needs a clear label, as do the columns. Separations between the bars must be distinct. The bars may be either vertical or horizontal, and often it is useful to note exact figures on top of or at the end of each bar. You may also find it useful to group bars when presenting data that falls together logically, such as a comparison by months, or males' and females' responses on the same subject, as shown in the following bar graphs:

Figure 5.2. Unemployment for March–April

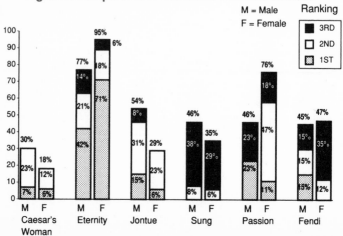

You may include additional information by segmenting the bars:

Figure 1. Comparison of Consumer Perfume Choices

Circle Graphs

Circle graphs (pie charts) divide whole entities into respective percentages to show such things as budget allocations, comparisons of revenue generated by the top six tire producers, and the U.S. holdings of the major foreign investors.

Your first step in designing a pie chart is to convert percentages to degrees, with each percent equaling 3.6 degrees. (Your percentages must, of course, total 100 percent for accurate presentation.) In setting up your graph, you will start at twelve o'clock and arrange sections from largest to smallest in clockwise order. All segments should have percentages and labels. The last segment may be listed as "Other" or "Miscellaneous." In distinguishing the segments, you may shade or computer-color them or leave them unshaded. If you use shading, select shadings that vary enough to provide clear distinction between sections. The following graph illustrates shading characteristics:

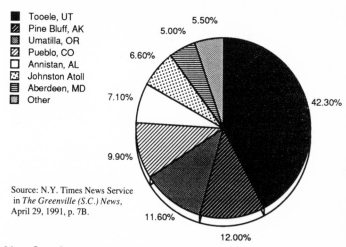

Legend:
- Tooele, UT
- Pine Bluff, AK
- Umatilla, OR
- Pueblo, CO
- Annistan, AL
- Johnston Atoll
- Aberdeen, MD
- Other

Values shown: 5.50%, 5.00%, 6.60%, 7.10%, 9.90%, 11.60%, 12.00%, 42.30%

Source: N.Y. Times News Service in *The Greenville (S.C.) News*, April 29, 1991, p. 7B.

Line Graphs

Line graphs illustrate trends over a given period of time. They are especially useful in presenting information such as figures on sales or production, perhaps, or accident or spoilage levels measured over a several-month or several-year period.

Because line graphs show upward, level, or downward movement, they are liable to encourage misrepresentation. Be scrupulously accurate about providing data at regular intervals and showing enough points to illustrate a real trend. Line graphs may include several lines, as shown in the following graph:

Figure ES2. Sources of Net Income for FRS* Companies

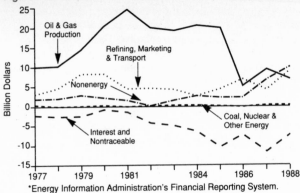

*Energy Information Administration's Financial Reporting System.

Source: Energy Information Administration, *Performance Profiles of Major Energy Producers, 1988,* 1990, xii

Illustrations

For illustrations, you may rely on the skills of a graphic artist, but you probably have simple drawing, boxing, and shading capabilities on your word processing or graphics program. Illustrations, drawings, and diagrams may be used for:

labeling segments of an object:

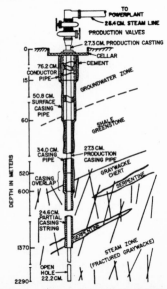

Source: U.S. Department of Energy, Division of Geothermal Energy, *Geothermal Power Plants of the United States: A Technical Survey of Existing and Planned Installations,* April 1978, p. 98.

▬▬ noting dimensions on a construction project:

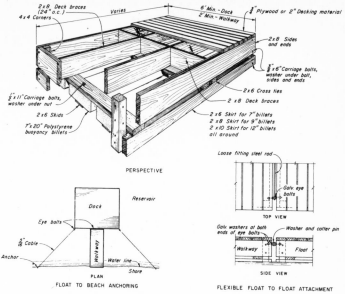

Source: U.S. Army Corps of Engineers, *Lakeshore Management Plan for Hartwell Lake Project*, January 1979.

▬▬ showing movement in a process or procedure:

HEATING SYSTEM SCHEMATIC

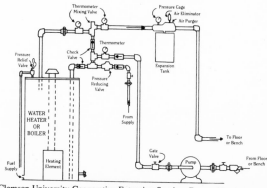

Source: Clemson University Cooperative Extension Service, *Energy Management with Root-Zone Heating*, October 1990, p. 8.

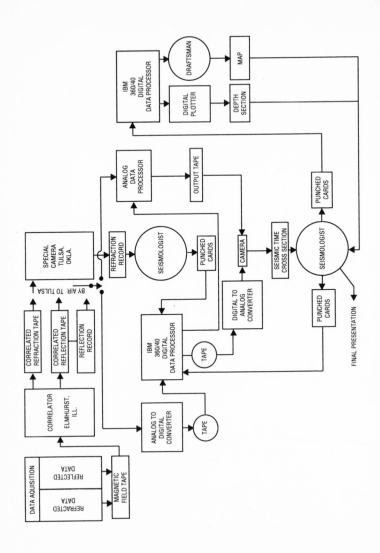

Source: Environmental Protection Agency, *Deep Tunnels in Hard Rock*, 1970, p. 163.

■■■ giving maps of regions, with inserts to show their larger contexts:

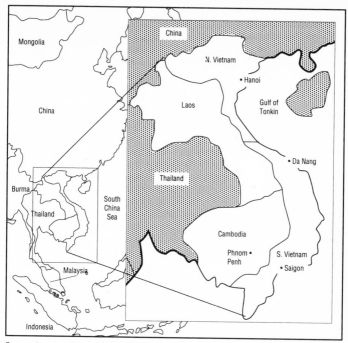

Source: *American History the Easy Way,* Wm. Kellogg, Barron's Educational Series, Inc., 1991.

In planning these visual elements, you should include all the information that you consider pertinent and necessary—based on your analysis of your audience's needs and level of knowledge. Be wary of assuming that your reader will know details such as the building's existing wiring or the location of a little-known country, or the direction the handle must be turned. Drawings clarify such details for a reader and are useful for giving instructions and describing processes, a topic that receives more detailed discussion in the next chapter.

CHAPTER PERSPECTIVE
Graphics are helpful in presenting data in reports, in directions and instructions, and in describing complex processes. They make material easier to understand by presenting it in visual form. Even simple graphics smoothly integrated into presentations are beneficial.

Procedures and Instructions

INTRODUCTION AND MAIN POINTS

Whether you are composing an instructional brochure to accompany your product, describing the installation of a water softener system, writing documentation for a software program, or outlining the steps of the grievance procedure, your readers or listeners must have clear information for understanding and carrying out the appropriate sequence.

Describing procedures often seems like a simple undertaking—that is, until you begin writing. Then you may realize that the process you are describing is actually quite complicated—or you may not become aware of that fact and give ambiguous or incomplete directions. The keys to giving successful instructions are carefully considering the process as a whole, seeing the process from the reader's perspective, detailing the steps in a clear and coherent progression, describing each stage fully, and illustrating complex steps in the process.

After reading this chapter:

■ You will be able to determine the depth of material appropriate to different projects and audiences.

■ You will recognize the need to organize the process into a clear progression.

■ You will be able to present directions with explicitness sufficient for a reader to follow them without questions.

■ You will be able to use graphics to clarify complex material.

BASIC REQUIREMENTS

Effective instructions and descriptions of processes depend upon basic elements.

Knowledge of the Process

Unquestionably, the most important factor in writing clear instructions is your own understanding of the process. If you are charged with describing a procedure that you do not thoroughly understand, you will need to gather more information before you attempt to explain the process to someone else. If any stage of the process is unclear to you, ask questions or work through the process yourself before beginning your discussion.

Sufficient Directions

The second requirement is that you give enough information and not assume too much knowledge on your readers' part, especially concerning those steps central to the procedure. Think through the process to see it as others would see it and give directions accordingly. It is better to give readers too much information rather than too little, to define too many terms instead of too few, to be repetitive rather than unclear.

A young college student taking electron micrography images, for instance, might not realize that all the photographs should be taken at the same power of magnification. A teacher or supervisor might assume this knowledge as a "given," but without previous experience in the procedure, an assistant should not be expected to know this important factor.

Anticipation of Questions or Problems

If you are able to view a procedure as a beginner would, you will find it easier to spot ambiguities and anticipate your readers' questions. For example, a consumer might have a question concerning the following directions for preparing a frozen entree:

- Drop bag into pot of boiling water.
- Return water to boil.
- Heat eight minutes.

Knowing that some directions call for lowering the temperature once the water is boiling, the reader may wonder whether to keep the water at full boil for the eight minutes or to reduce the temperature to simmer for that period.

In contrast, these directions for operating a shop vacuum include information that may seem unnecessary but it will eliminate questions:

> Your Shop-Vac Wet/Dry may be emptied of liquid waste by removing the tank cover. To empty, stop the motor and remove the plug from the wall receptacle. Remove the tank cover and deposit the liquid waste contents into a suitable drain. After the tank is empty, return the cover to its original position. To continue use, *plug the cord into the wall receptacle and start the motor.*

Source: Shop-Vac Corporation 1982.

Your directions may include comparisons to widely known objects or qualities—"The paste will be the consistency of gravy" —and you may mention ways to counter problems: "If grease pops during broiling, lower the temperature setting," or "If your chimney does not draw immediately, light a newspaper on top of the firewood to encourage a draft." Field-testing your instructions is helpful in locating potential ambiguities.

Clear Progression of Steps

Obvious directional signals benefit the person learning about a procedure. Whether you number steps or use words such as "next," "then," or "after you open the container," the progression of steps must be very clear. If a procedure is lengthy or complicated, you may choose to divide it into several sections, giving headings to the sections and enumerating the steps associated with each. This categorization will help the reader more clearly comprehend how the individual sections interrelate to form the whole process.

Familiar Language

Consider your audience's level of specialized knowledge to determine how much technical language you can safely use. If you are writing to or for people in your field, you may assume understanding of terms relevant to your profession. Your readers may be well aware of the meaning of "operations water" or "multiservice containers." If you are writing for a general audience, however, you need to define such terms within the text, in endnotes, or in a glossary:

> The product water-contact surfaces of all multiservice containers (containers intended for use more than one time)...shall be clean and adequately sanitized.
>
> ...
>
> Operations water: Water that is delivered under pressure to a plant for container washing, hand washing, plant and equipment cleanup and for other sanitary purposes.[1]

PRELIMINARY SECTIONS

Before going into the steps of the procedure, you may need to give some information on the purpose, scope, desired uses, anticipated results, and special cautions. Every description of a procedure needs an overview, especially if the material is new to the reader. You may mention applications of the process, information on related research findings, interconnection with other pieces of equipment or processes, or a list of topics to be covered:

> Many people want to learn more about the installation, operation, and care of wood heaters; how to obtain and prepare firewood; and the potential problems related to home heating with wood. This publication presents information in each of these areas with emphasis given to wood-burning stoves.

Source: Clemson University Cooperative Extension, *Home Heating with Wood*, September 1984.

Instructions for using an appliance may be introduced or rounded out via public relations-oriented comments that also give basic information:

> You are now the owner of a Shop-Vac Wet/Dry Vacuum…. Ideal for cleaning the patio or basement floors, tough enough to use in the garage or workshop. Gentle enough to be rolled out in the living areas of the home to coax the soil out of rugs and other floor areas. Amazing enough to say goodbye to mops by making quick work of spills, patio rain water, floor washing, wet basements, and kitchen accidents.

Source: Shop-Vac Corporation, 1982.

Diagrams of objects with all parts identified provide very useful preliminary material for people learning how to carry out a complex procedure. If you have included a fully labeled drawing at the beginning of the document, you can later refer to "the external ground connector," confident that if your reader has a question about the location of that part, the diagram can be checked for clarification:

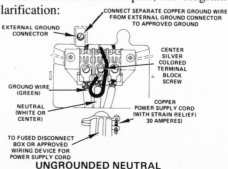

Courtesy Whirlpool Corporation

Identifying parts by number or letter, then referring to them in the text by the same code is a variation on the labeling method:

LOCATION OF CONTROLS

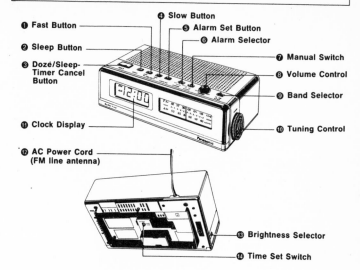

❶ Fast Button

❹ Slow Button

❺ Alarm Set Button

❻ Alarm Selector

❷ Sleep Button

❸ Dozé/Sleep-Timer Cancel Button

❼ Manual Switch

❽ Volume Control

❾ Band Selector

⓫ Clock Display

❿ Tuning Control

⓬ AC Power Cord (FM line antenna)

⓭ Brightness Selector

⓮ Time Set Switch

ELECTRONIC CLOCK

To set the correct time on the Clock Display⓫, use the following procedure.
1) Plug the AC Power Cord⓬ into an AC electrical outlet, so time digits will appear on the Clock Display⓫ and the time digits will flash continuously.
2) Set the Time Set Switch⓮ to "ADJUST".
3) Press the Fast❶ or Slow❹ Button until the correct time appears on the Clock Display⓫.
● The Fast Button advances the displayed time rapidly and the Slow Button advances it minute by minute.
   Make sure the AM or PM setting is correct.
4) Reset the Time Set Switch⓮ to "LOCK" to keep the correct time, otherwise the set time will be shifted.
● The correct time can usually be obtained by listening for time checks on the radio or from telephone time services.
5) To increase the brightness of the time display, set the Brightness Selector⓭ to "HIGH"; to decrease it, set to "LOW".

Source: Panasonic Corporation
Model RC

A drawing that notes installation points is useful for some kinds of instructions:

EXAMPLE OF ANTENNA GROUNDING AS PER NATIONAL ELECTRICAL CODE INSTRUCTIONS

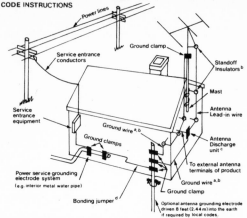

a. Use No. 10 AWG copper or No. 8 AWG aluminium or No. 17 AWG copper-clad steel or bronze wire, or larger as ground wires for both mast and lead-in.

b. Secure lead-in wire from antenna to antenna discharge unit and mast ground wire to house with stand-off insulators, spaced from 4 feet (1.22 meters) to 6 feet (1.83 meters) apart.

c. Mount antenna discharge unit as closely as possible to where lead-in enters house.

d. Use jumper wire not smaller than No. 6 AWG (13.3 mm^2) copper, or the equivalent, when a separate antenna-grounding electrode is used.

Source: Soundesign, Harrison Industrial Plaza, 1 Cape May Street, Harrison, New Jersey 07029.

A materials list is necessary to construction projects:

MATERIALS INCLUDED

- 2 side panels, marked *right* and *left,* each with a 45-degree angle cut on the top edge
- 2 roof panels, marked *right* and *left,* each with a 45-degree angle cut on the top edge, and a triangular rib on the underside to hold the panels in place
- 1 rear pentagonal panel
- 1 front pentagonal panel with cut-out for entrance
- 1 floor panel with left, right, front, and back markings
- 1 box of 1¼-inch wood screws

Warnings, cautions, or assumptions—concerning meeting government codes, maintaining certain climatic conditions, or methods of handling materials—are important to note at the outset:

IMPORTANT SAFETY INSTRUCTIONS

1. SAVE THESE INSTRUCTIONS. This manual contains important safety and operating instructions for GE Battery Charger Model BC4B

2. Before using battery charger, read all instructions and cautionary markings on (1) battery charger, (2) battery, and (3) product using battery.

3. CAUTION. To reduce risk of injury, charge only GE Rechargeable Nickel Cadmium type batteries. Other types of batteries may burst, causing personal injury and damage.

4. DO NOT put batteries in fire or mutilate them; they may burst or release toxic materials.

5. DO NOT attempt to short-circuit the batteries; may cause burns.

6. DO NOT expose charger to rain or snow. Shock hazard may result.

7. Use of an attachment not recommended or sold by General Electric may result in a risk of fire, electric shock, or injury to persons.

8. To reduce risk of damage to electric plug and cord, pull by plug rather than cord when disconnecting charger.

9. Make sure cord is located so that it will not be stepped on, tripped over, or otherwise subjected to damage or stress.

10. An extension cord should not be used unless absolutely necessary. Use of improper extension cord could result in a risk of fire and electric shock. If extension cord must be used, make sure:

A. That pins or plugs of extension cord are the same number, size, and shape as those of plug on charger.
B. That extension cord is properly wired and in good electrical condition.
C. That wire size is equal to or greater than #18 for lengths of up to 150 feet and #16 for lengths 150 feet or greater.

11. DO NOT operate charger with damaged cord or plug. Dispose of battery charger.

Source: General Electric Company, Nela Park, Cleveland, Ohio 44112

The preliminary section should contain all the information that you consider pertinent to the process as a whole—details that readers need to be aware of before they concentrate on the steps themselves.

STEP-BY-STEP DESCRIPTION

You may have chosen to categorize steps in groups or sections. In each section, then, you will carefully enumerate the steps, with each paragraph or entry representing a single step or stage in the process.

Both descriptions of processes and instructions benefit from illustrations, though sets of instructions may rely on them more substantially. The two kinds of presentations vary both in the way they are formatted and phrased. When describing a process, you will use paragraph form, give more purely informational material, and focus on the process rather than on the reader's actions. For example, consider the following description of the process of smoking venison:

> Nonresinous wood—willow, cherry, apple, maple, or hickory—should be used to produce the smoke. Soft woods will produce a smoke responsible for a bitter taste in the cured product. Fine shavings and sawdust produce the best smoke.

> Smoke movement and interior temperature are controlled by advancing or retarding heat from the hotplate by adjusting the opening of the smoke-hole in the top of the smoker. If cold smoking is desired, the interior temperature should not rise above 100°F during the three days of smoking. Smoke cooking involves smoking until the internal temperature of the product reaches 155°F.

Source: Extension Division, Virginia Polytechnic Institute and State University, May 1980.

In contrast to descriptions of processes, instructions focus on directing the reader's actions in carrying out a procedure. Such directions usually use short commands and relatively simple steps to increase clarity and ease of following:

FIGURE 1. FRONT VIEW OF VCR

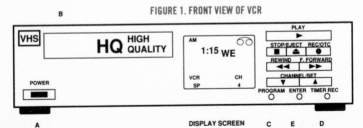

1. Turn the unit on by pressing the POWER button (A).

2. Insert a blank tape into the FRONT LOADING SYSTEM (B), hinged side forward. Push the tape into the VCR until the automatic mechanisms pull it in the rest of the way.

3. Press the PROGRAM button (C). The following display will appear:

Number of weeks

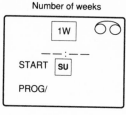

Day of week

USING ILLUSTRATIONS

Whether you do the final drawing yourself or refer it to the graphics department, your illustrations do make a difference. They move a step closer to actual demonstration of the process—whether that is installing a range, operating a lathe, repairing a television, or setting up a spreadsheet. As you add illustrations to your text, try to follow these principles:

Integrate Illustrations Smoothly

In supplementing directions with diagrams, establish the pattern of introducing the step, referring to the figure, and positioning the illustration nearby. If possible, keep this sequence on the same page. If discussion of a new step begins low on a page so that the corresponding diagram will be forced to the following page, move the entire entry to the next page to minimize the reader's page-turning.

Supply Ample Illustration

When you give directions, assume that if there is a way for your readers to get lost, they will. Illustrate any stage of a procedure that may be misunderstood. It is better to include too many drawings than too few. Some readers will find an illustration unnecessary and skip over it, but others will appreciate the additional directions.

Keep Illustrations Simple

Be careful not to overcomplicate diagrams. Describe and illustrate one step at a time, and if you are gearing your document to young readers, keep your directions especially clear, as do these instructions for operating a small outboard motor:

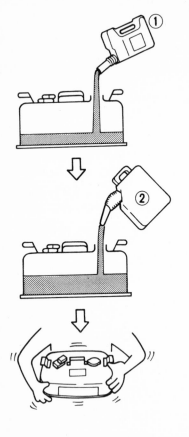

Mixture

1) First pour oil into the fuel tank, and then gasoline.
2) Mix the fuel thoroughly by shaking the fuel tank.

CAUTION

- Avoid using any oil other than that designated.
- Always use new gasoline.
- Use a thoroughly blended fuel-oil mixture.
- If the mixture is not thoroughly blended or the mixing ratio is incorrect, the following problems will occur.

Low oil
ratio: Due to lack of oil, major engine trouble such as seizure will result.

High oil
ratio: Fouled spark plugs, smoky exhaust, or heavy carbon deposits will result.

---

① Oil   ② Gasoline

Source: Yamaha Motor Corporation, U.S.A., Cypress, CA 90630.

Emphasize Warnings and Cautions

If your directions contain important warnings and cautionary notes, emphasize them within the text by bolding, capitalizing, boxing, or shading. Treat negative directions in the same way— "Do *NOT* plug in yet."

CAUTION

**RISK OF ELECTRIC SHOCK
DO NOT OPEN**

CAUTION: TO REDUCE THE RISK OF ELECTRIC SHOCK, DO NOT REMOVE COVER (OR BACK). NO USER SERVICEABLE PARTS INSIDE. REFER SERVICING TO QUALIFIED SERVICE PERSONNEL.

WARNING: TO REDUCE THE RISK OF FIRE OR ELECTRIC SHOCK, DO NOT EXPOSE THIS APPLIANCE TO RAIN OR MOISTURE.

The lightning flash with arrowhead, within an equilateral triangle, is intended to alert the user of the presence of uninsulated "dangerous voltage" within the product's enclosure that may be of sufficient magnitude to constitute a risk of electric shock to persons.

The exclamation point within the equilateral triangle is intended to alert the user of the presence of important operating and maintenance (servicing) instructions in the literature accompanying the appliance.

The symbols are located on the bottom (or back) of cabinet.

If two steps are to be completed simultaneously, highlight that detail: "While turning the handle, press down with the palm." If this important connection is overlooked and the instructions are misinterpreted, the customer experiences frustration, which may become a customer relations problem for your organization. Everybody's interests are served when intricate steps are made very clear to the reader.

Label Parts

If you included in the introductory section a full display with parts labeled, you may refer to that initial drawing as you describe the steps, or you may insert drawings for the separate steps. Referring to the full display works well if your directions are relatively simple:

Instructions

BEFORE YOU INSTALL YOUR SHOWERHEAD

Remove your old showerhead from the shower arm using a wrench if necessary. Your wall-mounted or hand-held Shower Massage unit attaches to any standard 1/2" threaded shower arm. If your present shower arm has an integral ball joint **B**, replace it with a shower arm having exposed 1/2" threads **C**, available at most hardware stores.

Before you proceed with installation, read the SPECIAL INSTRUCTION sections that follow.

SPECIAL WATER CONSERVATION INSTRUCTIONS

A flow regulator device has been installed in your showerhead to comply with mandatory water conservation measures in many states. If you live in California, New York, Maryland, Wisconsin, Oregon, Georgia, New Jersey, or another state having such laws, you must use the flow regulator to remain in compliance with your state water conservation policies.*

If you do <u>not</u> live in an area with water conservation laws, you may remove the flow regulator at your option. Refer to the following instructions.

Flow Regulator Removal

Unscrew the filter screen **H** by grasping the flanges with fingers or pliers and turning counter clockwise. Remove the filter screen from the pivot ball assembly **E**, and lift out the flow regulator device **F**. Reinstall the filter screen in the pivot ball assembly and proceed with showerhead installation.

*Other states may have passed water use regulations since this printing. Check with state or local authorities for more current information.

Wall-Mounted Unit

Hand-Held Unit

Source: Teledyne Water Pik, 1730 E. Prospect Street, Fort Collins, Colorado 80525.

Include Measurements, Distances, and Directions

In construction projects, you may want to note the measurements and sizes within the illustration.

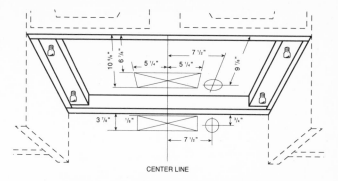

CENTER LINE

   I.   Install the hood with the top front edge flush with the front of the cabinet framework and centered in the cabinet opening. See Fig. 1 for dimensions used to locate duct opening and electrical cable opening.

Courtesy Whirlpool Corporation

In directing readers to specific locations, you may indicate distances between points:

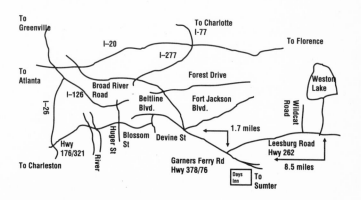

Source: Palmetto State Triathlon, Columbia, South Carolina 29250.

In describing installation, you may note direction of movement:

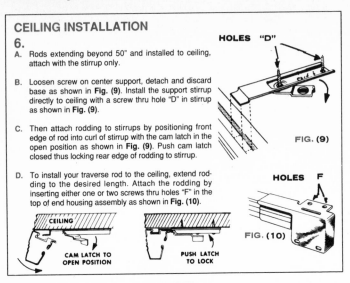

CEILING INSTALLATION

6.

A. Rods extending beyond 50" and installed to ceiling, attach with the stirrup only.

B. Loosen screw on center support, detach and discard base as shown in **Fig. (9)**. Install the support stirrup directly to ceiling with a screw thru hole "D" in stirrup as shown in **Fig. (9)**.

C. Then attach rodding to stirrups by positioning front edge of rod into curl of stirrup with the cam latch in the open position as shown in **Fig. (9)**. Push cam latch closed thus locking rear edge of rodding to stirrup.

D. To install your traverse rod to the ceiling, extend rodding to the desired length. Attach the rodding by inserting either one or two screws thru holes "F" in the top of end housing assembly as shown in **Fig. (10)**.

HOLES "D"

FIG. (9)

HOLES F

FIG. (10)

CAM LATCH TO OPEN POSITION

PUSH LATCH TO LOCK

Source: Sears and Roebuck, Chicago, Illinois 60607.

CONCLUDING PROCEDURE DISCUSSIONS

All process descriptions and instructions should end with some sense of completion. Occasionally the last step will give something similar to "Sand and finish your lamp base, following instructions for staining or antiquing." Frequently, however, you will need to add a sentence or two of closure: "Now your fire screen is complete and ready for summer use in your fireplace," or "Should you have any questions, contact your nearest Cayhill service representative."

CHAPTER PERSPECTIVE

Clear, substantive directions are necessary to people encountering unfamiliar areas, functions, and activities. Your role in giving directions is to simplify and streamline steps as much as possible, yet give enough details to clarify any questions the participant might have, supplementing your directions with illustrations at points of complexity. For these documents, more than for any other, you need field testing and double-checking to spot ambiguities.

FOOTNOTES

1 *Title 21 Code of Federal Regulations 129.3.*

Oral Presentations

INTRODUCTION AND MAIN POINTS

From one career stage to another you will accumulate a repertory of writing skills as you produce letters, memos, and a variety of reports—proposals, engineering analyses, sales projections. As your responsibilities increase, so will the likelihood that you will find yourself speaking about your ideas in internal presentations and in public contexts. Heading a project group in an architecture firm, for instance, you will need to show the drawings and models for the major renovation of an historic building, explain the advantages of your engineering solutions to particular problems, and persuade the senior partners that your efforts will sustain the firm's reputation and meet the client's requirements. You will also be ready to assure the preservation society that the landmark building will retain its legendary charm; you will persuade the zoning commission that adequate parking facilities will require a variance; you will show the Chamber of Commerce and local civic clubs how your renovation, though costly, will enhance the community image. Many professionals, then, find that they must be equally well prepared to express themselves in written and in oral presentations.

Both speaking and writing call for a sense of order, reasonable care in handling language, and an awareness of the audience's needs. Although both forms of communication seek the same goal of stating ideas clearly and persuasively, they sometimes pursue different paths to those ends. You will find that some natural advantages fall to the writer, others to the speaker. In writing, you can highlight key points through creative spacing on a well-formatted page, and in speaking, you can use a greater number of transitional phrases and other directional cues to keep your audience on track and in phase. If your reader has nodded over two or three paragraphs, he can turn back to an earlier point, but if your listener misses a key phrase because of an unfortunate word choice or a lapse of clear enunciation, he might lose a significant idea or an important connection between one detail and another. In some matters, the writer and the speaker anticipate the audience's needs in different ways.

This chapter, then, explores how you will prepare your message for oral delivery in a conference room or in a public forum. We will consider what you need to know about your audience from the beginning phase of your preparations, and we will discuss the special value that credibility—believability—holds for any speaker. You will also note a variety of useful procedures for preparing your notes and delivering your speech.

After studying the material in this chapter:

■■ You will know what you should ask about both the audience and the occasion when you accept a speaking invitation.

■■ You will recognize the importance of establishing your credibility early in your speech.

■■ You will consider how to use audiovisual aids without letting them overwhelm your spoken message.

KNOWING YOUR AUDIENCE

You have been asked to speak on a given subject because you have been involved in a particular project or you have earned a reputation for expertise. You know the details your audience wants to hear. In fact, those details are contained in the written report you have just completed. Why not simply carry a copy of the report to the meeting and read it? For good reasons, you should proceed otherwise.

A written report will probably have a closely defined readership for whom technical terms, acronyms, and other economies of language will create no problems. For wider distribution of an in-house report, you can add explanatory footnotes and a glossary. You can hope that the curious reader will keep a dictionary handy. If the reader's attention is distracted, he can always return to the page and later pick up the thread of your discussion. Too, the polished page often lends a sense of authority to its contents. In speaking, especially to those outside your firm, you cannot count on these advantages. In considering what compensating adjustments you might make in your oral presentation, we might usefully distinguish between in-house presentations and public speeches.

INTERNAL AND SPECIALIST-GROUP AUDIENCES

Presenting a project proposal to the executives who must approve it, you can assume familiarity with the raw materials and processes that you propose to bring together, perhaps into a new product line or an experimental method of assembling quickly needed temporary structures. You will not need to give an extensive review of the background of the issue at hand. You will be able to condense your reasoning for at least some of the steps. As Richard A. Underwood, a veteran of such presentations at General Motors, advises about the listeners at an internal meeting, "Those guys don't want you to fool around. They value their time. They want to hear your proposal and be out of there—to get on with something else. They want to know that you plan to do this, this, and this to produce that, that, and that, and it's going to cost this amount and will yield these results. Have your points ready—bim, bam, bam—with necessary justifications, and be ready for questions."

The likelihood of succeeding with an internal presentation might be enhanced by your position in the company (you have earned a reputation for solid work), but you should arrive not only with an outline of the points you must cover but also with some shrewd anticipations of the questions you might be asked. If you know that the Vice President for International Marketing will attend the meeting, you can bring a list of countries where your new product will be in the greatest demand. If you recall that another senior executive always asks what the competition is doing, you can have market share percentages and lists of rival brand names ready, and you can be prepared to argue that a market niche is open for your innovation. The impression of readiness might make the difference between approval and rejection of your proposal.

You will also find yourself treating certain other speaking occasions with the same conciseness you bring to the conference room. Once your proposal has received executive approval, for example, you will need to show and explain your innovation to representatives of an advertising agency, to members of the production and fabrication departments, and to other affected groups. You can practice economies when you speak before these specialists or those in any field—collectors, academic seminars, and convention committees.

PUBLIC AND GENERAL AUDIENCES

The sustained attention of a specialist group might derive from deep interest in the subject, and the in-house audience will be closely attuned to opportunities for profit, expansion, and the shared glory of a breakthrough. For larger, more general audiences, you can probably expect courteous initial attention, at least long enough for you to seize the listeners' collective imagination and carry it into the realm of your subject. You cannot know how to capture and hold their interest, however, without knowing the composition of your audience.

How much or how little will your listeners know about your subject in advance? If you are an accountant, what facts about the the most common errors in federal and state income tax returns will interest the Rotary Club? If you are an entomologist just returned from a year of collecting spiders in New Zealand, what details of your discoveries will intrigue a high school science club? In short, what aspect of any field will hold people's interest either because of its practical usefulness, its drama and color, or its potential to affect their lives? Play matchmaker between your subject and your audience, and you will soon find yourself plotting ways to draw a look of astonishment, a pleased smile, or a nod of recognition and understanding.

What kinds of people compose your audience, and what occasion brings them together? You have been asked to speak to this club or that professional sorority meeting in a certain place at a specified date and time. You need to know more than simply when and where to arrive. When you accept the speaking engagement, ask the questions that will facilitate your planning: Does the group want to be informed or entertained? How long should I speak? How many will attend? What program events will precede and follow my speech? Once you know these details, you can begin to make a mental outline and to store up likely verbal and visual enliveners. You will know what to include—and what to edit out because it is too obvious, too obscure, too suggestive, or too complex.

At this early stage of preparation, you have begun to match the audience and the subject. Before planning in closer detail, you need to bring another important factor into consideration: credibility. You will be introduced as a person of certain attainments, such as professional rank or rewards you have received. The recital of your attributes and accomplishments will raise the audience's expectations, but credentials alone do not assure credibility. No matter how solid your expertise, the audience needs to believe in the messenger before it will fully trust the message.

GAINING CREDIBILITY

Credibility is not an exterior quality like secondary factual detail or a backup anecdote you might decide to insert into your speech.

As a projection of an acceptable personality, your credibility will emerge from a sometimes subtle combination of elements and impressions. In planning your speech, you need to be conscious of those qualities that telegraph your interest in the audience—its understanding, its welfare—as well as in your subject. In other words, you will strive to be both interest*ing* and interest*ed*. You can show these attributes in many ways.

The audience will find credibility (or the lack of it) in your platform demeanor and suitable (or unsuitable) manner of dress, in your easy way of verifying your expertise in the subject (without either self-importance or false humility), and in your tone. Overusing irony can make you seem sardonic and even bitter; never shifting out of a strictly factual tone can make you sound literal-minded. An unenthusiastic recital of facts might satisfy your basic intention to inform, but your visible lack of excitement may come across as indifference or contempt. An audience's uneasiness about a speaker can be as damaging as an active dislike for an unpopular message—and the messenger.

You cannot write personal credibility into your delivery notes ("Be simpatico here"), but you can watch for and edit out any word choice, social reference, example, or other element that might sound smug, chilly, hyperenthusiastic ("too good to be true"), or condescending. For instance, watch for the accumulation of Latinate words ("expedite" for "send") that would give your delivery a stilted, bookish, pretentious air.

Let the nature of the occasion guide your handling of literary or historical allusions, precise numbers, and relative completeness of details. If your speech comes late in the noontime Optimists International meeting, after your audience has enjoyed a hearty lunch, you would be well advised to round off "254,672" to "a quarter of a million" or, even better, "thirty times the population of Centreville." Instead of listing your museum's full inventory of major Impressionists, choose half a dozen titles by widely known artists, unless you are speaking before an association of museum directors or art historians. And remember that allusions—hinting references—are worthless if they puzzle the audience. Referring to the club secretary as a Madame Defarge, always quietly recording names, will be a fine joke—if everyone is familiar with that sinister character in Dickens's *A Tale of Two Cities*. Allusions that pass over the heads of your audience will undercut the needed rapport between speaker and listener.

As you package details to be comprehended quickly, so you will tailor your word choices for immediate understanding.

During your speech on the dangers of high-altitude climbing, the listener should not need to labor at processing the phrase "*incremental* strain on the lungs" when you can dramatize the increasing pressure by asking each auditor to imagine adding "a ten-pound weight for each twenty steps you take" at a given altitude. As a hospital administrator speaking at a medical conference, you can brandish the phrase "acute trauma," assured of being understood, but for a public announcement of the hospital's plan to build the long-needed Acute Trauma Wing, you should be prepared to supply images of blood, broken glass, splintered bones, and unsteady pulses. Graphic as they are, these images will translate the professional term for the layman's understanding. Of course, you can do too much "translating" or too little paraphrasing, you can insult your audience by over-explaining, or you can leave your listeners in a fog of incomprehension. Here you will prove the great value of having asked about the nature of your audience when you agreed to make the speech.

Even your choice of personal pronouns can affect the audience's perception of your credibility. Unless your topic centers on a singular personal achievement such as your winning an Olympic medal or surviving a danger-filled Amazonian jungle trek, plan to minimize your use of "I" and "my." Shun pompous and self-important proclamations such as "I think that...." and "It seems to me that...." Simply state your idea, or shift to the "you" approach: let "I recall that...." become "You will remember how...." The "you" perspective is equally appealing to hearers and to readers, unless the topic or the context gives "you" an accusatory edge. For many subjects an even more effective approach will be to find the area or the angle of approach that will allow you to blend "I" and "you" into "we," so that the issue of "what *I* want you to do" can become the matter of "what *we* as concerned citizens can do" to solve a problem. "I regret the rapid cutting of the rain forests" is a static statement of personal opinion, while "We all lose in uncontrolled clear-cutting" is an implicit call to united protest and action. Similarly, if you are describing the operation of an emergency medical clinic, you might impress your audience more strongly by saying "We see upwards of thirty accidental poisoning cases a week" than in isolating your part: "I see five or six accidental poisoning victims per week." Use "we" to establish a sense of mutual endeavor with your peers and shared feeling with your audience.

A speech can scarcely be credible if the audience cannot follow it. For this reason, speakers have traditionally valued organizing sentences, frame words, and transitional devices. These words and phrases are like the switching and signaling system of a railroad; they let all concerned parties know what is coming from where, headed where. As you end the introductory phase of your speech, having established the scope of your subject and the thesis you propose, you can focus attention through an organizing sentence such as "You should make every effort to preserve the Greene River Bridge for three reasons: its historic value, its superior engineering, and the tremendous cost of any replacement structure." The middle section of your speech will explore these reasons in the order listed, and you will signal the beginning of each phase in one of several ways:

> The first reason is... .
> Next, consider... .
> The most important factor... .

For even more emphatic transitions from one phase of the subject to another, you can use internal summaries and previews: "We have noted three reasons for preserving the Greene River Bridge, which should be a viable structure for years to come. We should also note four reasons for rejecting the proposed replacement bridge." You can use the summary element ("We have seen") and the preview ("Now we will consider") separately or together.

When you have given the facts that support your argument, and when you have quoted the opinions of clearly identified experts, you will identify the beginning of your final appeal, the peroration, with a further signal: "Thus, three excellent reasons should persuade you to...," "In summary...," "The best of these choices is...."

Throughout the speech, in less structurally significant ways, you will emphasize parallels, contrasts, or progressions of thought with words and phrases like "however," "also," "on the contrary," and "thus." Incremental repetition, brilliantly illustrated in the echoing assertion "I have a dream" in Martin Luther King, Jr.'s historic civil rights speech, has long been a favorite unifying device of public speakers. The closing hope of Abraham Lincoln's Gettysburg Address—

> ...that this nation, under God, shall have a new birth of freedom—and that government of the people, by the people, for the people, shall not perish from the earth—

can scarcely be bettered in its sense of synthesis and closure, achieved through the essentially simple device of parallel phrases. Such devices emphasize similarity, contrast, or complementary relationships of elements and ideas.

Curiously enough, the opening of your speech will probably be the part you plan last, after the broad outline of the central sections has taken shape in your mind. It is also the part you might most likely leave open to spur-of-the-moment change, so that you can spontaneously accept the compliments of the introduction and the applause of the audience in greeting you. If appropriate to the subject and occasion, a moment of light banter with a friendly host or master of ceremonies will set both you and the audience at ease. Do not, like some speakers, feel obliged to begin with a contrived joke unrelated to the topic or the setting. This dubious procedure is often said to "liven up" the audience, but you can invite the audience to be "at home" in much more purposeful ways.

For example, referring to the announced topic, you can freshly define the scope of your discussion, perhaps asking your listeners to picture themselves in a place or situation related to your subject: "If you see that the person seated next to you is choking, would you know what to do?" That opener would be a very effective way of quickly drawing collective attention to the life-saving techniques everyone should be familiar with. Analyze your subject to find a starting point that is easy to portray with vivid, highly visual, or especially clear words and images. Then you can move into your discussion of more abstract ideas. Citing a family's wrenching choices about whether or not to have a sickly stray kitten or puppy "put to sleep," you can shift into weighing the medical and legal communities' arguments about the issues surrounding living wills and human euthanasia.

In planning your conclusion, refer once more to your purpose in addressing the group and to the celebratory nature (if any) of the occasion. While trying to avoid clichéd quotations, you can show the graduating seniors how they can find their proper niche in the world. You can remind your civic club listeners of their stake in human rights, animal rights, equal justice, a safer environment, or better government. You can urge Horizon Club members to see the remarkable countries you have described while those places are relatively unspoiled. Whatever your final advisement, you will briefly touch again on each of the main points in the body of your speech, and draw them together into a suitable peroration: Visit Greenland and see this and this and this;

or, forget all the reputed dangers of city water fluoridation and accept this scientific assurance, this credible testimony, and these proven benefits. If your arguments have flown high, bring them back into clear relation to your listeners' concerns and the natural desire for well-being. You will have earned credibility through your sense of humor, your wisdom, your humaneness, your adaptation of the material to the audience's understanding, and your care in directing your listeners from one point to the next.

PREPARING YOUR NOTES

Your speech now exists as a mental outline, already in the process of being fleshed out with well-chosen examples and key phrases. Next you will prepare the notes that will allow you to speak extemporaneously while maintaining eye contact with the audience. Your notes should be full enough to remind you of important ideas and examples, yet concise and well-spaced enough to be followed easily. If your first impulse is to find the largest note cards available and to fill each with closely scribbled notes, a second thought will convince you that this is self-defeating. Your eyes and your attention will be much too occupied in following each card line by line.

Use 3" x 5" or 4" x 6" cards and write on only one side of each (flipping cards from front to back creates a distraction for you and for the audience). Where you can, try to fit a brief segment of your speech on each card, and number each card so that, in case of a spill, you can reassemble the set quickly. Although you will transcribe selected quotations exactly, you should record all other ideas as key words and brief phrases separated by ellipses (...), dashes, or eye-relieving space, so that the card does not become too crowded for at-a-glance reading.

Bolding, underlining, and printing all-capitals are popular ways of identifying words that need voice emphasis—key words, ironic words, words that might be mistaken for similar words ("affect" and "effect"). For difficult or unusual pronunciations, you can write accented syllables in capitals and use spaces or small dots, dictionary-fashion, to show syllabification (syl•LAB•uh•fa•CAY•shun). Should you find yourself speaking of American songwriter Cole Porter's hometown, Peru, Indiana, you can remind yourself it is pronounced PEA•roo there.

Some speakers like to invent visual shorthand to remind them of the connections among points. Parallel columns of positive and negative details form economical groupings, and lines and arrows readily show the relationships of components:

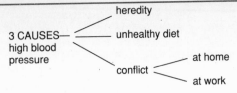

Using different colors of ink (and different widths or thicknesses of point) is a highly efficient way of distinguishing main points from supporting ones:

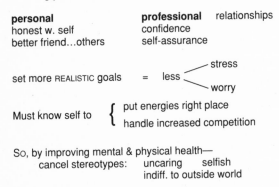

If your speech involves a series of oppositions, you might list the positive points in green, negative ones in black. Reserve red for audiovisual cues: "TAPE 2" or "Slide: Cost Projection." You will discover a wide range of ways to make your cards easy to follow without becoming traps for your eye and your attention.

If you use handouts, arrange distribution to minimize distractions. You may, for example, guide your audience through a portfolio, printed diagram, or travel brochure. If you have organized your speech around frequent reference to these materials, pass around your copies before you begin speaking, so that, once begun, your speech will not be interrupted by the logistics of distribution. On the other hand, if you are a travel adviser or an insurance agent who has brought brochures for listeners to take home and review, or if you have brought product samples to hand out, do not mention or distribute them until the end of your speech. Anticipation of them will compete with your spoken presentation, which should remain the primary focus of the audience's attention.

PREPARING AND USING AUDIOVISUAL MATERIAL

Any graphs, charts, or other visual material will benefit from the contrasting use of color and line. Whether you plan to sketch your pie chart on a portable chalkboard, project it from a slide, or show it drawn on poster paper, be sure that it is scaled large enough to be seen. Tack the poster sheet to a board, if possible, or bring it unrolled so that its ends do not curl and spring distractingly. Pointing out features of your graphic illustration as you continue talking, stand to one side of the screen or panel and, as much as possible without seeming to stand stiffly "at attention," keep your feet pointed toward the audience. In other words, avoid seeming to address an easel or a screen rather than the people who have come to hear you.

A common mistake is to leave a visual display in place after it has served its purpose. The same colorfulness that makes a chart or bar graph useful when you need it will also create a distraction when you go on to other phases of your subject. Audience members' eyes will continue to be drawn to the arching lines and splashes of color. Of course you will move quickly from one slide to the next in a travelogue or illustrated description of a manufacturing process, but in a less visually intensive presentation, turn the projector off (or use the remote control to move the slide tray to a blank slot) between one image and the next. Similarly, turn the reversible chalkboard over to its unused side or erase it when you no longer need to refer to your illustration. Remove the tacked-up poster from view and unobtrusively roll it up or lay it face down on the floor. If you have written out your note cards carefully and placed them strategically on the lectern, you will be able to maintain the pace of your discussion while performing these necessary housekeeping tasks.

GIVING YOUR SPEECH

If you have carefully planned the scope of your speech, prepared readable notes, and produced your supplementary materials with an awareness of the audience and the facilities available, your presentation should go smoothly. If you can, arrive early and check to be sure that your slide tray fits the projector, and be sure that the bulb and power source are functional. Having given your note cards a final review and timed your speech before arriving (and having assured yourself that the cards are in the correct numbered order), keep them in your coat pocket until your host begins to introduce you. Drop the binding rubber band into your pocket before you stand and move toward the lectern, and carry the small stack of cards unobtrusively. Make no particular attempt to hide the cards as you carry them, however; audiences understand that speakers need occasional prompting. Place your notes on the top of the lectern so that you have room to shift each card to the left, out of the way, after you have finished with it. Move from card to card without lifting each into the audience's view.

If your response to your host involves light exchange with an old friend or colleague, and if the tone of your opening requires a quieter, more neutral, or more sober mood, pause for a moment and establish clear eye contact with the audience. Look for three or five friendly faces—people who appear to be good listeners—and direct your remarks to them, shifting your gaze from right to left and from the nearby auditors to those further back in the room. Avoid the head-bobbing mechanical effect of alternately glancing at your notes, then at the ceiling or back wall. Again, your confidence in your material and your easily readable notes should allow you to sustain eye contact with the audience. If someone frowns, you can say, "Let me put that another way" or "You will remember that...." or "Of course you realize...." These personalizations of the material, prompted by signs of puzzlement or wandering attention, will carry your listeners through your connections and transitions. Pause immediately before or after a key point, and occasionally repeat an essential phrase, if you like. Although you should avoid a hill-and-dale or a sing-song effect, let your underscorings of important words and subtle adjustments of pace and volume give variety to your delivery. Keep hand gestures and bodily movement to a minimum except when you are miming the glide path of the Concorde or invisibly tracing the outline of your future world headquarters building. In short, avoid unconscious or nervous movement. Let your preparation lead you through an assured delivery.

CHAPTER PERSPECTIVE

Many would-be speakers waste too much psychic energy in worrying: "What if I fail?" "Will I lose my place in the middle of my speech?" If you become absorbed in self-conscious fretting, you will dissipate the mental and emotional powers you can more profitably direct toward success. Remember that you would not be asked to speak on a given subject if you were not expert, so you should not lack for something to say. You simply need to identify what incident, what angle, what astonishing fact, what cunning word choice will open your audience's imagination and draw it into your topic.

Approached with enthusiasm, the public speech and the internal presentation can be pleasurable, even exhilarating experiences. Your initial apprehensiveness will disappear as you focus your energies on the careful preparation that underlies success. Your early processes of defining your subject, your audience, the occasion, and your purpose will be translated into words and gestures as you speak, and you will be gratified to see the culmination of your efforts: winning project approval, changing people's minds about a public issue, or bringing pleasure, challenge or warm congratulations to your listeners.

Resume and Cover Letter Design

INTRODUCTION AND MAIN POINTS

Job-seeking is a stressful process in professional life. So much depends on first impressions and on predicting and reading other people's reactions. Frequently, the candidate who is hired is not the one with the most extensive training or the most impressive work record but the one who best projects suitability for the position.

This chapter discusses the ways to focus information on your training, work experience, and your personal strengths to convince a potential employer that you are *the* candidate for the particular position. Assessing your credentials is the first step, followed by designing the resume and composing the letter of application. The next chapter discusses job search, interview, and follow-up communications.

After studying this chapter:

▬ You will be able to focus on your credentials for presenting them in the resume and interview.

▬ You can design an attractive resume that strongly emphasizes your goals, strengths, and accomplishments.

▬ You can compose a confident, substantive letter of application.

ASSESSING YOUR CREDENTIALS

Before you can sell yourself successfully, you must determine what your selling points are. Your first step in the employment process, then, is assessing your personal and professional skills. Do not underrate yourself. Your self-evaluation is often the key to others' assessment of you. Evaluate your skills with honesty and confidence.

As you consider your strengths, focus on five or six of your major achievements—a time-saving improvement to a shipping procedure, an innovative solution to a sensitive personnel problem, a successful year as treasurer of an organization, completion of a difficult project, mastery of a computer program. How might these accomplishments apply to the work environment?

Did they center around work with people or ideas or equipment? Did they involve writing, speaking, lecturing, managing budgets, supervising, or coping with deadline pressures? Did they involve:

___physical activity	*or*	___mental activity?
___outside work	*or*	___inside work?
___direction from others	*or*	___self-direction?
___solitary work	*or*	___group work?
___supervision of others	*or*	___supervision by others?
___generation of ideas	*or*	___follow-through on details?
___familiarity in routine	*or*	___variety in routine?
___high stress level	*or*	___low-moderate stress level?
___work for a salary	*or*	___work on commission?
___regular schedule	*or*	___flexible schedule?
___extensive travel	*or*	___little travel?
___work in a city	*or*	___work in a suburban, small city, or rural environment?

What are your personal and professional qualities? Are you well-organized, motivated, inventive, responsible, competent, conscientious, flexible, positive, tolerant? Can you lead? Can you communicate your ideas? Many of the questions you will be asked in the interview will center on your professional goals and personal skills— "What are your major strengths?" "What are your major weaknesses?" "What can you offer my company?" "What kind of working environment do you prefer?" and "Where do you see yourself in ten years?" If you think about the answers to these questions, you can make a stronger first impression than you can by giving impromptu answers.

This self-assessment should show you which positions to apply for, which skills and accomplishments to highlight in your resume, and which credentials to emphasize in the interview. After you have completed this step, you are ready to look at resume design.

DESIGNING THE RESUME

A resume is not a life history but rather a sales brochure designed to be read in thirty seconds or less. Its primary purpose is to gain you an interview, not a job offer. Your resume offers specific details on your goals and accomplishments. Every entry should highlight your skills and emphasize your suitability for the particular position. The resume is a place for positive information. Do not include negative details. You are not obligated to mention a low college GPA or indicate that you were dismissed from a job (if either is true). If you are asked questions on these subjects in the interview, you should answer the questions honestly and point to any extenuating circumstances that might have caused the difficulties—but do not volunteer such negative information in the resume.

First impressions are very important. Make your resume the best self-presentation you can produce. (Most business executives, however, look unfavorably on the glossy and readily identifiable products of resume shops.) To project a professional impression, your resume should be typed, word-processed, or printed, with no penned-in changes.

Typed or word-processed resumes offer the distinct advantage of individualizing your career objective and details of your work record to target particular positions. Printed resumes, on the other hand, offer a more sophisticated look, but, because they are produced in quantity, they allow you little opportunity to refocus your resume without paying for additional typesetting. Resumes laser-printed on high quality stationery now provide a very satisfactory compromise between printshop printing quality and the word-processing ability to individualize resume details.

Resumes should be printed on white or pastel stationery. Among the pastels, yellows, grays, and creams seem to create a more favorable response than do blues and greens. The letter of application should be typed on stationery matching the resume, so when you print your resume, purchase an ample supply of matching stationery and envelopes.

Resumes must be free of significant errors. With the large numbers of resumes that arrive in personnel offices each week, a flawed resume is usually passed over—unless the candidate has outstanding credentials otherwise. The most common resume flaws are errors in grammar, punctuation, and word usage, excessive length, disorganized information, poor typing or printing, pompous styling, and sparse credentials. A resume should be detailed, brief, positive, action-oriented—and accurate. A candidate should never falsify resume information on training or work record. Doing so provides grounds for automatic dismissal from a job and damages one's professional reputation.

Resumes should always be accompanied by letters of application. Some personnel departments route resumes and application letters as a packet. Others separate them, asking personnel to rank the two documents individually. If a candidate has both a strong resume and letter, he or she will receive further consideration for a position opening.

The standard formats for resumes are chronological and functional. Recent college graduates and professionals with a steady upward direction to their careers usually use a chronological format, while those people with varied kinds of experience frequently consider a functional arrangement more advantageous to their work record. Use the format that best illustrates your credentials. Figures 16-1 and 16-2 show examples of both chronological and functional resumes.

THE CHRONOLOGICAL RESUME

Formatting is important to your resume. Position headings such as <u>Career Objective</u> and <u>Work Experience</u> either at the left margin, as shown in Figure 16-1, or in the center, as shown in Figure 16-2. Emphasize the most important entries—your name and the major headings—by using all capitals, underlining, bold-facing, or a combination of these techniques, but avoid using so much highlighting that you create a cluttered look. The reader's glance should be drawn downward on the resume, with easy movement from section to section and emphasis on the important points. The resume should have clean lines and a pleasing balance of material on the page. Text may be placed to the right of the heading or under the heading:

WORK EXPERIENCE   Office Assistant   Summer 19__
                              Phillips Pest Control   Alton, Iowa

                              Handled incoming calls, wrote business correspondence, completed weekly payroll, and performed other office functions.

or

WORK EXPERIENCE:

Office Assistant, Phillips Pest Control, Alton, Iowa. Summer 19__. Handled incoming calls, wrote business correspondence, completed weekly payroll, and performed other office functions.

The usual sections for the chronological resume are the name and address, the career objective, education, work experience, affiliations, and references. Accomplishments, personal data, and a list of publications are optional.

FIG. 16-1. *Sample Chronological Resume*

TODD M. BAKER_____

5590 Appleton Street
Linden, New Jersey 07036   201-803-6590

OBJECTIVE   A position in a progressive construction or construction management firm, utilizing my training and experience in building science and management.

EDUCATION   Ohio State University   Columbus, Ohio
B.S. in Building Science and Management, May 19__. Minor in Financial Management. Major GPA: 3.0/4.0

COMPUTER EXPERIENCE   Lotus 1-2-3, AutoCAD, Primavera Project Planner; work with Microsoft programs, Apple Macintosh, and IBM-compatible computers.

RELATED COURSES

Investment Analysis	Corporation Finance
Contract Documents	Business Ethics
Formwork and Concrete Design	Estimating
Construction Economics	Risk and Insurance
Personnel Management	Safety in Business

WORK EXPERIENCE   **Tri-Built Construction**   Irvington, New Jersey
Construction Manager   June 19__-present
Execute bids and estimates for $50,000–$1.5 million commercial contracts. Supervise on-site construction as a project manager and coordinate subcontractor work schedules. Have gained experience in office and job site management and have observed a variety of commercial contracting methods.

Framington Instrument Company Paterson, New Jersey
Engineering Assistant   Summer 19__
Prepared job estimates for electrical and process control instruments. Participated with field engineer in installing electrical and pneumatic instruments for industrial use.

MVC Construction Company   Linden, New Jersey
Construction Laborer   June 19__-July 19__
Participated in all phases of residential and light commercial construction. Completed several projects featured in construction and architectural publications. Generated a broad base of construction knowledge and developed disciplined work habits.

AFFILIATIONS American Institute of Constructors
Association of General Contractors

FIG. 16-2. *Sample Functional Resume*

TERRI A. BROWNLEE
3421 Crown Apartments
Richardson, Texas 75080
721-607-5432

CAREER OBJECTIVE
To obtain a position with a financial institution offering experience and advancement opportunities in financial analysis and internal operations.

EDUCATION
University of Texas at Dallas, Bachelor of Science in Financial Management, August 19___. Paid 60 percent of college costs through part-time employment.

Special project: Forecast 19___ financial statements for Southwestern Bank, using the computer-based Interactive Financial Planning System (IFPS) in conjunction with that institution's Profit Planning Division.

WORK EXPERIENCE
MANAGEMENT:
  Resident Manager, Crown Apartments
  Blake Blanding and Associates, Inc., Richardson, Texas

  Oversaw maintenance and grounds upkeep. Showed apartments to prospective tenants. Handled rental collection and accounting. Initiated social activities for tenants in 82-unit complex. August 19___-August 19___.

REAL ESTATE:
  Reservations Manager, Sales Office
  White Rock Lake Development Corporation, Dallas, Texas

  Arranged business appointments for seven real estate agents at resort community. Prepared sales documents. Interacted with marketing department concerning advertising and follow-up. Accounted for reservations revenues. May 19___-August 19___.

BANKING:
  Teller, Richardson and Northeast Dallas Branches
  Southwestern Bank, Dallas, Texas

  Gained experience with banking operations, security, customer service, and employee motivation. May 19___-May 19___.

RETAIL:
  Sales Assistant
  Melton's Department Store, Carrollton, Texas

  Assisted customers with purchases, arranged displays, and maintained inventory control in women's apparel. November 19___-May 19___.

ACTIVITIES
Financial Management Association, Rotary International, Toastmasters.

Name and Address

Your name—typed either in all capitals or upper and lower case, bold-faced or underlined—can be positioned in the center or at the left margin. You may use your whole name if each name is relatively short, such as John Michael Shaw or Elsa Marie Brown. Or you may use your first name, middle initial, and last name for a professional sound: John L. Houghman. If you are called by your middle name, it is best to use your whole name, for example, Bertina Anne Layton, rather than your first initial and middle name, B. Anne Layton, to avoid an affected "J. Alfred Prufrock" sound. Your professional name should sound smooth and pleasing, and the form you select should be the one you use throughout the employment process.

In the name and address section you also include your complete address and telephone number. (If you have two addresses, as a college student does, list them separately with headings for each: "Campus Address" and "Home Address.") List your full address, including zip code and telephone number with area code. Don't abbreviate Road, Street, or Avenue, but you may use the abbreviations Apt. and Blvd. You may use postal abbreviations (with no periods) for the state if the name of your city is long.

Career Objective

The career objective is the focus of the entire resume. All the resume information should relate to it. Some professional people suggest omitting the career objective on the resume and including it in the application letter, but regardless of where you place it, it is an important entry. Confused or uncertain career goals are a major reason for a candidate's rejection.

Phrase your career goal as specifically as possible without limiting your options. If you are applying for a certain position, state your goals in terms of the position announcement: "Desire position as systems analyst. Am particularly interested in marketing and finance applications. Prefer to serve as systems consultant to several departments." If you are not applying for an open position, use less precise phrasing. Indicate your area of interest and the skills you can offer a company— "A marketing position that can utilize my skills in personnel relations, in problem-solving, and in completing projects on time." Avoid self-focused statements such as "A position that can provide me with varied experiences in banking." Emphasize instead the skills and qualities you can offer to the company.

Indicate your long-range goals, too, if doing so does not weaken your position. You would not, for instance, want to indicate that you intend to enter law school in three years. Even though the average period of employment at the first position is one to three years and the second three to five years, your potential employer wants to believe that you may remain with the company for some length of time. And once you begin your employment with the company, you may change your mind about going to law school and decide to stay.

Education

Most resume designers present details of education after the career objective, although someone who has been employed for five or more years may choose to list work experience next. Use <u>reverse</u> chronological order for your educational background. For each entry, indicate certification or degree you obtained, date you obtained it, college or institution, and location of the institution. If your GPA was 3.0 or above, include that information: "GPA: 3.0/4.0," which indicates a 3.0 GPA based on 4.0 scale. If your cumulative GPA was below 3.0 but your major GPA above, you can list your major GPA: "Accounting GPA: 3.1/4.0" without referring to your cumulative grade point average. And you may include information on both cumulative and major GPAs.

You may include "Computer Experience" in this section as a subheading and list experience with computer languages, systems, and software. You may use an entry like "Computer Experience: BASIC, FORTRAN, Word Star, Word Perfect, Lotus 1-2-3, and dBASE III." You may also include relevant information under subheadings such as "Related Courses," "Certifications," "Grade Level Achieved," and others that you find appropriate.

If you have attended several colleges or technical schools or institutes, you will list the schools and dates of attendance and may include degree or computer or coursework information under each entry. Omit high school information, since it becomes less important as you gain professional training and experience.

Work Experience

Work experience is the central section of your resume. All your entries should directly relate to your career objective to show you as qualified for the targeted position. Present your experience in reverse chronological order—unless an early position relates to the career objective more clearly than does a recent one. In that case, present the strongest entry first and place the date in a less conspicuous position.

You may begin entries on work experience in one of three ways:

1. by date: **Summer 1988**
                 Assistant Store Manager
                 Betsy's Boutique, Conway, Arkansas

2. by company: COLGATE-PALMOLIVE Greenville, NC
                 Office Manager   Summer 1989

3. by position: **LEGAL ASSISTANT**—Summer 1988
                 Smith, Blaine, Roark, Attorneys
                 Tulsa, Oklahoma

If your work record shows a steady rise in level of responsibility, you may choose to present your work experience chronologically. If the companies that you have worked for have high name recognition, you may want to focus on the company. If your positions entailed a high level of responsibility with lesser-known companies, you may find that emphasis on the positions best shows your work experience. Use the arrangement that best presents your record. Many recruiters prefer resumes with a clear focus on positions because they can quickly assess a candidate's professional experience. Some personnel directors want to see position titles highlighted and placed in the left margin alongside the company, date, and duties information for quicker scanning:

LEGAL ASSISTANT   Smith, Blain, Roark, Attorneys.
                       Tulsa, Oklahoma. Summer 1988

                       Duties included....

In describing your work responsibilities for each position, try to use the verb + object pattern. Action verbs such as *coordinated, demonstrated, scheduled, improved, maintained, supported, reviewed, delegated, adapted, organized, analyzed, originated, launched* underscore your strength and leadership ability. You may, however, choose the phrasing "Responsibilities included" or "Duties:" followed by a listing of functions you carried out in the respective positions. You will probably use one of the following formats:

> Supervised the work of five employees. Installed computerized billing schedule. Maintained stockroom inventory.
>
> Responsibilities included supervision of five employees, installation of computerized billing schedule, and maintenance of stockroom inventory.
>
> Duties: supervised five employees, installed computerized billing schedule, and maintained stockroom inventory.

Whichever pattern you choose, try to remain consistent throughout the Work Experience section because parallel structure provides the smoothest styling.

In describing your work experience, do not undersell yourself. Clearly outline your responsibilities and accomplishments in each position. Mention projects you initiated, grants you received, conferences you planned, leadership positions you held, programs you implemented, increases in sales, and recognition for outstanding performance. Note your experience with writing, speaking, developing budgets, supervising, organizing, and coordinating projects.

Include all full-time work experience and any significant part-time experience. If you have held several short-term positions in a given field and prefer not to list them individually, you can list some of them generally with phrasing like "Various positions in construction in Kansas City, Missouri area, 1986-89."

Accomplishments or Skills

You may want to add a section outlining your accomplishments or skills to illustrate your credentials. An entry such as this is optional, and it may precede or follow the work experience section. You can list in bulleted form the skills that you have developed through your career training, work experience, and organizational involvement. Focus on those accomplishments that would be useful to the position you are seeking. Your entries might be similar to one of these:

ACCOMPLISHMENTS: • Selected by management to
                       improve program for schedul-
                       ing part-time employees.

- Increased production line efficiency in department by 5%.
- Taught safety training program that contributed to 30% reduction in accident frequency.
- Decreased absentee rate in department by 3.5% in one year.

SKILLS:
- Fluent in French and German
- Adept at public speaking
- Strong leadership and organizing ability
- Able in personnel relations

Publications

Publications are important to academic positions and some to management positions. Cite in this section monographs, articles, bulletins, books, and other kinds of publications, as well as papers presented at conferences. Alphabetize entries in the group if you have only a few entries or alphabetize within categories if you have a large number of entries. Their form will follow the bibliographic form discussed in Chapter 12.

Affiliations and Activities

In this section, you will note awards and honors you have received, as well as organizations you are affiliated with. List all your professional organizations and some service associations (Lions Club, Rotary International, Business and Professional Women's Organization, League of Women Voters, and the like). Some organizations may need identification. Use full names rather than initials or acronyms. For each entry, list any offices you have held and committees you have chaired. Affiliations that you should probably exclude from your list—in your own best interest—are religious and political associations.

You may also choose to add "Interests:" to this section. Some people consider this information unnecessary while others believe it provides a valuable clue to the candidate as a person. If you choose to mention your leisure-time activities, try to show a blending of active and more introspective pastimes: golf, flying, playing the guitar, and reading science fiction, for example.

Personal Data

Including personal data is optional. If there are several languages in which you are fluent or if you have computer experience or have traveled extensively, by all means include it. Information on marital status, date of birth, health and weight are usually not included. Do not volunteer any information that would decrease your attractiveness to an employer—your avid interest in hang gliding, your intention to apply to graduate school in two years, or your role as a parent of several young children.

References

In the reference section, you may simply note that references are "available upon request," although such a statement may be unnecessary. One alternative is to list the references on a second page, using the same heading format and stationery. Then you can give the interviewer a copy if you are asked for it.

Ask all referents' permission before you list their names on your resume or on any application form. Referents most valuable to the employer are present and past employers, then academic advisors and business associates. Your referents should know you well enough to comment specifically on your career goals and work performance.

For each recommender, list the person's full name, position and company (or relationship to you), complete address, and phone number, including area code. Phone numbers are helpful because many employers telephone for references rather than requesting letters. A typical reference entry may read like this:

> Mr. William Cole, President
> Cole Manufacturing Company
> 5406 Blanton Avenue
> Lansing, Michigan 48911
> (517) 884-6590

THE FUNCTIONAL RESUME

If you are well into your career and your work experience is varied, a functional format (illustrated in Figure 16-2) may show your credentials better than would a chronological format. A functional resume is arranged by experience or skills—*Public Relations Experience*, *Teaching Experience*, *Management Skills*, *Computer Skills*. With this format, you can choose the appropriate headings and relate them to your career objective. You will indicate dates for each work period, but place them near the end of the entry. You do not have to present the entries in chronological order, and you can include unpaid work experience. Thus, the functional format gives you much more versatility than does chronological order. Except for the *Work Experience* section, however, the functional resume follows the same format as the chronological.

Many resume-formatting variations are available, and only you can determine the format best for your credentials. Regardless of the format you choose, the most important qualities are clear focus on your goals and accomplishments, logical arrangement of details, professional style and appearance, and facts that distinguish you from other candidates. First impressions *are* important in both the resume and letter of application.

COMPOSING THE LETTER OF APPLICATION

In the application letter—which should always be sent with a resume—you have a chance to elaborate on resume details and project a sense of your personality. The tone of your letter should be enthusiastic, congenial, and confident, and the more the letter sounds like you, the better it is.

Unlike the resume, which may be printed in volume, each application letter should be typed or word processed individually. You will undoubtedly use some of the same information in successive letters, but your focus will vary as you write to the different companies.

Throughout the letter, emphasize what you can contribute to the company. To adapt John F. Kennedy's famous remark, ask not what the company can do for you but what you can do for the company. Make knowledgeable comments about the company's current activities—an expected expansion, a recent merger, or the introduction of a new product line. Researching the company will require some time on your part but will show your interest.

Apply for a particular position, if possible. Avoid the "I'll take anything" approach, which suggests desperation or lack of marketability. Indicate in the opening paragraph how you learned of the position for which you are applying. The strongest source is a referral from someone within the company or industry, since 85 percent to 90 percent (or more) of the positions in industry are filled through personal recommendations or referrals. If this is the means by which you heard of the opening, mention the name of the contact person early in the letter and indicate that the person recommended your applying for the position. If you learned of the opening through a trade journal or newspaper advertisement, name the source.

If you are sending an unsolicited letter without knowledge of an actual opening, stress your interest in the company and your desire to become a part of it. Be sure to include information that indicates you have done research on the firm. Mention product names, employee benefits, pending major contracts, or other "recognition" details.

In the middle paragraphs, elaborate on your qualifications for the position. Generally, you will present information on your work record first, emphasizing the kinds of experience you gained in your various positions. Avoid simply repeating resume details; instead, discuss the professional skills you developed in each position, especially those you expect to use in the position you are applying for. After you discuss your work record, you can elaborate on your training and education: computer experience, technical skills, languages, specialized training. In addition, you may focus on experience you have gained through other avenues, perhaps through travel or as part of an organizational, community, or college project. You may also elaborate on your experiences in professional or community organizations and their value to the position, perhaps in organizing and executing projects, handling budgets, and coordinating programs.

The last paragraph provides the opportunity to ask for an interview. If you plan to be in the particular city on a certain date, state that fact. Indicate your date of availability. Courteously but confidently request the opportunity to talk with the personnel director (or president or department head) to discuss the position and your credentials. You may ask the person to call or write you if your credentials are appropriate for the available position. Be sure to include your phone number in the letter, because the resume may be routed separately.

If you are applying for a leadership position, you may choose to take the initiative and indicate that you will call the executive's office during a given week to discuss the possibility of an interview. If you use this approach, be careful not to say you will call "to set up an interview" since this is the employer's prerogative, not yours. Your making the next move is a more assertive approach than is waiting for the employer to call you. The likelihood exists, too, that you may speak directly with the employer. By calling, you also encourage the employer to make a clear decision about your candidacy.

Close your letter confidently and congenially. Avoid making flattering statements here (or anywhere in the letter). Again, the more clearly your letter represents you, the more effective your letter. Figures 16-3 and 16-4 show samples of application letters.

FIG. 16-3. *Sample Application Letter*

344 Blake Point Drive
Richmond, Virginia 16783
January 15, 1991

Mr. Thomas Hale
Senior Partner
Sandy and Babcock Architects, Inc.
54134 Bayview Drive
Tampa, Florida 36611

Dear Mr. Hale:

During the recent AIA convention in Chicago, Ms. Robin Walker, a member of your design staff, informed me of an anticipated opening for a conceptual designer in your Clearwater office. I am interested in exploring the possibility of obtaining that or a similar position within your firm.

I received my Bachelor of Science degree in Design from Virginia Commonwealth University in December 1990. In addition to taking a broad range of courses, I concentrated my independent studies on rendering and architectural delineation. The spring semester of my junior year I spent in Charleston, South Carolina, where I was instructed by the renderer Joseph McCaskill, FAIA. During my internship with Williams-Young and Associates, I prepared presentation drawings suitable for publication in various competitions, including the Builder's Choice Home Awards, the South Atlantic Regional AIA design competition, and *Southern Living*'s design awards competition. Most recently, I spent a week as a team member of the AIA's centennial celebration in Richmond. Under the direction of John Whitney, FAIA, I prepared various sketches, including a bird's-eye view of the city of Richmond that was used in the centennial publication. These and other details of my background are described in my enclosed resume.

Sandy and Babcock's reputation in the AIA is strong, and I very much want to be associated with your firm. I would like to talk with you, Mr. Hale, about your upcoming opening and my qualifications for the position. May I call your office the week of February 1 to discuss the possibility of an interview? I look forward to the opportunity of speaking with you.

Sincerely,

James A. Johnston

Enclosure: Resume

FIG. 16-4. *Sample Letter of Application*

9812 23rd Avenue South
Seattle, Washington 98105
March 15, 1990

Mr. Harold Preston
Vice President, ISS, Inc.
18956 Rainier Avenue South
Seattle, Washington 98105

Mr. Preston:

When Larry Barton, an employee in your Engineering Subroutines section, and I were recently discussing my upcoming graduation from the University of Washington, he suggested that you might have an opening for an entry-level programmer. As of May 15, I would be available to assist you in the updating of the third release of your Logistical Software package to the U.S. Navy scheduled for early November.

My bachelor of science in computer science training at the University of Washington has focused on various computer languages, including C, which you now use, and my department's emphasis on software design and efficiency has prepared me to write clear, concise programs and subroutines. My experience in the Division of Information Research taught me how to write software for large multiuser systems similar to the package you are now developing. Additionally, my experience as a tutor and consultant has taught me how to communicate technical ideas and concepts to both technically trained and nontechnical employees in a logical, comprehensible manner.

At your convenience, I would appreciate the opportunity to discuss my qualifications with you. You may reach me at 659-2006 after 3:00 p.m. or at my home address. I look forward to talking with you about your programming position and the possibility of becoming a part of the ISS team.

Sincerely,

Henry A. Clarke

Enclosure

CHAPTER PERSPECTIVE

In this chapter we have looked at the personal and professional points of information important to emphasize in a resume and letter of application and the options available in resume design. In the following chapter, we will focus on the subsequent stages of the employment process—setting up a job-search plan, gearing up for the interview, and completing essential follow-up communications.

Job Search Techniques

INTRODUCTION AND MAIN POINTS

Composing the resume and letter of application were the focal points of Chapter 16. This chapter discusses equally important stages: mapping out the job search strategy and anticipating the interview. After you have completed your work on the resume and cover letter—or while you are still in the midst of it—you will make some major decisions on how to approach the job search. You have heard stories of people who sent out 200 or 300 resumes and still wound up driving taxi cabs or working construction jobs. You can avoid such consequences if you logically plan the job search and intelligently prepare for the interview.

After reading this chapter:

- You will be able to outline a productive and results-oriented job search strategy.
- You will be able to plan a professional, dynamic interview presentation.
- You will know how to complete necessary follow-up communications.

OUTLINING THE JOB SEARCH

Candidates often distribute resumes *en masse* in the belief that they must cover as many bases as possible. This expensive and time-consuming approach, however, is one of the least productive ways to learn of openings, obtain interviews, and gain positions. Rather than distributing resumes in this haphazard manner, you can produce better results by planning a selective search process.

The best job search techniques are cultivating contacts in the industry, using the services of college placement offices and employment bureaus, searching the employment sections of professional journals, and reading newspaper advertisements. You may use a variety of these techniques rather than any single one.

Personal contacts offer one of the most productive avenues for learning of position openings and getting interviews. An overwhelming majority of the openings in business and industry are filled through personal recommendations and referrals, indicating that you should contact acquaintances who work in companies you find desirable. Find out about existing or expected position openings, and ask questions about the company to learn whether it provides a working environment you would find satisfying and challenging. Attend your professional meetings, too, and introduce yourself to other participants. Forming a solid network of colleagues and industry professionals is important to you, not only in the employment process but throughout your career.

Employment agencies can provide valuable assistance. Realize, however, that such agencies are working in the interests of the company. The agency's primary concern is finding a person to fill an opening, not finding the best position for you. If the agency makes a successful company-candidate match, though, both of you benefit. Remember, too, that before you sign a contract with an agency, you need to know whether you or the company will pay the agency's fee, usually a percentage of the first six months' or first year's wages. If you decide to use the services of an employment agency, check with the Better Business Bureau concerning the agency's reputation and choose an agency carefully.

Trade and professional associations, with their annual or semiannual meetings, also offer employment support. Industry journals often carry display ads and classifieds for position openings, and associations may offer special employment bulletins, especially in the weeks preceding trade shows or job marts—meetings that provide convenient interview situations.

Classified newspaper advertisements can also supply information on position offerings—if you want to work in a particular city or area. As you read, carefully take notes on positions, responsibilities, and salaries over a period of several weeks so you will have a realistic basis for evaluating job opportunities.

College placement offices are helpful if you are nearing graduation or have just graduated. About 75 percent of graduating seniors utilize placement services, interviewing with a wide range of major companies. (Many smaller companies do not have budgets adequate to support college campus visits, so you may have to contact those companies directly.) For six months to a year after graduation, most placement offices offer alumni the same benefits as they do seniors—company information, employment workshops, information on job listings, and interviews on campus. Many universities offer, for a slight fee, additional services for a longer period of time. You will probably have to clarify details such as these with your particular placement office.

Candidates sometimes use more direct approaches to finding jobs. Some arrange to visit companies they find attractive to get a feeling about the work atmosphere. If you choose to do this, try to talk to as many company employees (secretaries and professionals) as possible. You will gather an impression of the company's team image, the formality of the company hierarchy, and employees' satisfaction with their work. You may also learn of existing or expected openings. One young woman who wanted to work in Denver came up with an original approach. She went to the downtown business section, entered the tallest corporate building, and talked with employees on various floors of the building. In the process she heard of an opening, applied for it, and got the job. This approach is unusual, but it shows that candidates can and should be innovative and assertive and should aim for results.

Sending resumes to companies or individuals is necessary but is best combined with one of the other search methods—referral, response to an advertised position, or follow-up to a personal conversation—rather than being used alone. Concentrate on ten or so companies you would like to work for. To focus your energy on those companies, gather a substantial amount of information on each, try to meet people who work for them, and visit the plant sites, if feasible. Logically, of course, a company must have a position available before its representatives can consider your application. However, if you convince an employer that you can contribute significantly to the company, your application will be remembered and reconsidered when an opening does materialize.

PLANNING FOR THE INTERVIEW

If your job search has led you to a position opening for which you are distinctly qualified, and if you have persuaded the employer that you deserve a second look, you will probably be offered an interview. Weeks before you reach the meeting itself, however, you need to think through the interview to determine how to make the best impression and show that you are a strong candidate.

Getting an interview is your first goal in the job search process. It is in your meeting with the company representative that you have the chance for the personal dialogue and interaction that come into play in marketing your credentials. Here your confidence in your abilities, your commitment to your career, and your potential for success must shine through. For a successful outcome, plan for the interview and approach it with the assurance that you are the right person for the job.

After a successful first interview, you have a strong chance of being asked to a second interview, and perhaps a third. Understand that the interview process is lengthy; recruiters and candidates complete many interviews to reach one hire. Offers are not made at first interviews but at second, third, or even fourth interviews. A good match is important—both you and company representatives must be convinced that you are the right person for the job. Otherwise, you or the company personnel officer (or both) will soon be thinking of your leaving the company.

Background Preparation

In preparing for the interview, you need information on both yourself and the company. Your period of self-assessment should have focused on your skills, goals, and personal qualities. You will also need to do some research to gather background information on the companies with which you want interviews. If you go into an interview with little idea of the company's products or services, its representatives will be unfavorably impressed and will not want to spend much time on the interview.

Learn the company's full name (3M is Minnesota Mining and Manufacturing), its primary products or services, location of the home office and regional branches or plants, its industry position, problems the company or industry is facing, age of the company, price of its stock and its earnings, and changes in the company's focus or structure. This information is available in business periodicals, personnel or placement office brochures, annual reports, and reference sources such as *Standard and Poor's Register of Corporations, Directors & Executives, Dun & Bradstreet's Million Dollar Directory*, or Moody's manuals. You can also learn a great deal from conversations with people in the company or industry.

Once you have completed your background research, you can consider the more immediate aspects of the interview—desired candidate qualities, professional dress, and interviewer and interviewee questions.

Desired Candidate Qualities

Recruiters and managers are looking for candidates who can fit comfortably into the company and contribute to its goals. Strong communication skills are essential. The ability to speak and write clearly and to communicate with people with various personalities, backgrounds, and attitudes is a plus for any candidate.

Other qualities important to employers are (1) expertise in the chosen field, (2) leadership and initiative, (3) common sense and problem-solving capabilities, (4) public relations skills, (5) the ability to fit into the company as a team player, and (6) enthusiasm, strong work ethic, and the willingness to work extra hours to get the job done. The more of these qualities you possess, the stronger your candidacy for the position.

Professional Dress

You will dress much as you expect the interviewer to be dressed: navy, taupe, or gray suit (for both men and women), white or pastel shirt or blouse, little jewelry, restrained hair style, polished shoes, and little or no cologne. Men should wear knee socks and women should wear natural-color hose with pumps. Before the first interview, you should coordinate your ensemble and wear it at least once. The more comfortable you feel in your clothes, the more confident you will feel going into the interview.

Interview Preliminaries

You want to project a professional image in the interview, and your choice of clothes is a primary factor in establishing this. You should always take with you materials that show your preparation. Take a portfolio containing two copies of your resume and list of references, copies of any of your reports or papers that relate to the position you are applying for, a notepad, and a pen. If you have a copy of the company's annual report or other company information, take that to the interview, too, so you can ask pertinent questions on the reports or brochure.

Arrive at the interview fifteen to thirty minutes early. Allow yourself time to catch your breath, collect your thoughts, and survey your surroundings. Do not rush into this meeting. Your early arrival will also give you the opportunity to meet the secretary. Realize that as you talk informally with the secretary you are making an important impression because managers value their secretaries' assessments of candidates.

Interview Formats

Interviews usually last about thirty minutes. Interviewers have their days blocked into thirty-minute segments, so if they exceed the time period, they are probably interested in the candidate. Interviews may be tightly or loosely structured.

Most are structured with a series of questions and answers. The first five minutes allow time for ice-breaking small talk. Interviewers usually prefer to set the interviewee at ease, believing that a relaxed candidate shows a more accurate picture of himself or herself than does a tense one. The central twenty minutes of the interview provide time for ten to twelve questions and responses, with most of the questions coming from the interviewer. The last five minutes or so offer the candidate the opportunity to ask questions.

Some interviews are loosely structured, with a "tell me about yourself" opening request. In this kind of interview, you would discuss your credentials, preferably in an organized fashion. You can best prepare for this kind of interview by focusing on your major accomplishments and personal qualities. Provide examples of both, referring to projects you have worked on, programs you have initiated, and conferences you have coordinated. Look also to the list of questions that interviewers frequently ask candidates, and prepare answers to them. Although the "tell me about yourself" device may be used for an opener, the interviewer will probably move to asking questions once you have made initial comments. The primary purpose of this kind of request is to measure your poise and ability to express yourself.

Interviewers' Questions

Interviewers' questions most frequently center on accomplishments, qualities, and goals: (1) What can you offer our company? (2) Where do you see yourself in five years? in ten years? (3) What are your major strengths and weaknesses? (4) How do you spend your leisure time? (5) What have been your most significant accomplishments? (6) Why are you interested in our company? (7) What courses did you like most and least in college? (8) How would you describe yourself? and (9) How would you change this organization?

You should compose answers to these questions in advance so you will not have to give impromptu answers in the interview. If you are asked what you can offer the company, cite four or five major skills—your computer expertise, your competence in working with people of different ethnic and cultural backgrounds, your familiarity with business functions associated with the position you are applying for. If you are asked why you are interested in this particular company, focus on those accomplishments that you became aware of through your research—rapid growth, strong industry reputation, opportunities for middle managers—and provide details to illustrate.

If you are asked about your major strengths and weaknesses, elaborate on four or five of your strengths with specific illustrations: your willingness to make decisions, your ability to work well with others, and your innovative approach to problem-solving. As for your weaknesses, settle on one or two weaknesses that might be considered strengths for the company—a tendency toward perfectionism, impatience with people who do not meet deadlines, a tendency to overwork. What you admit to, of course, must be honest, but be selective in the weakness you cite. Don't admit to one that is self-damning.

If you are asked how you spend your leisure time, mention a variety of activities (if true) rather than only one. Cite active pastimes such as team or individual sports, along with quieter or more introspective hobbies such as photography, painting, music, or collecting art objects. Your answer should show a wide range of interests as well as excellent physical and mental health. Your list also gives the interviewer clues to your personality and temperament.

The subject of salary makes many candidates anxious. Do not introduce the topic of salary yourself. Even though salary is vitally important to you, it should not appear to be the focus of your interest. If you are asked what salary you expect, you may cite the salary range noted in the *Occupational Outlook Handbook* (available in the reference section of the library) or in employment outlook sources (available in placement or personnel offices). You may also hedge with comments such as "a salary commensurate with my training and experience." If the subject of salary is not introduced until late in the interview, you may negotiate a better salary if the recruiter wants to entice you to the company with a more attractive offer.

Your interview responses should be brief but substantive. Provide examples and give additional information when it seems appropriate. Be careful, however, not to appear overly aggressive or too talkative. If you need to jot down any information during the interview, do so but don't take copious notes. You may also note related questions to ask at the end of the interview.

Interviewee Questions
Your own questions may pertain to the amount of travel associated with the position, the nature of additional training, the amount of supervision you should expect, the average age of middle man-

agement, and follow-up clarification from the earlier points. At the close of the interview, double-check the spelling of the interviewer's name, and give the interviewer a firm but not bone-breaking handshake as you prepare to leave.

Interview Logs

You should keep a record of your interviews with the names of companies and recruiters, dates resumes were sent, number of interviews, impressions of the companies, and any other information you believe is pertinent. You might set up a table such as the one illustrated below to use for recording factual information. You might also want to keep a sheet on each company, noting more substantive details about the interview.

Company	Contact Person	Method of Contact			Interviews			Offer		Impressions
		Resume	Call	Intview	1	2	3	Y	N	

HANDLING FOLLOW-UP COMMUNICATIONS

After you have completed the interview, you may need to follow up with several kinds of letters and phone calls: expressions of appreciation, inquiries, refusal of an offer, or acceptance of an offer. These communications are brief, but they keep your name in the employer's mind.

Sending a note of appreciation to the interviewer is not mandatory but is advisable if you are interested in the position. The layout of the letter is simple. In the first paragraph you will express appreciation for the interview and may comment on your interest in the company. In the second paragraph you may note your impressions of the company and restate your potential contribution. In the last paragraph you may simply close with congenial remarks. None of the paragraphs need be longer than two or three sentences, but your statements should flow smoothly and logically to avoid any abruptness in sound or meaning.

I appreciated the opportunity to talk with you on March 15 about my qualifications for your accounting position and a potential career with Holtzendorf's.

Your company has an enviable reputation in the Midland region for production and distribution of office supplies. With my computer and accounting experience, I am confident of my ability to contribute to your organization, and I would like to be a part of your team.

I look forward to speaking with you further concerning your position. Please call me at 992-909-3209 if you have any questions.

An inquiry letter or telephone call may be necessary if in three or four weeks after the interview you have not received any communication from the company. Primarily you need to determine the status of your candidacy, but you may also indicate any changes in your credentials that have materialized since the interview.

Thank you for the February 18 interview. I appreciated learning more about Milner's Manufacturing Company and the shipping department director's position you have available.

I am most interested in the position and am writing (calling) to inquire about the status of my application.

Most of the information relative to the position is outlined in my resume, but I will be happy to provide you any additional information you may need concerning my credentials or references. I anticipate hearing from you soon.

Once you have written what seems to be numerous thank-you letters and made as many inquiries, you should receive one or more offers. Then your task is to indicate your response in a professional and positive fashion.

An acceptance letter is the easiest follow-up to write because your enthusiasm is natural and your message will probably be brief. In the first paragraph, you will state your acceptance and comment on the prospect of being a part of the company. In the second you may confirm the agreed-upon salary and starting date and offer any information pertinent to your accepting the position and moving to your new location. This paragraph may be quite short or relatively long, depending on the number of details that you feel need to be noted. In the last paragraph you can make some congenial comments to close, unless you need to request some action on the part of the employer. If so, you will need to indicate the date by which you need the action completed.

> I am pleased to accept your offer of the directorship of the C. R. Roberts quality assurance program and welcome the prospect of being a part of your team. To confirm our agreement, I accept the salary of $58,000 and expect to begin my employment July 1. The signed contract is enclosed.

> We have begun the necessary steps for the transition. Our home is on the real estate market with some likely prospects for selling. I have written the Seattle Chamber of Commerce asking for real estate and other information. My wife and I intend to come to Seattle the week of June 1–5 to look for suitable housing and anticipate making the move in late June. I will appreciate your sending me any information that you consider useful to us.

> It will be my pleasure to greet you in June. Please convey my warm thanks to Ted Williams and Julia Robbins for their coordination efforts and hospitality during my visit May 5.

A rejection letter is more difficult to write because of the need to be diplomatic as you decline an offer. In the first paragraph, you may thank the person for the interview(s) and make some complimentary comments about the company. In the second you can state that you have taken a position with another company and may give the reason(s), if you can do so diplomatically. In the last paragraph, you will simply close congenially and positively. Do not criticize or alienate the person to whom you are writing. You may want to work for this company some day or you may later have this person as your supervisor.

> Thank you for your consideration of my candidacy for your store management position. I very much appreciate the time you have afforded me, as well as the opportunity to become more acquainted with the Bryson-Mahon organization and the Phoenix area.

After much consideration I have decided to accept a position as store manager of McCovill's in Houston, a position that brings with it the opportunity to move into district management. The decision was a hard one to make because of the strong growth that you at Bryson-Mahon are experiencing, your secure organizational structure, and your notable reputation in public relations.

My impressions of your personnel and work are purely positive, and I welcome the opportunity to work with you and your representatives on future occasions.

CHAPTER PERSPECTIVE
In this chapter (as well as in the preceeding one) we have discussed many of the facets of employment that are definable, and yet even those are subject to differences of opinion. Certainly personal chemistry plays its part, but as you prepare for a job search, you have the obligation to yourself to project the most positive and professional image you can. The information in these chapters should help you to accomplish that purpose.

International Communications

INTRODUCTION AND MAIN POINTS

With the increasing globalization of business and industry and rising income levels that finance international communication and travel, a large segment of our society can reasonably expect to travel to countries outside our continent. These trips may be short jaunts or extended stays, and their purpose may be business or pleasure.

When you contemplate such a trip, your initial concern may be about language barriers. Then, realizing that English is rapidly becoming an international language, you might assume that no other barriers exist. The fact is, though, that cultural and social differences may be even more important than language. The aim of this chapter is to focus on some of the differences between American customs, attitudes, and beliefs and those of other countries. The objective is not to serve as a guide to any one area but to illustrate the need for awareness of other nations' cultural diversities.

After reading this chapter:

- You will realize the importance of increasing cultural awareness regarding the customs of other societies.
- You will recognize the major differences in beliefs, attitudes, and customs that influence business and social interchanges.
- You can use advice from experts to improve your own communication with people from different cultures.

THE NEED FOR CULTURAL AWARENESS

Ethnocentricity—that sense that one's own culture and customs are right and all others are "foreign" and perhaps wrong—is a universal characteristic. A person's native culture leaves an indelible imprint upon his or her perception of self and others. This culturization runs deep and causes people to resist change. Visitors in foreign countries, for example, may alter behavior during their stay abroad but will usually revert to their native country's customs and attitudes as soon as they return home.

The same attachment to our own culture also leads us to assume that other cultures mirror our own—that people in other societies think and act as we do. When foreign visitors charge into international situations unaware of significant differences, they may seem insensitive and self-centered. They may unintentionally insult their hosts, create embarrassing situations, and, if they are involved in a business enterprise, lose money in ventures that go awry. Because many Americans lack sensitivity to other cultures, we have acquired an unfortunate reputation for being bombastic and egocentric.

Business people contemplating international investment usually focus on such factors as the target country's economic environment, its currency, government restrictions, contractual customs, and trade laws that affect the venture—but some place little emphasis on learning about the culture. "Cultural differences," says David Ricks, author of *Big Business Blunders*, "are the most significant and troublesome variables for the multinational company. The failure of managers to comprehend fully these disparities has led to most international business blunders."[1]

VALUES AND ATTITUDES

Societal attitudes, being deeply held, are most susceptible to accidental insult and misunderstanding. To avoid transgressions, major or minor, potential travelers need to be aware of the values particular to their target country or countries.

Family

People in the United States and other countries perceive the family very differently. With our willingness to move from one city or region or even country to another, "family" is considered the nuclear unit of father, mother, and children. Even that definition has been changing in the last decade, with single-parent households and unmarried individuals now being classified as families. In many other cultures, however, the family is extended to include the grandparents, uncles, aunts, and cousins, and all or many of them living in close proximity, perhaps even in the same dwelling. In Mediterranean and Latin American countries, one's most important membership is the family: a person's status and acceptability are based on the family's respectability and social rank. Roger Axtell, author of *Do's and Taboos Around the World*, advises visitors to Middle Eastern and Asian cultures to mention their families, both to indicate their own stability and to show recognition of the importance those societies place on families.[2]

Individualism

Emphasis on individualism is another area of difference among cultures. We appreciate entrepreneurship, encourage early independence in our children, and appreciate people's self-motivation and drive for excellence. In many countries, however, group needs take precedence over individual needs—in, for example, the Netherlands, the Scandinavian countries, and many African, Asian, and South American societies. The Swahili language of East Africa, for instance, has no verb equivalent for "to own," and milking rights to a cow are passed daily or weekly from family to family, depending upon respective families' needs. The ownership of property is collective rather than individual.[3]

Work

German sociologist Max Weber noted that the most economically developed societies are those with a strong work ethic, and Americans are blessed—or cursed—with such an attitude toward work. For us, "time is money." We evaluate people according to their contributions to society and are critical of the rich playboy or the welfare recipient who is unwilling to work. In fact, retirees frequently assume worklike activities—teaching at universities, volunteering for literacy programs, and contributing to community service projects. Because our attitudes toward work are so deeply ingrained, we expect that other people share them, but not all countries do. People in India, for example, value living the simple life, and inhabitants of many Asian countries feel so uneasy when their incomes start to rise that they reduce their workload.[4] In a similar vein, Buddhists and Moslems feel that hard work is futile when their lives are controlled by forces so much greater than their own, and Buddhists also believe that desire for material possessions and self-fulfillment leads to suffering.

Role of Women and Relationship of the Sexes

While we pride ourselves on our liberated attitudes toward women's equality and sexuality, we should realize that, in the world view, we are definitely in the minority. In Saudi Arabia, for instance, there is little public social interaction between males and females; men and women are strictly separated in educational situations and social ones such as dinners. A single woman may find real difficulty being admitted to the country and doing business. One woman who encountered this barrier started wearing a wedding ring, registering at hotels as married, and taking her meals in her room and thus successfully handled her business.[5] In spite of restraints on the business and social involvement of women in these male-dominated societies, however, women managers from the U.S. and Europe (but not from Japan) have achieved success in Brazil, Saudi Arabia, and Egypt. In recent years, affluence generated by oil money has led to more education and power for Arab women, and in Kuwait women can now own shops, serve on corporate boards, and even run companies.[6]

CUSTOMS

Learning something of a country's language is vital to a person planning an extended stay. If your schedule is "If it's Tuesday, it must be Belgium," obviously it is impractical to learn the language of every country. But, if you can become acquainted with some of the key phrases, the *pleases* and *thank yous* and some of the customs of a culture, you can compensate remarkably for not knowing the language.

Some countries rely more than others on customs and traditions. The following scale, illustrating cultures' dependence on contextual cues, is based on the writings of Edward Hall (1976) and L.R. Kohls (1978):[7]

HIGH CONTEXT

Japanese
Chinese
Arab
Greek
Spanish
Italian
English
French
American (U.S.)
Scandinavian
German
Swiss German

LOW CONTEXT

Differences between high context and low context peoples may become evident in many business and social interactions[8]:

TABLE 16-1 DIFFERENCES BETWEEN HIGH- AND LOW-CONTENT CULTURES

Factors/Dimensions	High Context	Low Context
Bonds between people	Strong	Fragile
Involvement with people	Deep [Strong]	Low
A person's word	Is person's bond	Not to be relied on. Get it in writing.
Lawyers	Less important	More important
Speaking at close distances	Comfortable	Uncomfortable
Superior's responsibility	Responsible for subordinate's mistake	Less responsible for subordinate's mistakes
Competitive bidding	Not effective method	Effective method
Hard work as success	Belief weaker	Belief stronger
Industry	Busy not healthy	Busy natural
Future improvement	Little confidence	Great confidence
Change	Slow	Easy and fast
Space	People breathe on other	Bubble of private space/resent intrusions
Time	Polychronic—everything must be dealt with in terms of its own time	Monochronic—time is money. Linear—one thing at a time
Negotiations	Lengthy—purpose is to allow parties to know each other	Proceed quickly

We in the U.S. de-emphasize ceremony and nonverbal cues to emphasize the spoken word, but residents of many other countries place much value on the symbols and rituals that accompany words. Learning to use the courteous gestures of a culture, especially in countries that particularly prize them, does much to bridge language barriers and to lessen prejudices. Axtell, for example, encourages visitors to Muslim countries to sprinkle their conversations with expressions of *Inshallah*, "God willing," which is used as commonly as *okay* in the U.S.: "See you tomorrow, *Inshallah*."[9]

The custom of giving gifts in greeting visitors is important in many societies as a symbol of one's respect for the host (and hostess). The process should be handled with finesse. The host should take the lead in giving, no visitor should appear to outdo the host, and most peoples do not open gifts immediately. Some of the best gifts for Americans to give are lighters, pens, cigarettes, American brand-name articles (with such well-known names as Bloomingdales, Tiffany, Levis), Americana items (Indian pottery, Vermont maple syrup), and gifts for children (yo-yos, magic markers, Disneyland T-shirts). Gifts not suitable for giving are alcohol (particularly in Muslim countries), clocks in China (they are a symbol of bad luck), red roses in France and Germany (they are a symbol of love), and any article that looks cheap or seems too personal. Gifts of food are not welcome in the Middle East because they suggest that the hosts are unable to provide enough food to satisfy the occasion.[10] In Japan and Germany the wrapping is as important as the gift. And when you receive gifts, you should send your host (or hostess) a prompt thank-you note written on personalized stationery, with names and addresses correctly written.

Bribery is closely akin to gift-giving in many parts of the world. Although we in the U.S. look askance at such a practice, it is common in some countries such as India, where gifts of money may provide the only way to get something accomplished. In countries that do not collect income tax, civil servants are paid so poorly that under-the-table payments are considered part of their wages. Whether it is called *dash* (in Africa) or *kumshaw* (in Southeast Asia) or grease, modest payments to officials to speed bureaucratic actions are accepted means of cutting through red tape.[11]

Eating customs vary across cultures, and flexibility here can be a major facilitator. We have replaced formal dining with quick lunches and snacks, but people in other countries consider dining an occasion. Most societies devote hours to dinners, with multiple courses, toasts, and prescribed rituals. Some peoples, such as the Japanese, expect to blend business and dining, while others, such as the Germans, resent business talk at meals. Even if the prospect of eating unfamiliar foods makes you uneasy, most experienced travelers would recommend that you try at least a bit of every food you are offered. Instead of asking what you are eating, say to yourself, "It tastes a lot like chicken."

The exchange of business cards at the beginning of both social and business occasions is a custom that is more significant in other cultures than in ours. Business cards give a person status by indicating rank and company association, and the printing also helps with the pronunciation of unusual names. If you are going to a country where English is not widely understood, ask a local printer to add a translation of your business card information to the back of your card.[11]

Prospective travelers should learn the protocol surrounding bowing in Japan, the sauna in Finland, and business meeting styles in Japan and Arab societies. The sources noted at the end of this chapter provide valuable information on customs particular to individual cultures. Certainly it is clear that going abroad without doing such research is a mistake.

NONVERBAL CUES

It has been estimated that only about 30 percent of our communications are verbal.[12] Anthropologist Edward T. Hall calls the nonverbal 70 percent "the silent language." Those nonverbal cues that we readily understand and accept in our society frequently do not transfer with the same meaning to other cultures.

Time

One of the major adjustments American travelers must make is to other people's time perspectives. We feel an obligation to stay busy, to use our time efficiently, to remain productive—and we have generated a fast-paced lifestyle. In traveling, however, we find markedly different attitudes toward the use of time. On one end of the scale, the Japanese, Germans, Swiss, Swedes, and Norwegians prize punctuality and expect an apology for lateness. At the other end are the Greeks and Spanish, who close their offices from early to late afternoon.[14] Latin Americans, who expect about a thirty-minute delay for meetings and social occasions, are surprised when people arrive on time. Likewise, the Arabs do not like to schedule activities because by doing so, they feel pressured.

Use of space also varies among cultures and may cause uneasiness, as happens when an American talks to someone from the Middle East. Arabs prefer to stand only nine or ten inches from a person when speaking—a distance Americans find more appropriate to an intimate discussion. As the conversation progresses, the American backs away and the Arab moves to close the gap. In general, people from the Mediterranean and South America tend to stand much closer than do northern Europeans and North Americans. As for the Japanese, they employ a concentric arrangement, with the central positions being the most important. Thus, the window area is not the prestigious location in Japanese business environments.

Attitudes toward touching generally follow the same lines as use of space. People in Mediterranean cultures, Arabs, Israelis, and eastern Europeans tend to be high-touch groups, while the

English, Germans, northern Europeans, and people in many Asian cultures de-emphasize touching.[15]

Eye contact also differs markedly, with the highest levels of steady gazing being found in Arab and Latin American peoples and the lowest among inhabitants of India and northern Europe. Some societies teach the avoidance of eye contact in certain social situations. For instance, in Japan, a person engaged in conversation focuses on the Adam's apple rather than on the other person's eyes, and in parts of Africa one is taught to avert the eyes when speaking to a person of superior status.[16]

Reactions to silence also vary. Americans find silence disconcerting and attempt to find some topic of conversation to fill the void. In fact, we insult Africans when we rush in with "yes" or "I know," even though we are expressing agreement. The Japanese also use silence as a natural part of their negotiations. Because they, like other Asians, are reluctant to express disagreement and rarely say "no," they maintain long periods of silence as they wait for all members to come to agreement.

Gestures pose travelers problems because of the assumption that a gesture's meaning in one country is the same in another. A classic example of this misconception is the "OK" sign formed by the thumb and forefinger, which is a positive sign in the U.S. but means "worthless" in France, money to the Japanese—and is an obscene gesture in Brazil. A man reacting to seeing a pretty girl also uses different gestures in different countries: the American raises his eyebrows, the Italian screws his forefinger into his cheek, the Brazilian places an imaginary telescope to his eyes, the Frenchman kisses his fingers, the Arab tugs at his beard, and the Greek and Spaniard stroke their cheeks. The multitude of gestures particular to individual counties complicates the traveler's understanding of casual conversations, but information gleaned from sources such as the Axtell, Ricks, and Ferraro should prove useful to the prospective traveler.

TRANSLATIONS

Translations between languages often cause blunders that may be humorous or embarrassing—or costly. Situations that have a social orientation—advertisements, public relations ventures, social encounters—rely substantially on idioms and conversational language, and so these messages are especially vulnerable to mistranslation. Some of the classic mistakes are amusing to us but were not to the companies whose representatives made them. Senator Paul Simon cited some of the most well known examples:

Body by Fisher, describing a General Motors product, came out "Corpse by Fisher" in Flemish, and that did not help sales.... *Come Alive With Pepsi* almost appeared in the Chinese version of the *Reader's Digest* as "Pepsi brings your ancestors back from the grave."... A major ad campaign in green did not sell in Malaysia, where green symbolized death and disease. An airline operating out of Brazil advertised that it had plush "rendezvous lounges" on its jets, unaware that in Portuguese, "rendezvous" implied a room for making love.[17]

Americans visiting Great Britain also encounter some differences in terminology, for instance, *lorry* (truck), *boot* (trunk of car), *hire* (rent), *petrol* (gasoline), *queue* (line up), *biscuit* (cracker), *loo* or *w.c.* (bathroom), *lift* (elevator), *chemist* (druggist), *flat* (apartment), *underground* (subway), *coach* (bus), *ground floor* (first floor), and *pillar-box* (mailbox).

POINTS OF ADVICE

When you anticipate travel to another country, you can help minimize difficulties by developing some cultural awareness and simplifying your speaking situations. The major recommendations are to:

▬ Learn something about the culture and customs of the country you are visiting. Learn some of the standard phrases and courtesies important to business and social interactions. Respect other countries' traditions.

▬ Speak and act in a restrained manner. Americans have the reputation for being brash, aggressive, and hasty in their actions. People in many cultures are offended by slaps on the back, casual use of the first name, failure to use people's professional titles, and ignorance of ceremony and ritual.

▬ Keep verbal and written messages short, language simple and standard. Minimize use of idioms and slang.

▬ Don't try to use humor; it is too culturally based to transfer well from one culture to another.

▬ Don't discuss religion or politics. Discuss, instead, the country's accomplishments, arts, or literature.

▬ Take plenty of business cards for exchange and gifts for giving.

▬ Allow time for people to ask questions to clarify misunderstandings, and ask questions to make sure your message has been accurately comprehended.

CHAPTER PERSPECTIVE

The most costly blunders made by individuals and representatives of corporations have come from lack of knowledge of a country's customs. Granted, doing pre-travel research will not eliminate every awkward moment in international exchanges, but it should keep mistakes insignificant and, as Franklin Root notes, increasing one's knowledge of other cultures offers further benefit:

> Only when we come into contact with persons of other cultures who have different perceptions and behavior traits do we become aware of cultural differences and in that way of our own cultural uniqueness.... In a nutshell, those who know no other culture cannot know their own.[18]

FOOTNOTES

1 *(Homewood, IL: Dow Jones-Irwin, 1983), 7.*

2 *2nd ed. (New York: John Wiley & Sons, Inc., 1990), 24.*

3 *Gary P. Ferraro,* The Cultural Dimension of International Business *(Englewood Cliffs, NJ: Prentice Hall, 1990), 96.*

4 *John D. Daniels and Lee H. Radebaugh,* International Business: Environments and Operation, *4th ed. (Reading, MA: Addison-Wesley Publishing Co., 1986), 97.*

5 *Daniels, 84.*

6 *Vern Terpstra,* International Marketing, *4th ed. (Chicago: The Dryden Press, 1987), 107.*

7 *Ferraro, 56.*

8 *Gretchen N. Vik, Clyde W. Wilkinson, and Dorothy C. Wilkinson,* Writing and Speaking in Business, *10th ed. (Homewood, IL: Irwin, 1990), 515.*

9 *Axtell, 22.*

10 *Vik, Wilkinson, and Wilkinson, 508.*

11 *Axtell, 121.*

12 *Axtell, 8.*

13 *Ferraro, 68.*

14 *Alan Tillier and Roger Beardwood,* International Herald Tribune Guide to Business Travel: Europe *(Lincolnwood, IL: Passport Books, 1989), 30.*

15 *Ferraro, 86.*

16 *Ferraro, 80.*

17 *Ferraro, 8.*

18 *Franklin R. Root,* Entry Strategies for International Markets *(Lexington, MA: D.C. Heath and Company Lexington Books, 1987), 239.*

Selected Bibliography

Books

Axtell, Roger. *Do's and Taboos Around the World*, 2nd edition New York: John Wiley & Sons, Inc., 1990.

Committee for Economic Development. *Transnational Corporations and Developing Countries: New Policies for Changing World Economy*, April 1981.

Daniels, John D., and Lee H. Radebaugh. *International Business: Environments and Operations*, 4th edition. Reading, MA: Addison-Wesley Publishing Co., 1986.

Ferraro, Gary P. *The Cultural Dimension of International Business*. Englewood Cliffs, NJ: Prentice Hall, 1990.

Hall, Edward T. *The Silent Language*. Garden City, NY: Doubleday & Company, Inc., 1959.

_____. *Beyond Culture*. Garden City, NY: Anchor Books, 1977.

Ricks, David A. *Big Business Blunders: Mistakes in Multinational Marketing*. Homewood, IL: Dow Jones-Irwin, 1983.

Root, Franklin R. *Entry Strategies for International Markets*. Lexington, MA: D.C. Heath and Company Lexington Books, 1987.

Terpstra, Vern. *International Marketing*, 4th edition. Chicago: The Dryden Press, 1987.

Tillier, Alan, and Roger Beardwood. *International Herald Tribune Guide to Business Travel: Europe*. Lincolnwood, IL: Passport Books, 1989.

Vik, Gretchen, Clyde W. Wilkinson, and Dorothy C. Wilkinson. *Writing and Speaking in Business*, 10th edition. Homewood, IL: Irwin, 1990.

Guides

AAA Travel Guides
Fodor's Travel Guides
Michelin Tourist Guides

Glossary

bibliography an alphabetized list (by authors' surnames and by the titles of unsigned works) of research sources; sometimes designated Works Cited (only those sources expressly contributing to the document) or Works Consulted (all sources reviewed in the research project)

citation formally credited research source

clause a subject, a verb, and any other structural words needed to complete a statement. A viable sentence must have at least one main (independent) clause. A subordinate (dependent) clause must be attached to a main clause.

colloquialism language accepted in casual conversations but too informal for most business communications ("a lot of" for "much" or "many")

data concrete facts or details. A single fact is a datum. "Data" properly indicates a group, a collection, or a series of details, not an isolated detail.

direct pattern organizational strategy in which the major idea is stated first, followed by supporting details and reasons for acceptance

documentation credit given to research sources, usually in the forms of internal references, footnotes or endnotes, and a bibliography

enclosure a supplementary item enclosed in a letter

endnotes source references gathered at the end of a research document or at the end of a major division thereof (a chapter, for example)

ethnocentricity belief in the superiority of one's own ethnic group

executive summary a review of a full report's key ideas, placed at the beginning of the report

figure (1) in rhetoric, a metaphoric expression, a "figure of speech"; (2) in graphics, any type of graphic display including graphs, charts, maps, lists, or diagrams

footnotes source references cited at the bottom of a page on which the research borrowing occurs. A raised[1] or parenthetic (1) number in the text signals the presence of a corresponding footnote below.

homonyms words that are similar in sound but different in meaning

idiom, idiomatic phrasing habits in a language. The English idiomatic expressions "to catch the train" and "to catch the 11:00 news" make little sense when translated literally into other languages. The Spanish idiom "Hace calor" (literally "It makes hot") is usually paraphrased into idiomatic English as "It is hot."

indirect pattern organizational strategy in which justifying details and persuasive statements lead to a major conclusion of fact or advocacy

internal references source references incorporated into a research report text, usually through mention of the contributing author's surname (or an abbreviated title for unsigned sources) and a page number

jargon the specialized or technical language of a trade or profession

kinesics the study of gestures and body movements that transmit messages without words

metamessages messages transmitted nonverbally through gesture, posture, look, and tone of voice

oxymoron a self-contradictory or paradoxical word, phrase, or idea: "bittersweet," "the living dead"

parallelism similar grammatical and syntactical form given to words, phrases, or statements of similar kinds, values, or degrees of importance; often expressed as compound elements ("heart and soul") or a-b-c series ("heart, mind, and soul")

paraphrase rewording to achieve clarity, precision, or freshness of expression

peroration the conclusion, especially of a public address; a closing argument or appeal

phrase a distinct cluster of words but less than a clause. "In the morning" is a prepositional phrase; "riding to work" is a verbal phrase

plagiarism "literary theft"; failure to credit research sources clearly and fully

proxemics study of the way people need and use space in business and social situations

quota sampling sampling a population in a manner that reflects the demographics of the population

random sampling sampling a population in a manner that insures that each member of the population has an equal chance of being selected

redundancy unnecessary reinforcement: "free gift," "return back," "new innovation" (The "nova" element in "innovation" means "new.")

rhetoric the planned use of written or spoken language to achieve anticipated effects such as assent, sympathy, or other audience response

sentence a statement containing at least one main clause

sentence fragment a phrase or a subordinate clause mistakenly (or deliberately, for effect) punctuated as if it were a full sentence

sexist language expressions which imply discrimination on the basis of gender

stub side labels in a table used as a visual aid

syntax a language's way of arranging words to form ideas

"through" line a notation (in a memo's heading) of an intermediary between the sender and the recipient

transactional analysis the psychological theory concerning the existence of an interrelationship between three roles that people play—parent, child, and adult

verbal (1) expressed in words, as in "verbal agreement"; (2) in grammar, a word or phrase formed by converting a verb to other uses as a noun (gerund or infinitive) or a modifier (participle)

voice (1) active voice—sentence construction in which the subject is the actor: "Our company bought General Tool." (2) passive voice—sentence construction in which the subject receives the action: "Our company was bought by General Tool."

Index